ARIAN:

oBELKVE !
.

DO.llen

How Basketball Can Save the World

HARMONY

NEW YORK

How
Basketball
Can Save
the
World

13 Guiding Principles for
Reimagining What's Possible

David Hollander

Published in the United States by Harmony Books, an imprint of
Random House, a division of Penguin Random House LLC, New York.
HarmonyBooks.com

Harmony Books is a registered trademark, and the Circle colophon is a
trademark of Penguin Random House LLC.

Library of Congress Cataloging-in-Publication Data
Names: Hollander, David Adam, author.
Title: How basketball can save the world : 13 guiding principles for
   reimagining what's possible / David Hollander.
Description: First edition. | New York, N.Y. : Harmony Books, [2022] |
   Includes bibliographical references.
Identifiers: LCCN 2022040280 (print) | LCCN 2022040281 (ebook) |
   ISBN 9780593234907 (hardcover) | ISBN 9780593234921 (trade paper-
   back) |
   ISBN 9780593234914 (ebook)
Subjects: LCSH: Basketball—Social aspects. | Basketball—Psychological
   aspects. | Teamwork (Sports) | Self-actualization (Psychology)
Classification: LCC GV889.26 .H65 2022 (print) | LCC GV889.26
   (ebook) |
   DDC 796.323—dc23/eng/20221013
LC record available at https://lccn.loc.gov/2022040280
LC ebook record available at https://lccn.loc.gov/2022040281

ISBN 978-0-593-23490-7
Ebook ISBN 978-0-593-23491-4

Jacket design: Kaitlin Kall
Author photograph: Kerri Anna Smith
Chapter-opening art: Shutterstock.com/Danny E Hooks

1st Printing

10 9 8 7 6 5 4 3 2 1

First Edition

For Lola

CONTENTS

INTRODUCTION

It's like this.

I walk by a basketball court, any court, I stop. Full stop. If they're playing, I'll hang out for a while—just to watch, to hear basketball sounds. Lose myself. Forget time.

Merely seeing the word *basketball*—anywhere, in any format—heightens my senses and raises my level of engagement.

With the object in my hands, I'm like Arthur pulling Excalibur from the stone. I am transformed. I am someone else, somewhere else. And in that space, the space of basketball, life is somehow more and I am better.

You think this is all a bit much? Let me go further. I don't see basketball simply as part of my identity. I see it as an existential matter, as if without it I'm not really even here.

So many understand this. Yet it takes one to know one. And when we meet, it only takes a moment before one of us asks the other: "Do you still play?" This is our handshake. This is our measure. It is our check against whether and how, and how much, we really are still here. We ask because we know the value of playing.

Introduction

We know what's at stake when you stop playing. And now, as old as I am, I know I'm getting closer to not playing. And that possibility brings fundamentally important things into sharp focus: basketball, my life. Whether and how I remain cosmic. Whether I am still free.

Basketball is an "ever since" thing for me. Ever since my dad put a twelve-by-twelve-foot blacktop in the backyard before I was born. Ever since I spent thousands of dusks on that blacktop practicing, which always ended with the same plea: "Just one more shot, Mom!" Ever since CYO and Summer League championships. Ever since varsity, coaching, and countless public courts from Alphabet City to Shanghai, Nashua to the Negev, Toronto to Las Terrenas. From wherever I could find some decent run. Later, off the court, as a person in the world, celebrating the game in classrooms, boardrooms, and back rooms with league commissioners, power brokers, producers, present and future Hall of Famers, sneaker executives, playground legends, and cultural tastemakers. All this time, *basketball and I* have never let go of each other.

Basketball stays with me. It's what I return to. It's where I feel my whole self integrated, where I find balance. Where the world makes sense, where my relationship with other people gets right. It is my sanctuary. My truth. It is a lifetime pass to a universally shared space and consciousness, bonding me with all who know, have known, and will know what I know. And I know I'm not alone.

Many, including Franklin Foer in his excellent *How Soccer Explains the World,* have used sport as a lens to view culture, conflict, and social conditions. But what if basketball could actually *save* the world by helping us think differently about solving world problems?

Introduction

On an intuitive level, I feel that it can. But on a deeper level, I also *know* that it can. Basketball is just so different from other sports. Its basic playing space, fifty feet by ninety feet, is much smaller than a soccer or football field, which can be up to four times as long. Basketball players, like people in the world at large, must navigate shared space. In so doing, they must closely observe and successfully understand each other. With no equipment and playing basically in undergarments, they are exposed to one another—teammate to teammate, teammate to opponent, and participant to spectator—up close and clearly. And in basketball, all participants do all things. No one is prohibited from going to any particular place on the court, or doing more or less than anyone else. Not so in football, where player positions and functions are strictly defined, specialized, and differentiated. Baseball is ultra-positional, particularly when it comes to the pitcher. Even in soccer or hockey, where the principles of movement somewhat approximate basketball, defensive players typically don't spend much time in the offensive area, and the uniquely positioned goalie has radically different powers than the other players. In basketball, players switch between offense and defense in an instant; there's no separate unit to do one or the other.

In life, as in basketball, we often must change our position—fluidly and without warning—to meet changing circumstances. In other large field and court sports, it's possible that over the course of the game, certain players may never even come near one another. That's not possible in basketball. In basketball, everyone on the court is intimately—in a relational and spatial sense—tied to everyone else.

I'm not saying other sports don't teach us wonderful things.

Introduction

I'm saying this sport is particularly good at showing us how to be in this world with each other and make it better. I'm making an objective observation: The game is more *human* in size, interaction, structure, and participatory experience. As a result, applying basketball as a worldview would be a lot more apt to solving the problems of *humanity.*

In 2019, I finally got the opportunity to test the idea of basketball as a philosophy with a course I began teaching at New York University called "How Basketball Can Save the World."

The genesis of the class took the form of a question: Isn't it time to look to new systems of thinking, leadership, problem solving, efficiency, fairness, and equality? For thousands of years, the world has been led by the same kinds of leaders—monarchs, generals, clergy, politicians, economists, lawyers, and captains of industry. Those leaders and thinkers created societal practices and schools of thought—*isms,* like capitalism, socialism, communism, nationalism, isolationism, utilitarianism, theism, and so on—to manage and make sense of the world. Century after century they based their policies and plans on these great *isms* believing they made the world more just, more efficient, more productive, more meaningful. The result, after millennia of the same kinds of leaders continuing to employ the same kinds of thinking, is a world more broken, more confused, and more conflicted than ever. Why not look to a ubiquitous global phenomenon that has continued to grow faster in popularity, relevance, influence, and impact than almost any other human activity over the past century: basketball.

The 13 Principles that underlie this book are a numeric homage to the original 13 rules of basketball devised by James Nai-

Introduction

smith. They are distilled from what Naismith intended the game to be, how it has operated globally ever since, and what the world has told us the game means. I explicitly wanted to elevate the study of basketball to the same plane as political science, history, music, or any other academic major.

In the years since the class began, I have been honored to host a revolving congregation of Naismith Basketball Hall of Famers, award-winning filmmakers, Pulitzer Prize–winning journalists, bestselling authors, global tastemakers, peacemakers, playground legends, anthropologists, sneaker mavens, league commissioners, artists, photographers, urban planners, entrepreneurs, leaders of indigenous peoples, and even a former star player turned globally acclaimed mezzo-soprano. The very first class met on the court at Nike's New York City headquarters, every student holding a ball. We visited the legendary Dunlevy Milbank Center in Harlem and "The Cage" at West 4th Street, and we enjoyed VIP access to the 2019 NBA Draft at Barclays Center. We helped sway the Vatican to recognize the first ever Patron Saint of Basketball! With each guest and each experience, we analyzed, validated, elucidated, and enlivened those 13 Principles.

Now, in this book, I state my case. *How Basketball Can Save the World* proposes a new story, a new frame through which to see our meaning, a new *ism*. This world—*our world, right now*—needs new inspiration, new paradigms, new foundational principles. Therefore, we must look to a new source of ideas for fairness, problem solving, sustainability, and growth to meet this new era. I insist we look at basketball.

Modern government is broken. Competing worldviews of

democracy and authoritarianism are ferociously, irreconcilably at odds. The economy is broken. We are now seeing the greatest disparity in wealth, throughout the world, since the Gilded Age. Brokenness abounds from eroded trust in the media to right-before-our-eyes climate destruction, to the vanishing of privacy, to the deterioration of our social fabric, now threadbare. So many feel increasingly desperate and alone, and the great many stand divided.

We live in a world of intense division. From the derisive social critiques of Gen Z–Millennials to the taunts of "OK boomer," the generations share little but mutual contempt, blame, and condescension. The #MeToo movement powerfully exposes the brokenness in gender relations. And what of racism and othering? What of hate? What of the vulnerability and unchecked persecution of stateless ethnic groups: Kurds, Rohingya, Yazidis, Uighurs? What of homophobia, Islamophobia, xenophobia, transphobia, and the resurgence of overt, normalized, global anti-Semitism?

These conditions result from old prevailing *isms,* recycled century after century. All of it is *systemic.*

Young people in particular sense this. Jia Tolentino, in her essay collection *Trick Mirror,* writes that her generation suffers from an inescapable "ethical brokenness," which she describes as a Millennial's Hobson's choice: "I have felt so many times that the choice of this era is to be destroyed or to morally compromise ourselves in order to be functional—to be wrecked, or to be functional for reasons that contribute to the wreck. It's a powerlessness that makes us complicit."

Philosopher-historian Yuval Noah Harari calls this moment an "age of bewilderment." It is forcing us to reexamine all of our fundamentally held assumptions: "When the old stories have collapsed, and no new story has emerged so far to replace them. Who are we? What should we do in life? What kinds of skills do we need? Given everything we know and don't know about science, about God, about politics, and religion what can we say about the meaning of life today?"

Today, basketball is a global force sui generis that continues to fascinate and unify. It opens closed worlds. It gives sanctuary to the outsider and the other. It appeals equally to the urban and the rural. It has been and continues to be compelling, operative, and influential in major societal discussions of race, access, gender, immigration, culture, and commerce. No other pastime sells more footwear, activates more social media, and interests more young people. The game flourishes nearly everywhere on every continent.

Basketball's capacity to do all that it has done—and its potential to do even more—traces directly back to the intention and foresight of its inventor, James Naismith. Naismith was a right-place, right-time, free-thinking individual in the world of 1891, who had a particularly special mix of personal qualities and lived experience. He was a Canadian immigrant in the United States, an orphan from a young age, and an intellectual misfit-wanderer. A divinity school graduate who forsook the ministry in search of a higher calling, leading him to create an eminently physical manifestation of his spiritual aspirations. He just wanted the world to be a better place.

Employed at Springfield College, a gym teacher's academy in

Massachusetts, he was tasked with coming up with a nonviolent indoor physical activity to occupy "incorrigible," violence-prone students in the winter months. Naismith's challenge in the fall of 1891 was a microcosm of the challenge facing the world. The brokenness that Naismith saw in the tumultuous, conflicted, inequitable Gilded Age looks an awful lot like the brokenness that we face today.

Basketball was Naismith's vision for society as he wished it to be—for those incorrigible men in his gym class and for the world at large spinning out of control. Naismith looked at that gym, at those men, and knew he had to create something new. Old ideas would not fix that brokenness. And thus, his 13 original rules became the framework for a new way of play. *Basketball worked.*

The 13 Principles presented in this book are inspired by and deeply connected to Naismith's vision, and to the phenomenal impact that has sprung forth from that vision. My hope is that these principles, though not explicitly stated in any rule book, codify what is inherent to the game.

Meg Barber, the coach of the NYU women's basketball team, once said to me, "What you're trying to do is make the word *basketball* mean something else." That's right. That word—and the game it signifies—has always meant something else to me, and to so many others. And to Meg. For those who experience the game, we hold these truths to be self-evident. They just needed to be said out loud. This book and these principles give those truths language and voice.

The 13 Principles are not complicated. They're not hard to understand. It's simply time for new thinking and a new consciousness to take action to fix things and move us forward.

Introduction

No more of the same old mistakes, from the same old thinking, by the same old leaders. No more being trapped by old definitions, limited by old meanings and old vocabulary. Those systems have demonstrably failed. Basketball has given us a nearly century-and-a-half proof of concept.

Basketball works.

PRINCIPLE
1

COOPERATION

You have to give everybody space to be their best; to operate. The more you play, the more you just have a feel. I understand the types of passes a teammate can make—how hard or how fast—and where I need to be in order to receive it. I understand if Breanna Stewart has the ball, I need to give her space, let her operate, do what she does best. If somebody else has the ball, maybe I need to go get it, because they're not a ball-handler, or we're being pressed, and I need to close down that space. If you're too crowded, you know you're going to hurt your teammate. It's fascinating when I think of myself on the court in that way. Backpedaling my way out, sprinting over here or coming over there. There's definitely a spatial negotiation constantly happening and it's always for the betterment of the team. Same thing when I'm out in public: I know exactly how far you need to be and I know exactly where I'm going.

—Sue Bird, four-time WNBA champion, five-time Olympic gold medalist, five-time Russian National League champion, five-time EuroLeague champion, two-time NCAA champion, New York State high school champion

I can still recall how I snapped my fingers and shouted, 'I've got it!'" That was James Naismith's eureka moment, for himself and for all of us. His premise was basic: "If he can't run with the ball, we don't have to tackle."

Naismith knew that the boys in his class at Springfield College only liked games that involved tackling and rough physical contact. Those students had already chased two previous Springfield College class instructors out of their jobs for trying to introduce nonviolent recreation. What would hold the attention of these "incorrigible" ruffians? To get them to cooperate, Naismith offered them a vehicle of cooperation. Incredibly, during a single night of hard thinking by the lamplight at his desk, he wrote the 13 original rules of basketball.

If the players of his new game couldn't run with the ball, then what?

"The next step," thought Naismith, "was to see exactly what he could do with it." The solution? Pass to a teammate.

This was Naismith's quantum leap. He eliminated ball-movement-by-running and replaced it with passing, completely eschewing the entrenched, one-dimensional principle of individuals running with a ball toward a goal, trying to evade or plow through would-be tacklers. This was a profound shift in form and consciousness. Naismith's new game introduced the core necessity of team cooperation in place of the core worship of the single player versus the world.

If you wanted to advance up the court and score, you had to pass or share the ball. That was his first rule. His second rule radically expanded the scope of cooperation: Any player can pass in any direction—forward, backward, laterally—to any other player. Naismith delimited cooperation in form, direction, and variety. "In my mind," he said, "I began to play a game and visualize the movements of the players."

Naismith posted his 13 rules on the gymnasium bulletin board the next morning, explicitly stating in rule 5 the nonviolent intention of the game: "No shouldering, holding, pushing, tripping, or striking in any way the person of an opponent shall be allowed."

It didn't start off exactly as he drew it, though. "The boys began tackling, kicking, and punching in the clinches," he recalled in *Basketball: Origin and Development*. "They ended up in a free-for-all in the middle of the gym floor. Before I could pull them apart, one boy was knocked out, several of them had black eyes, and one had a dislocated shoulder. It certainly was murder." But each time a brawl broke out, Naismith patiently redirected them. And sometime that afternoon, in that YMCA gym in Springfield, Massachusetts, it happened: The boys took to the game and its rules so entirely that they didn't want to leave the court to go to their next class.

James Naismith created a new game that replaced individual possession with interdependent cooperation as its basis and foresaw how the game would prove utterly compelling because of it. Basketball felt good, and he knew it. And his students knew it. And if you have played the game, you know it, too.

Cooperation

It's not just that the value of cooperation in basketball is intrinsic and self-evident, it's also enjoyable. Basketball also provides fundamental cooperative pleasures like the give-and-go or the pick-and-roll. Or the perfectly executed switch on defense to defend against the pick. Or a rotation to help on defense—cooperatively named "help defense"—where you leave your man to help another.

Or the ultimate cooperative-basketball transcendental meditation: the three-person weave. Pass, cut, catch. Pass, cut, catch. Again and again and again. The three-person weave patterns like a figure eight, but it's more accurate to think of it as an infinity symbol. As if the way to live infinitely is to let go of the ball, then come back around to get it again. In the human utopia of the three-person weave, you trust in seamless, continuous, rhythmic cooperation. You know the ball is coming back even as you let it go. It is a rapturous exercise.

How deep in the human psyche can this cooperative joy be found? Many take it back to 1200 BC Mesoamericans—Mayans and Aztecs—who participated in a ritualistic "ballgame" that looked an awful lot like basketball. On a sunken court, with elevated circular hoops at each end, the game was played by teams who advanced a bouncy solid rubber ball through repetitive, cooperative, circular team movements. These circular movements were meant to honor the coming harvest; the patterns symbolized the changing seasons, the sky and the underworld, life and death, harmonizing with the spinning earth, becoming one with the vast and endless cosmos.

For the Mesoamericans, this ballgame was about cooperating with the universe—not declaring dominion or separateness from it, not plundering it, but, through the game, sanctifying their necessary symbiosis with it. This basic principle of cooperation may have even deeper roots, predating humanity entirely. Suzanne Simard, a University of British Columbia scientist, has gone a long way in demonstrating that trees—yes, trees—cooperate, especially when they are part of a team: the forest. They communicate, reciprocate, show selflessness, and share resources with other trees. Trees give-and-go, pick-and-roll, and shore up each other's weak sides through active, independent mycorrhizal networks. For the sake of the forest, trees cooperate.

Naismith so embedded cooperation into his game that even the greatest individual players must embrace the principle in thought and action in order to reach the highest of achievements. Phil Jackson, who amassed eleven rings as an NBA coach and player, wrote in his basketball bestseller *Sacred Hoops,* "Good teams become great ones when teammates trust each other enough to surrender the Me for the We." This was true even for Michael Jordan. There would have been no first dance, or last dance, if he hadn't learned to cooperate with Scottie Pippen.

PLAYERS UNDERSTAND

Bill Russell is the most successful individual player in NBA history in terms of championship rings. He won eleven championships in thirteen seasons, far more than any other player. Again and again, he famously bested the Goliath of his day, Wilt Chamberlain. Years later another Hall of Famer, Sonny Hill, asked him on a sports radio show how he might stop Shaquille O'Neal, who was at the time (ca. 1994) seemingly undefendable because of his physical dominance. There was a brief silence, then Russell answered, "I wouldn't stop him. My team would."

Russell could not conceive of himself without the cooperation of his teammates. When he paused before answering, it was likely him thinking, "Me stop Shaq? . . . Wait, the *me* part here does not compute." Any question about a basketball stratagem, for Russell, could only be answered from a cooperative team standpoint. As soon as he thought of himself doing something on a basketball court, he instantaneously thought of the other four players on the floor, and what they would be doing in concert with him. Russell was known to believe so strongly in the basketball cooperative that he consistently resisted the notion of being named to Halls of Fame, All-Star teams, or winning MVP awards on a variety of "it's not about me" grounds.

Echoes of Russell's ethic surfaced two generations later when Ja Morant, perhaps the most spectacular individual talent of this decade, immediately gifted his 2022 NBA Most Improved Player Award trophy to teammate Desmond Bane. Morant posted on his Instagram: "@_dbane1 i left your award in your kitchen gang, you deserve it killa."

Another modern-era espouser of the cooperative style of play was Bill Bradley, who, along with being a two-time NBA champion, was also a Rhodes Scholar and a US senator. In "A Sense of Where You Are," future Pulitzer Prize–winning author John McPhee observed Bradley as an All-American college basketball player at Princeton, already intellectualizing the cooperation principle. "The depth of Bradley's game is most discernible when he doesn't have the ball," noted McPhee. "He always knows where the ball is but is not immediately concerned with getting it." In other words, Bradley was cooperating.

Bradley's own words testify to the importance of cooperation to him personally. In his seminal basketball memoir, *Life on the Run,* published during his NBA playing career, he wrote that cooperation itself is what he's really after, not basketball or anything else. "The press and public approval mean little to me. What is important is my own judgement as to whether the team plays according to my estimation of how an ideal team should. It is a more complicated process than simply playing or being a star."

And in his second book, *Values of the Game,* published after his retirement, Bradley further articulated his basketball-istic commitment to the cooperation principle: "Part of the beauty and mystery of basketball rests in the variety of its team requirements . . . a high degree of unity only attainable through the selflessness of its players . . . it is in the moves that the uninitiated often don't see: the perfect screen, the purposeful movement away from the ball, the deflected pass." In basketball, cooperation is not the means to an end, but the means *and* the end.

To many in basketball the cooperative orthodoxy is nonnegotiable, not even for the sake of overdue financial advancement. A few years ago, the Women's National Basketball Players Association president Nneka Ogwumike (league MVP, league champion, and All-Star) was pitched the idea of a WNBA one-on-one tournament—a marketing vehicle to attract more consumers to the women's game. The plan combined sports betting with reality-show drama and lucrative sponsorships. Nneka could see this would potentially shine a spotlight on underappreciated women players, but there was a fundamental problem with the idea. "Most of the women in our league don't like one-on-one. That's not our game. That's not *the* game. We believe we are playing not just the purest form of basketball, but the purest form of team sports play in the world."

This is what can happen on a basketball court: a shift in your understanding of what cooperation can mean. John Edgar Wideman, an All–Ivy League basketball star at Penn and two-time winner of the PEN/Faulkner Award for Fiction, said it best. In his peerless basketball memoir *Hoop Roots,* he wrote: "I learned, among other things, to recognize and be grateful for a helping hand, learned it might not be exactly the kind of hand I wanted, maybe it would be a rough hand, a bitter pill, but I was learning to appreciate different hands on their different terms. Above all learning not to be so intent on moving forward I turned my back on the ones behind who might need my hand or have one to offer."

THE SPACE OF EMPATHY

In 2013 and 2017, Google conducted two rigorous internal studies. The goal of these studies was to identify the company's best employees and their defining qualities, ranking from one (most important) to eight (least important). As it turned out, STEM skills, the core competency of Google's enterprise, was *last* on the list at number eight both times. So what were the top five? Being a good coach, communicating and listening, insight into the values and points of view of others, empathy, and support of colleagues—the kind of cooperative skills you need to work with other human beings. In other words, the most valuable people at Google are the most cooperative people.

Right after the 2017 study, Google's head of industry, Paul Santagata, told *Harvard Business Review*'s Laura Delizonna that one of the ways to make his employees more cooperative was to run them through a reflection exercise called "Just like Me." The exercise made them consider their co-worker/counterpart in the following ways:

- This person has beliefs, perspectives, and opinions, just like me.
- This person has hopes, anxieties, and vulnerabilities, just like me.
- This person has friends, family, and perhaps children who love them, just like me.
- This person wants to feel respected, appreciated, and competent, just like me.
- This person wishes for peace, joy, and happiness, just like me.

What Santagata was trying to teach is the cooperation superpower: empathy.

In our everyday interactions, the cooperation principle is best expressed through empathy—not just understanding where someone else is coming from, but actually experiencing a palpable psychological or physiological feeling that mirrors what another person is feeling in a given time and place. Chamique Holdsclaw, who won three consecutive NCAA championships at Tennessee and is a six-time WNBA All-Star, describes in Robin Layton's photo essay *Hoop: The American Dream* how basketball is a participatory textbook that teaches empathy skills. "Basketball taught me some basic principles of life: learning how to work with people and how to accept different backgrounds and cultures. It taught me how to work with someone who is different from me."

Pulitzer Prize–winning poet and MacArthur Fellow Natalie Diaz played against Holdsclaw in the NCAA Final Four; one of her four trips to the tournament playing for Old Dominion. She later played professionally in Europe and Asia. Diaz explained to WNYC's Tobin Low and Kathy Tu, "I could be on a court with any four other players, like in a pickup game, and I could not know them, but suddenly I have to find ways of knowing them." When she stopped playing and turned to poetry, she recognized how the game informed her deployment of language. "These words are being used as a powerful gesture of naming, of saying I exist, of saying I am here in this space. . . . It's a way of enacting a type of family even among strangers." That happens in the space of a basketball court. And creating that kind of basketball space makes all the difference.

Basketball's cooperation principle is tied to a requirement of intimate physical space. Basketball is intrinsically about humans sharing that physical space. Shared physical space is where empathy develops. Shared space allows humans to solve problems cooperatively not only because it fosters socially intelligent interactions, but also because the experience of exercising social intelligence and empathy is a vital, nourishing part of the human experience. It's enjoyable. We like it. We seek it. It's life-giving. We feed off one another's social cues when we are placed in the intimate basketball-istic space to do so. And that's how we learn to be excellent at cooperation.

But that kind of spatial interaction is getting harder and harder to come by. Professor Scott Galloway, at the NYU Stern School of Business, says the pandemic accelerated developing consumer and workplace trends, pushing us into a new societal construct he calls "the Great Dispersion."

The physical shift to remote working may be irreversible. Long commutes are eliminated, as is unused office space. The downside, however, is that people no longer work closely and regularly in the same space, which in turn will eliminate those crucial social intelligence-building interactions that knit a workforce together.

And this trend is not just in the workplace. We no longer go out to brick-and-mortar retail stores; we order from Amazon. Home streaming has replaced theater-going. Likewise, instead of going to the supermarket, we can order online and have our groceries delivered. Instead of going to the doctor's office, we do telehealth. Students don't go to school; they do remote learning. In a world of dispersion, when do we run into each other?

Real personal interaction, not digital dispersion, is how we can achieve meaningful cooperation and how we build the ultimate cooperation skill: empathy. When we share space, we see each other. We humanize each other, because of all the micro-interactions. It's about building social intelligence, person to person, interaction to interaction, thus creating a more socially intelligent, empathetic society and global community at the macro level. A million virtual meetings filled with the best cooperative intent and spirit will never come close to in-person, face-to-face, social-intelligence-building basketball-istic meetings. It will never equal the thousand subtle things—what Bill Bradley called "the moves that the uninitiated often don't see"—that happen between people sharing close-up basketball space, where immediately you begin to build trust and empathy through your actions and interactions.

Understanding how to share limited physical space with others is a necessary corollary of the basketball cooperation principle, an indelible condition in basketball's cooperative social contract. Why must there be a *social* contract—a binding agreement not imposed or legislated by authorities, but understood and accepted between people? Because we are people, and we are not alone. The planet is chock-full of people who are not you, your family, or your friends. We are stuck here *together.* Martin Luther King, Jr., said, "We are caught in an inescapable network of mutuality." Basketball believes that's the point. That's the right conceptual framework for our life vis-à-vis other lives. That's the game itself.

Powerfully, it may also be a way to move our world forward from the most intractable noncooperative human conflicts that have mired us for centuries.

PEACE

After graduating from Catholic University in the summer of 2000, Sean Tuohey went straight to Northern Ireland to play professional basketball and operate basketball clinics for Protestant and Catholic children in Belfast. The clinics showed Sean that basketball could help overcome deeply entrenched barriers between the two groups. (Basketball was also one of the few politically neutral sports in the region.) A police chief in Belfast who befriended Sean suggested that what worked in Northern Ireland might also help in postapartheid South Africa. So, equipped with a basketball and seven thousand dollars raised by his parents' friends, Sean packed a bag and traveled to Durban, a city on the east coast of South Africa. He recruited his older brother Brendan, who had also played basketball professionally in Ireland, and together the Tuoheys established PeacePlayers International (PPI) in 2001.

PeacePlayers, in the organization's own words, "uses basketball as an innovative tool to unite a critical mass of diverse leaders around the globe who work together to dismantle structures of conflict and inequity in their societies and beyond." Their global mission is to "challenge the hate that is driven by the fear of our differences" through basketball, developing young leaders who will create a more peaceful world, bridge divides, and help to change perceptions.

"I call it conflict transformation, not conflict resolution," Brendan told our NYU class. "What's the way that that transformation happens? When we find a way to *see each other as human beings.*" He elaborated: "I believe in sport for development, period, but basketball is a sport like no other. It's unique because of its intimacy. The basketball court is probably as small as any other playing field that there is. It's five on a side, not eleven, so what you do affects others no matter what. It's positionless, you go anywhere on the court, and so the game creates ideal relationships for truly seeing each other and getting quickly past just seeing 'the other.'"

Brendan does not claim basketball itself is enough. It's more that basketball is especially good at creating what Brendan called a "new, shared unwritten language," so there's a starting point for growth.

"We're not saying that 'Hey, the active playing of basketball together is going to, on its own, be the answer.' But it creates the foundation. It creates that 'All right, I can see you; I can relate to you. Now, can we look to maybe have deeper conversations or form a friendship?'"

From their own experiences as competitive siblings playing basketball with each other and with other kids, the brothers came to the conclusion that people who can play basketball together can learn to live together.

"My brother is a year and a half younger than me and, you know, we had a contentious relationship growing up," Brendan remembers. "We actually played basketball against each other in college, and that did not go well. My mom is still scarred from it. So the fact that the two of us work together on anything—much less an organization around conflict—is fairly amusing to people that know us. And to people that still know us, because it's not like that relationship has changed all that much."

Because of their natural competitiveness, the Tuohey brothers wisely created a geographic division of labor. While Sean led PPI's efforts in the field, Brendan built the organization from Washington, D.C.

After two decades of tireless work, the sheer scale of PPI's reach is tremendous: 260 partner schools and nonprofits, two thousand coaches trained, and over seventy-five thousand participants. In addition to South Africa and Northern Ireland, they run PPI in two other geopolitical hot spots: Israel and the West Bank, and Cyprus. In 2017, PeacePlayers launched a multiyear partnership with Nike to unite communities in the United States with a specific focus on strengthening relationships between youth and law enforcement. They took on the toughest urban areas: Baltimore, Brooklyn, Chicago, Los Angeles, and Detroit. Through their Sports and Peace Innovation Network consulting arm, PPI handles another twenty-two projects in countries across five continents. They've received top honors and awards including NGO of the Year: Peace and Sports Award, the Arthur Ashe Courage Award (ESPYs), the Oklahoma City National Memorial Museum's Reflections of Hope Award, the Robert Wood Johnson Foundation Sports Award, and the Laureus Sport for Good Award.

The recognition is certainly nice, but for the Tuohey brothers it's more about the data. In December 2020, PeacePlayers published an eight-year randomized controlled trial (RCT) led by top researchers from New York University and the Berlin Social Science Center (WZB). The study involved eight hundred Arab and Jewish participants ages eight to sixteen from more than twenty communities throughout Israel. Brendan insisted on the rigor of the RCT method, typically used for medical research, which randomly divides people into experimental and control groups, because "it is the only research method that is able to prove a cause-and-effect relationship between participating in a program and achieving its intended outcome."

The findings? The PeacePlayers Middle East program works. It does what it intends to do. It transforms Arab and Jewish young people into agents for peace. As a result of sustained participation, PeacePlayers's young leaders acquire the positive attitudes, personal resources, and strong motivation needed to influence their peers.

Four key findings from the study showed, quantitatively and qualitatively, that PPI's basketball program achieved its goals. Specifically, the programs succeeded in (1) building cross-community friendships, (2) reducing prejudices, and (3) developing leaders who (4) actively advocate for peace.

Undeniably, the study showed that basketball's cooperation principle is a proven effective tool to change the world—its status quo, its perennial unsolvable conflicts—by transforming people who then transform others. Basketball's cooperation principle can move the world forward. It can fix what's broken. It can bridge human divides, which is the necessary precondition to having people work together to build bridges, roads, hospitals, schools, clean and potable water sources, a safe environment, and whatever else this world needs.

The effectual power of the basketball cooperation principle is more than just a theory. In the case of PeacePlayers, just follow the science.

UBUNTU

In 1984, Mark Crandall, a high school junior from Amagansett, Long Island, was selected for a local Rotary Club exchange program that sent him to live in Zimbabwe. It turned out to be a life-changing experience. After college he returned to Zimbabwe, and together with native Zimbabwean Ngoni Mukukula co-founded Hoops 4 Hope in 1995. Hoops 4 Hope is a youth sports-and-education program whose mission is to help kids think critically, plan for their futures, and take accountability for their actions. Twenty-five years later, through determined effort across continents, Hoops 4 Hope has established seventy-five programs in Zimbabwe and South Africa, with 750 kids attending daily afterschool programs, totaling more than 7,600 annual participants. Hoops 4 Hope has been chronicled by the Discovery Channel, became the life-skills curriculum partner of NBA Basketball

Without Borders Africa, and received awards from the United Nations and International Olympic Committee for their remarkable grassroots work.

Crandall tailors the curriculum of Hoops 4 Hope to the different real and present dangers that exist in each of the local communities where they work: HIV/AIDS awareness, substance abuse, gender inequality, teenage risk management, conflict resolution, Ebola, and Covid-19. But no matter where they are, the physical classroom is always the same: a basketball court.

Their pedagogical methods are eminently basketball focused. Instructors, peer mentors selected from the local communities, employ "Circle Time." "Circles are powerful," the curriculum states. "The key is that a circle has no beginning or end, no one is bigger or smaller than anyone else." In the circle, they engage and encourage young people to discuss common challenges and to seek solutions. Hoops 4 Hope's peer mentorship model allows the learning process to occur in participants' own languages. This makes it more like an exchange or facilitation of activities rather than a top-down distribution, thus modeling the cooperation they teach. The conceptual framework that ties together their mission is the "7 Tools of a Champion": (1) Integrity, (2) Responsibility, (3) Sense of humor, (4) Self-awareness, (5) Self-esteem, (6) Focus, and (7) *Ubuntu,* which flows through everything taught and learned.

Ubuntu is an ancient philosophy found in every African country south of the Sahara. It is often translated as "I am because we are" or, more simply, "humanity." Most popularly found in the Zulu language, Ubuntu has a linguistic equivalent in twenty-one other African languages and countries.

Cooperation

Archbishop Desmond Tutu, in his book *No Future Without Forgiveness,* explains that Ubuntu is not "I think therefore I am." It says rather: "I am a human because I belong. I participate. I share." In essence, I am because you are.

At the 2018 Nelson Mandela Annual Lecture in Johannesburg, on the anniversary of Mandela's one hundredth birthday, Barack Obama invoked Ubuntu as Mandela's "greatest gift . . . his recognition that we are all bound together in ways that can be invisible to the eye; that there is a oneness to humanity."

Ubuntu, *I am because we are,* has been incorporated all over the world through political science, diplomacy, criminal justice, social work, and much more. It's a powerful, global healing message. And Hoops 4 Hope found basketball to be a particularly compatible messenger. To play basketball well is to see your teammates as you see yourself. Ubuntu is a beautiful, all-encompassing synonym for the basketball cooperation principle: the constant, intentional, interpersonal transmission of social intelligence and empathy.

Through basketball's unique spatial intimacy, Mark Crandall has created a program that cultivates an appreciation among young people for others *who are not like them.* Call it empathy, call it social or emotional intelligence, but Crandall's Hoops 4 Hope graduates are walking down the street navigating the myriad interactions of the human experience, seeing other human beings as if they are seeing themselves.

In a May 2020 BBC report, Hoops 4 Hope kids explained Ubuntu consciousness in their own words: "It means one hand cannot wash itself. . . . I am not standing here because of my own likeness, I am who I am because of other people. . . . It makes us help the elderly, other children, people from other communities. . . . Oneness: different people, different cultures, difference, norms; and we play together in the form of basketball."

Not only has Ubuntu, in the form of basketball, brought measurable positive change to the next generation of African young people, but it has even helped bring together the opposing interpersonal relationships in another of the world's conflict-prone areas: NBA superteams.

In 2008, the Boston Celtics created "the Big Three" by boldly trading for future Hall of Famers Kevin Garnett and Ray Allen to join their team leader, Paul Pierce. That summer, before the season began, Celtics coach Doc Rivers knew he had a challenge on his hands. It was going to be hard enough to foster harmonious teamwork among three superstars, but he also needed to make sure the rest of the team did not feel any less important. At an NBA clinic in Africa that summer, Rivers met Hoops 4 Hope South Africa director Kita Matungulu and shared his worries. Kita knew the answer. "That's easy, Doc. We do it every day." On the first day of Celtics training camp, Rivers brought Kita to Boston as an assistant coach to impart the guiding wisdom of Ubuntu to the entire team. Doc, the Big Three, and every other member of the Celtics team fully embraced Ubuntu. That season, the Celtics won their first championship in twenty-two years. UBUNTU was engraved on their championship rings.

In a 2020 documentary film about Hoops 4 Hope, *Hoops Africa: Ubuntu Matters,* Doc Rivers described how the Ubuntu consciousness actualized on the court. "You saw Ray move over for Paul, Paul move over for Kevin, and Kevin move over for everyone—wanting and encouraging their success and so as everyone on the team was successful as they [the Big Three] were successful themselves. That's the Ubuntu meaning. We lived it. And it changed our team."

Like learning life skills in Hoops 4 Hope, Paul Pierce explained how Ubuntu became the catchall word for cooperating with each other on and off the court: "Everything from who pays for dinner, who borrowed something and needed to return it, to who forgot a man assignment, or missed an open cutter, we would say to each other, 'Ubuntu!'"

As the Big Three would attest, the space requirement of basketball's cooperation principle is transformative. We must get together in the same place. We must deal with each other. That's how we connect most deeply on a neurological level. Sharing physical space builds effective and ultimately pleasing empathic socially intelligent relationships.

The cooperation principle is the starting point of a new model, to fix a broken world. We cannot start at the point of division, exceptionalism, nationalism, nativism, tribalism, or localism. We can no longer just take the ball and run.

It sounds so trite: *cooperation*. But it's a profound choice we're given every day. It's a conscious fork in the road, presented to us every morning when we wake up, in every action and interaction from that point forward. Cooperate or not. The direction of the world hangs on that choice. And if we take that as our existential basis, commit to cooperation as our duty to one another—person to person, business to business, nation to nation—and adopt it as our chosen individual and collective consciousness, our social contract, then the bliss of being *here with each other* will not only be the concrete societal dividend from the cooperation each of us puts forward, the mending of the world's broken things, but also the personal happiness that comes from living together cooperatively in that world.

Call it *Ubuntu*. Or have your own moment of awakening, like Naismith had, late that night in Springfield, when he snapped his fingers and shouted, "I've got it!"

PRINCIPLE 2

BALANCE OF INDIVIDUAL AND COLLECTIVE

Basketball's defining challenge, once you get past the physical stuff, is social. More than any other American sport, it is a game of civics. Every player, on every play, has to find the proper balance between self-interest and self-sacrifice—a threshold that moves with just about every bounce of the ball. The game is fluid, with everyone shifting roles and responsibilities more or less constantly. The calculus between selfishness and self-sacrifice can be crushingly complex. A properly balanced team can make that calculus feel manageable. An unbalanced team can make it hopeless.

—Sam Anderson, *Boom Town*

On a basic level, the game of basketball was meant to solve an immediate workplace problem: find an indoor game to occupy "incorrigibles"—students who only wanted to play games characterized by possession and physical domination. Naismith's solution was a game where everyone on the team was equally entitled to possess the ball, equally empowered to score, but only one person could hold the ball at a time.

In basketball that means 80 percent of the game (100 percent when we talk about defense) is about what you do without the ball in your hands. And that has everything to do with what good things happen, or don't happen, for your team. For every individual basketball player, the game is a constant balancing act in concert with teammates for the benefit of the individual and the collective. Ball or no ball, everything you do on the court matters.

This was James Naismith's game: a microcosm of social balance that stood in opposition to nineteenth-century society. Mark Twain and Charles Dudley Warner dubbed this era the Gilded Age, for its glittering surface hid the massive wealth disparity and corruption that lay underneath. Naismith, no doubt, believed in the Muscular Christianity movement—sound, mind, and body elevates the spirit—that animated the work of the YMCA at that time. But had he only been interested in religious proselytization, he would have taken his divinity school degree and joined the ministry, not a gym teacher's college. Naismith had a more ecumenically humanistic drive and perspective. He humbly stated on his Springfield College application, "To do good. . . . Wherever I can do this best, that is where I want to go." For Naismith, that meant wherever he was standing in the real world, rather than limiting himself to a pulpit and congregation.

By the time Naismith arrived at Springfield College in 1891, the United States in which Naismith stood was, according to Stanford University historian Richard White, "transformed by immigration, urbanization, environmental crisis, political stalemate, new technologies . . . the creation of powerful corporations, income inequality, failures of governments, mounting class conflict, [and] increasing social, cultural, and religious diversity."

Naismith's writings do not indicate references to corporate monopolistic practices or oppressed workers. However, Robert B. Cheney, who edited *Basketball's Origins*—published in 1976 and lodged deep in the Springfield College archives—offers an intriguing analysis of what may have been Naismith's underlying thoughts on his creation.

In his semi-polemical preface, Cheney writes, "Naismith emerged from a turbulent adolescence with a desire to help other people live healthy and wholesome lives. This motive was instilled to some extent by what he perceived to be the deleterious effects of urbanization and industrialization." Cheney noted that like any great innovator, "Naismith perceived *'the trouble is not with the men but with the system that we are using.*'" Or, as Phil Jackson famously said, "Not only is there more to life than basketball, there's a lot more to basketball than basketball."

More than a game, it is the issue of systemic balance in American life where Cheney finds Naismith's invention to be of central and enduring value. Cheney proceeds to identify the historic transformation America was going through in 1891, when every rural worker faced traumatic upheaval. In Cheney's words, the American working man's life changed from one in which "no man was his superior; by his own decisions he determined his fate. His voice could be heard at the town meeting, and there his vote counted," to the "rude jolt" where that same man was "compressed into the city with all the problems of urban congestion. Now he works under the lights: crowded in a factory, exchanging his hours of labor for another man's money. His political voice is drowned out by loud machinery. He himself is lost under mammoth corporate skyscrapers. He is nameless, close to the bottom rung of the ladder of 'success' and wealth. Before, he shared his green acres with plants and animals; now he shares his grey block with the city, the nation, the world."

Cheney's interpretation that Naismith's creation was an unverbalized but intentional response to the Gilded Age is plausible and compelling. The YMCA itself was a direct response to the imbalanced life of the urban man cramped in factories. The game of basketball, born in the YMCA training school (Springfield College) and consistent with its mission, purported to restore balance to individual lives by creating a model for healthier relations between men. The game also provided a counterpoint to popular

American games of the era: the take-the-ball-and-run-past-or-over-others idea of football, or the celebration of individual performance that was the hallmark of baseball.

In *Basketball: Its Origin and Development,* Naismith acknowledged the rule changes that had evolved since the game's inception, but continued to emphasize basketball's five fundamental "unchanging factors," including this one: "No Man on either team shall be restricted from getting the ball at any time that it is in play."

That is an explicit anti-hierarchical principle if there ever was one.

THE DRAYMOND GREEN MODEL

Basketball teams have consistently shown that winning championships is about players adjusting themselves in order to achieve a collective end, regardless of what they may give up in individual attention, spectacle, adoration, or gratification. Watch Draymond Green, and witness a modern paragon of basketball's principle of balance between individual and collective.

On offense, Green sets screens for his sharpshooting teammates like Steph Curry. This leads to either Curry scoring or the defense adjusting, which results in space opening up elsewhere. If it's the latter case, then Curry can pass to another open teammate, or, if the defense has already adjusted to that, then Green adjusts to their adjustment by rolling off the screen to score himself. Green makes a thousand brilliant decisions every game that create space for others to flourish in a way that maximizes their abilities. Green can handle the ball and lead the break, or he can reliably fill the lane. Either way, he creates an advantage. He can score inside and relieve pressure on his perimeter teammates, or stretch the defense by hitting a three. He is a gifted and aware passer, always dishing the ball to the right person at the right time. And my god, can he rebound!

On defense, he stops things from happening. He can guard both perimeter and paint. He shuts down smaller players and confounds bigger opponents. He seamlessly switches off screens, which never results in a mismatch. Rather, it is his opponents constantly finding themselves caught in a mismatch, outmaneuvered, outmuscled, outhustled, outrun, outthought. He is often the first to grab a loose ball.

There is a whole game Draymond Green plays, and that game is the whole game of basketball. His stats aren't always eye-popping or even consistent. But there's more to it than that. The situational decisions he makes to create and close space for himself and others—a tipped ball, a deflection, the assist that leads to an assist, boxing out not for his own rebound but for a teammate's, the flustering of an opponent who has been stopped in his progress or denied the ball altogether—all of this adds up. There's more. The preventive message of his obvious physicality. Not just the screen he sets but his chosen angle of the screen—the way he cheats geometry for a little more space, increasing the odds of the shot converting. This is the subtle, often unseen, and measureless accumulation of a superior basketball IQ: an active, fluid, and deliberate understanding of creating invaluable balance.

Draymond Green is always balancing his individual actions with those of his teammates in order to achieve their collective goal: a championship, which his team has won four times. Green operates at such a high level of this basketball principle that even those who claim to know the game don't know what he knows. But that's not his problem.

"Most people will never learn the game of basketball," Green once told Seerat Sohi of Yahoo! Sports. "They think they know, but don't have a clue. It is what it is. I enjoy being one of the not-so-many people that actually know the game, as opposed to watching and thinking they can dissect it because they realize who hit a shot. It's fine."

Green says it's fine. His is an approach of individual responsibility in the service of collective gain. He says *I* will make sure *we* get that rebound, that the floor is properly spaced, that the pick is set, that the tipped ball goes in the right direction, that the offensive putback goes in, that the lane is filled. This way, Steph, Klay, and (once upon a time) KD (lately Jordan Poole and Andrew Wiggins) can maximize their talents and the whole team wins. In a healthy society—a society that prioritizes appropriate, goal-achieving balance between the individual and collective, a basketball-istic society—what Draymond does is valued at a premium, equal to what Steph, Klay, and KD do.

Green is not unhappy with his work. He does not see his lack of points as a less-than role. He sees what he does as equally valuable to what Curry does. They enrich each other. Green is happy for Curry, for Thompson, for Durant, only if they are also contributing toward the common goal. Each are stakeholders with different resources and core competencies, trying to appropriately balance their contributions, or give way to others to create the appropriate balance in order to get to the promised land.

In college, Michigan State coach Tom Izzo didn't see Green's potential until his senior year. But once he caught on to all Green had to offer, he tried to persuade NBA scouts to get on board, too. "I used to say this: I know all his intangibles don't add up," Izzo told Yahoo! Sports. "You can tell me all the things he can't do, but I'm gonna tell you all the things he can do: whatever it takes to win."

The Warriors drafted Green in the second round, and he sat on the bench until David Lee got hurt. Once he came in, though, the Warriors won sixteen of their next eighteen games. And Green never came back out. Three championships and a Defensive Player of the Year award later, Green's done arguing. And the basketball world is starting to listen.

In 2021, Seerat Sohi, an insightful NBA reporter based in Toronto who had joined Yahoo! Sports in 2018, filed a Draymond Green trend analysis: "The Draymond Generation: Why Undersized Bruisers Are Ideal in Today's NBA." Look at them all: Tony Allen, Patrick Beverley, Grant Tillman, Luguentz Dort, Grant Williams, and Eric Paschall. Now every GM wants a Draymond Green. But, as one NBA scout put it, "Draymonds don't grow on trees." Their value now is at a premium.

In 2020, NBA player Spencer Dinwiddie tried to make the case for his own potential value to a Brooklyn Nets team stacked with superstars Kevin Durant, James Harden, and Kyrie Irving. He said at a press conference that he'd like to be "the Draymond Green, the glue." Describing his balancing effect as "sometimes, I get ten boards, sometimes I get ten assists. Sometimes, I score a little bit . . . I'd be blessed to fill that role this year and try to win a championship."

Draymond Green is the balance beam on which the other elements can perform their cartwheels. Without his structural support, they fall off. Green widens that beam, understanding what is needed when and for whom. Inside basketball they know: with a player like him on your team, perfectly balancing the individual and the collective, you stand to win championships.

MR. THUNDER

A basketball-istic society understands acts of balance between individual and collective not only as acts in service of the highest good, but as goodness itself. As Sam Anderson laid out in *Boom Town,* his book about the insane creation of Oklahoma City, valuing those acts as such can be the difference between democracy and anarchy.

Oklahoma City was founded in a moment of sheer human chaos, the Land Run of 1889, where after a whistle blow thousands were allowed to run into the demarcated city limits and claim property. Anderson explained that the Land Run was "unique in human history. A place has never started like this before. You had [a] chaotic pile-up of people claiming plots all over what is now downtown Oklahoma City. The place went from zero people to 10,000 residents in a few hours and the next day everybody kind of woke up and looked around and it was like, 'What is this place?! How are we going to live here?' There's no roads, there's no anything. It's just a bunch of tents next to each other. So, they had to figure it out from there and kind of make it up."

From then until now, OKC has been trying to figure out its individual-collective balance. Anderson looked at how the new city was "like a laboratory for the unavoidable American problems. What does an individual gain, and what do they lose, when they become assimilated into the group? How does something messy as a mass of people ever organize itself into a functional system?"

His prism to explain that balance was the city's eventual landing of their sole professional sports franchise, the Oklahoma City Thunder. Their existence in the city, Anderson wrote, was no small thing: "The new basketball team [was] entangled in every other aspect of the place—its politics, its history, its economics, its weather. . . . Inextricable . . . from the fundamental tensions in the DNA of democracy itself."

Anderson was asked in our NYU class if the Land Run might be equated to the first-ever civic pick-up game in history. "That's a good one!" he chuckled. "I haven't heard that before. I've heard all the Oklahoma jokes, but that's good! Civic pick-up game: yeah, that's a good way to think about it."

"Everything I could ever want to say about anything was somehow in the Oklahoma City Thunder; in this mixture of weirdo personalities and super-charged talent," he explained to our class. "All working together, but also kind of pulling against each other in certain interesting ways. And to see if and how that could possibly work just struck me as a perfect test of humans trying to coordinate and make each other better, dealing with all the little obstacles that can get in the way of that, and that of course instantly—as your class teaches—becomes [like] a metaphor for all of human society."

What Anderson showed brilliantly was that society's struggle to attain productive, functional, pleasing balance is the essence of what happens on a basketball court. "Balance is so precarious," he told us, and then turned to his co-speaker, retired OKC player Nick Collison. "Nick was the human embodiment of balance."

Collison deflected credit, telling the students: "Well, you know, those guys [Kevin Durant, Russell Westbrook, James Harden] came in three staggered years. Kevin was the first one and was incredibly talented, but all those guys were . . . there was a lot of process. I looked at it like I was trying to play my role, do my job, and try to do my best to help these young guys out, and we just kind of built it each day in practice, went through the highs and the lows and learned a lot. I was always trying to just help out when I could, do my job on the court, things like that."

Anderson had to cut in: "Nick is being humble. I mean, what you had on that team was this absolute torrent of offensive firepower. You had one of the greatest scorers in the history of human beings in Kevin Durant, and a second one in James Harden, and then you had Russell Westbrook, who was just his own thing, who wants the ball at all times and wants to dunk on every defender on the floor and his own teammates probably, too. So you need a guy like Nick who is the consummate balancer. If you watch a highlight video of Nick, this is what you're going to see: Nick taking charges, Nick's face bleeding, Nick diving for loose balls, Nick boxing people out and getting defensive rebounds, playing tough post defense, and my favorite Nick thing, which is throwing backdoor passes. Every game, Harden, Durant, Westbrook would get these easy dunks from just backdoor cutting; when a guy wasn't expecting it, Nick hits them perfectly in stride with a bounce pass.

"He's setting screens, he's doing all the things that are not scoring in a basketball game that you can do, and he's doing all that happily."

Collison knew how to balance his teammates, and because of that OKC—with Durant, Westbrook, and Harden—made its only trip in franchise history to the NBA finals in 2012. Collison holds another "only" for the franchise. *He is the only retired OKC Thunder jersey.* Not Westbrook or Durant. And he earned that highest honor while amassing the following per-game stats: 5.9 points, 5.2 rebounds, 1.0 assists. It's not that Nick Collison wasn't a scorer. He could score. He was the leading scorer on a University of Kansas team that made two consecutive trips to the NCAA Final Four. He left college as the Big 12 scoring champ. But Collison looked around and saw one ball, four other players on the floor with him, and one collective goal.

"I remember talking to him about this in our first conversation," Anderson shared with the class. "About sacrificing for the good of a group; that all those three superstars would have to do it in certain ways. And Nick was like, 'Okay, I'm not a super elite scorer here so I'm going to be elite at everything else . . . I'm going to be the plus/minus king of the NBA.'" That's why they value Nick Collison. That's why he—and no one else—will be forever known in OKC as "Mr. Thunder."

A student followed up, asking: "At this moment of reset and reimagining in American and global society, are there principles for us to apply from your study of Oklahoma City through the lens of basketball?"

"Yeah," Anderson replied. "Something we should understand is that balance and health are synonyms or overlapping concepts. Civic health, stability, virtue—all of these positive things are not just passive elements that survive by themselves; they're active parts of a process. So, I think daily goodness, as modest or humble or as unexciting as it sometimes seems . . . and balance is a heroic endeavor. Nick Collison—part of the reason he's so beloved in

Oklahoma City and the NBA, in general, among basketball fans, is because we saw him doing that incredible grind. Day-to-day, minute-to-minute on the court grind, not for the glory of pouring in buckets and getting stats, but for this virtue of goodness and balance and winning, and keeping his community together." He looked over at Collison, "Maybe Nick is embarrassed right now, and I'm overstating it, but really I think that's what appeals; there's such a dignity, just a goodness in it. And I think what I would love people to learn and think about and practice is, to just bring that kind of goodness to your world and your community, and don't expect that it just happens automatically. It is a daily grind and there will be forces that oppose it on every side and I think that's what we've seen in America, where many thought 'Oh, we have a fine, stable status quo. Yeah there are malevolent actors, but it'll all get worked out in the end.' But it doesn't. Without a positive force of goodness, of balance, it just doesn't."

Finally, a student asked Anderson whether he made anything of Oklahoma City being founded and basketball being invented at almost the same time. Just a coincidence, or was there something more there?

"Really?" he exclaimed in surprise. "Had I known I would have done something with that."

THE GILDED AGE REDUX

History is repeating itself, and that's not a good thing. The innovators of the first Gilded Age promised more productivity and a better life for all, but it really only benefited the select few at the top. The same exact thing is now happening in the second Gilded Age, in which we currently live. In the first Gilded Age, technological advances took ownership of a person's day and their means of production; work became separated from home. Today's Gilded Age separates work from people and people from people. In both Gilded Ages, the advocates of new technology promised more democratization, more convenience, and a better quality of life for everyone. But just like before, technology only delivers a better life for the few. And those few cling to their dominance, walling off the rest of society.

When Naismith sat at his desk and thought up basketball in 1891, the country was malfunctioning socially, politically, and economically. In his 2017 history of this era, *The Republic for Which It Stands,* Richard White writes: "The Gilded Age was corrupt.... Corruption suffused government and the economy."

Politicians bestowed lavish favors to businesses in scandal after scandal. Major government contracts and subsidies went to giant private corporations. Businessmen amassed wealth on a scale never before seen in American history. Later dubbed robber barons, these titans of industry were more rapacious monopolists than innovative entrepreneurs; they were unscrupulous speculators and corporate buccaneers who took advantage of the system wherever and however they could.

Like now, the tech barons of the late 1800s claimed these imbalances were temporary; they were for the good of transforming the United States into a more unified and prosperous country. The truth, however, of what Americans were experiencing in their everyday lives did not match the promise of industry leaders. Instead of joyful societal change, America erupted in angry societal backlash—in streets, in the courts, in the legislatures. Tech titans and monopolists had not created a better life for all. The result of the first Gilded Age, the age of unchecked imbalance, was a nation torn apart, its institutions distorted and its social fabric shredded.

According to Professor White, divisions ran deep throughout the United States: "Political parties were less about ideology but tapped deeper loyalties that arose out of the Civil War and religious, ethnic, and sectional identities."

Today, as in Naismith's time, we are experiencing one of the greatest imbalances in wealth in human history. The tension is global. People have dared to march against oppressive economic imbalance all over the world, from Beirut to Belarus. In 2020, the Oscar for best picture went to *Parasite,* a nightmarish rendering of South Korean economic inequality. It became the first foreign-language film to take Hollywood's top prize. And in late 2021, the South Korean–produced television series *Squid Game,* inspired by the real-life problems of spiraling debt, became the top Netflix show of all time, watched internationally in nineteen different languages. When it comes to crushing debt and the wealth gap, everybody around the world is speaking the same language. The balance is way off.

In the United States, the similarities between the socio-economic imbalances of the late 1800s and the present day are impossible to miss. The variety of ways to measure wealth inequality are as creative as they are numerous. But they're all deeply troubling.

Oxfam's 2019 report states that 162 billionaires own and control half the wealth of all of humanity. Across the globe, 2,153 billionaires hold more combined wealth than 4.6 billion people—or 60 percent of the world's population.

The Bloomberg Billionaire Index (2021) reports that due to extraordinary top-of-the-pyramid gains during the pandemic, there are now five "centibillionaires" (Bernard Arnault, Mark

Zuckerberg, Bill Gates, Elon Musk, and Jeff Bezos), individuals whose net worth exceeded $100 billion.

The 2022 World Inequality Report stunningly reveals that "the poorest half of the global population barely owns any wealth at all, possessing just 2% of the total" while "the richest 10% of the global population own 76% of all wealth." According to the report, global billionaires increased their share of global wealth in 2021 from 2% to 3.5%, the steepest increase on record.

Seeing a world unmoved by dramatic and unprecedented statistical measures, Oxfam released a report ahead of the May 2022 Davos World Economic Forum entitled "Inequality Kills." Oxfam International Executive Director Winnie Byanyima plainly told the Associated Press, that extreme global wealth inequality is quite simply and unacceptably "out of control."

The Upswing, by Harvard professor Robert D. Putnam and social entrepreneur Shaylyn Romney Garrett, meticulously analyzes American life across multiple fields of study from the first Gilded Age to the second. Putnam and Garrett sum it up like this: "The story of the American experiment in the twentieth century is one of a long upswing toward increasing solidarity, followed by a steep downturn into increasing individualism. From 'I' to 'we' and back again to 'I.'" The authors share one particularly telling illustration of how America's culture of self-centeredness took over the past two generations: the frequency of the pronoun *I* in American books *doubled* between 1965 and 2008.

Which takes us to the 2020s, the era of "late capitalism": a period of hyper-economic, advancement-focused individualism guided by the popular expression "You do you." And how's that working out for everybody?

How Basketball Can Save the World

The United States seems to be suffering greatly from an imbalance of priorities. We are so preoccupied with material success that we are witnessing a new social malady known as workism. Daniel Markovits's *The Meritocracy Trap* asks two questions that get to the heart of the problem. What, exactly, are we working toward? And why are we working so hard that we can't even enjoy what we manage to achieve?

Unmoored from any reasonable balance between individual and collective interests, late capitalism from the United States to Denmark to southern Europe to East Asia has become a global existential crisis. It's even stifling human reproduction.

Anna Louie Sussman wrote in a data-rich, upsetting 2019 *New York Times* Sunday Review cover story, "The End of Babies," that "around the world, economic, social and environmental conditions function as a diffuse, barely perceptible contraceptive." The culprit, according to Sussman: "'late capitalism'—that is, not just the economic system, but all its attendant inequalities, indignities, opportunities and absurdities—has become hostile to reproduction." Intentional or not, she sees it as "a profound failure: of employers and governments to make parenting and work compatible; of our collective ability to solve the climate crisis so that children seem a rational prospect; of our increasingly unequal global economy." Late capitalism makes "having fewer children … less a choice than the poignant consequence."

We seem to have created a society that prizes individual advancement over continuation of the species. This cannot logically be seen as a reasonable balance of individual and collective when the end result is extinction.

By the start of 2022, so many were fed up with the absence of meaning that in search of a new work-life balance, the so-called Great Resignation resulted in over 25 million voluntarily leaving the workforce.

Basketball was James Naismith's articulation of his view of the appropriate balance of wealth and purpose. As Robert B. Cheney noted, Naismith looked at his incorrigibles as he looked at the entire polarized spectrum of American society: *The trouble is not with the men but with the system that we are using.* The game was Naismith's *new* idea of how the world ought to work—in his Springfield College gym and everywhere else.

The game was lighting the way again in the summer of 2020. Amid the paralyzing Covid-19 pandemic, Sam Anderson, one of the few reporters who got access to the NBA bubble, noted that what he was witnessing at that time was a national treasure: one of the only functioning institutions in the United States during that summer of chaos and conflict. And as he focused on the game and its players in a piece for *The New York Times Magazine,* he took a long view. "They remind me that basketball is not simply a game: It is a nearly mystical blend of individual and collective excellence— one of America's great cultural inventions."

Draymond Green stands as a defiant, proud new understanding of the way forward. Basketball values the balancer as much as the scorer. A basketball inspired society would value everyone in the chain—not just the innovator-entrepreneur, the tech titan, the famous influencer. The dignity in a basketball-istic society is not in the most clicks or the most likes. The dignity is in the work, the individual commitment to collective contribution, to the end point—even if unseen. Draymond Green represents the new vision for the kind of societal actor that creates appropriate balance of individual and collective and a society that highly values those actions.

If we do not learn from the past, we are surely condemned to repeat it—or three-peat it. How do we emerge from this second Gilded Age and avoid a third one?

Professor Richard White's masterwork, written before the pandemic and included in *The Oxford History of the United States,* said the Gilded Age had been typically treated as "flyover territory in American scholarship" and not taken seriously for its lasting impact. In contrast, his work shows clearly that that period in American history not only has had profound national formative impact but has rippled into national lessons unlearned and mistakes being repeated today. And in that crucial era, a solution, a pebble in the pond—basketball—may have been the talisman engraved in our world teaching us how to break free from a damaging historic cycle.

OPEN RUN = OPEN DEMOCRACY

Open run is a phrase commonly used to describe a period of time in which anyone can come to a designated court and play pick-up basketball. It also operates a lot like the idea of open democracy. Both open run and open democracy offer systems of governance transparently dedicated to balancing the individual and collective and getting that balance right.

Anyone can show up to a public court to play pick-up basketball. And when you do—when you enter an open run—it's essentially a random deliberative group thrown together for a common good. Each individual in the group serves no party, no tribe—only the game and the team's collective aim.

In that process, each must acknowledge the others and what each brings. This involves communicating and understanding and accommodating and balancing. It involves realizing some are great scorers, some do the other stuff like rebound or play defense well, while others set screens—but all count, all are valued in the playing process, and all arrive to the game in the same way. There are no scouts, no coaches, no gatekeepers, no recruitment, no campaign fund, no preestablished status requirement—just equally valued citizenship, like in an open democracy.

In open democracy, a transformative shared governance idea expressed by Hélène Landemore in her book *Open Democracy,* people serve in government to represent who they are, not a tribe or party. Like five people joined together on a team in open run, open democracy is a random deliberative group of people who jointly contribute and solve the challenge of what is before them.

"Democracy is a living ideal," says Landemore, currently a professor of political science at Yale, where she has been teaching since 2009. "American democracy started over two centuries ago as a minimalistic sense of that ideal." Now, she says, we are decidedly somewhere else.

Explaining it to Ezra Klein of *The New York Times* in a podcast, Landemore said, "We have been privileging the idea of people's *consent* to power over that of people's *exercise* of power. People want more authentic control. We ought to center people's rights, not institutions or offices."

She's not arguing for no democracy, but something "more of a democracy and less of a republic." She's arguing for a basketballistic rebalancing of the individual and collective. In Landemore's open democracy, anyone and everyone can be chosen to serve. It works like jury duty. Your number comes up and you are randomly selected to serve for a fixed term with others also randomly selected. Then the randomly selected public servants all assemble together to listen, learn, deliberate, legislate, and solve the people's problems. When your term is up, you go back to your life and others are randomly chosen to replace you. No more "elections."

Landemore's premise is that the best intelligence is a function of diversity. Group diversity, not the individual intelligence of group members, produces a better outcome. Elections in American representative democracy, she argues, have not produced a diverse body of representation and therefore are not even close to a representation of the people's will. This is especially true in the Senate, but it also holds in the larger House of Representatives.

Landemore says our current elections reinforce prevailing societal prejudices favoring the tall, eloquent, white, male, charismatic, and loud—and, of course, the wealthy. That's not who we all are. That's not who most of us are. Elections separate us and systemically close off the shy, ordinary, weak, inarticulate, and invisible. Why should the latter not have any power to shape how we are ruled? The reason our current representative democracy produces bad results for us is because the representatives are not at all *us*.

How can these elected officials possibly understand regular people when there is not one among them?

Open democracy is not about representing party or partisanship. There are no campaign contributions. In open democracy those who are randomly selected to serve reflect the true range of public interest. They look like what we are. The randomly selected body of public servants honestly reflects the variety of goals and needs that matter to the broad and diverse *us*, not the narrowly funneled, homogenous, inaccurate elected representation the current system produces. "The thing about random selection," Landemore told *The New Yorker,* "is they don't represent me, my vote or my affiliated interest necessarily but together, with others randomly selected they represent a more completely informing cross-section of many voices that compose the country."

Landemore calls her governing bodies "mini-publics" comprising anywhere from 150 to one thousand people. The key principles are diverse groups, random selection, deliberation, crowd-sourced responses and input, and porous information coming in and out.

"There's still room for experts—we're not getting rid of all the time-saving and professionalization that the governmental system already has," said Landemore. "It's just that at the crucial junctures—the moments of decision-making and agenda-setting—we make sure that there's an openness to citizens. The point is to let the system breathe."

Landemore insists we must trust ourselves, trust *us,* as a societal safety measure to do the right things and keep each other in check—rather than relying on a competing, simplistic, and compromised two-party system. For her, two-party system elections every four years have manifestly not been a clear or complete expression of people's will. With open democracy we won't miss the unheard arguments. Even though Landemore concedes that there's "more noise and more mess" this way, aren't we worth it?

In open democracy, members of the mini-publics have an incentive to respect, educate, and listen—not to serve party and special interests. It's like a pick-up game, where the randomly formed team together serves the interests of the game they're trying to win. In order to succeed together, they must balance their interests.

According to Landemore, today's homogeneous, privileged elected officials arrive at their office with a sense of entitlement, whereas randomly selected representatives come in with a humility to serve as best they can. Like a pick-up game, a selfish and self-important individual player will quickly lose the trust and cooperation of their teammates. You are judged in a pick-up game by your respect of team and game (your fellow citizens and societal needs), and your respect of the overall institution of that local court's custom (the welfare of the country and commitment to true democracy)—not self-centered, single-issue-interested, self-aggrandizement.

When you look at the homogenous social, economic, physical profiles of today's elected officials, it is akin to having a team of only high scorers. There are no balancers, no Draymond Greens. If you only have a group of high scorers, elected officials with exclusive perspectives, you're not able to solve problems for the diverse collective, for the team. On an entitled team of ball hogs, who sets the picks, gets the rebounds, and dives for loose balls? Nothing will really get done.

The 1977 Portland Trail blazers, an eclectic open democracy-esque assembly of Bill Walton, Maurice Lucas, Bobby Gross, Dave Twardzik, Lionel Hollins, and Johnny Davis, found the right answers together for a surprising (to most) 4–2 NBA title over the stacked, star-studded Philadelphia 76ers: Julius Erving, George McGinnis, Lloyd (World B.) Free, Doug Collins, Bobby Jones, and Darryl Dawkins.

The 2004 Detroit Pistons—an open democracy of Ben Wallace, Chauncey Billups, Richard Hamilton, Rasheed Wallace, and Tayshaun Prince—governed over the Los Angeles Lakers, who had storied incumbents Shaquille O'Neal, Kobe Bryant, Gary Payton, Karl Malone, and Derek Fisher, achieving a stunning 4–1 NBA title.

Gregg Popovich and Tim Duncan came together at the San Antonio Spurs in 1997 and stayed together for nineteen years, contending for winning the NBA championship five times across three different decades. That team culture reflected values of Landemore's open democracy; it encouraged "people's *consent* to power over people's *exercise* of power" and prized diversity (not individual stardom) for the best results. Spurs players and coaches came from all over the world—including the NBA's first female coach, Becky Hammon. Duncan and other core members of the Spurs made the choice year after year to make less individual money through free agency in favor of staying together. "These guys have given up real money with every new contract to stay together," Popovich told *The New York Times*'s Harvey Araton. "They care about quality of life, and it falls into the way they play." Their care for quality of life and for each other translated into winning championships on the court, which is about adjusting yourself in order to achieve the collective end, regardless of what you may give up as an individual. The ultimate embodiment of the Spurs ethos was Duncan—a first-ballot Hall of Famer, five-time NBA champion, two-time NBA MVP, and fifteen-time All-Star—whose selfless devotion to team objectives and doing the basic little things (ergo his nickname, "the Big Fundamental") led the media to call his play (and his team's play) "boring." What's so boring about five NBA titles?

In basketball your individual title or status does not matter. It's the way you represent the entire body politic.

In open run, as in open democracy, every player of every kind of contribution in the randomly formed group is valued no more and no less than every other. And if you've ever participated in some open run, you know that it promotes prosocial, improved-citizenship behaviors long after you've left the court, as it would for participants in open democracy. This prosocial effect, Landemore explains, happens because "for some period of their lives, they'd be forced to learn the political process from the inside, compelled to think through influential political decisions in collaboration with random Americans who disagree." The experience stays with you.

The same thing happens when you play pick-up with someone, a stranger, and then a week or a month later you see them on the street, in a deli, or at a laundromat, and you give each other a nod. There's a higher level of understanding, of trust, because you bonded while experiencing the basketball principle of balancing individual and collective, together in action, and you know it can be done.

"Once you force people into a context where they have to get past the posturing and commitment to ideas, where they have to address real-life problems with people like them—even if they think differently—you solve a lot of issues," Landemore explained. That's exactly like joining a random five to play pick-up. Work well together, and the winner stays on. And when your term is up, like in a pick-up game, it's about "Who's got next?"

STEVE NASH THEORY

At the beginning of the 2005–06 NBA season, Steve Nash let it slip in a *New York Times* interview with Liz Robbins that he was reading *The Communist Manifesto* and the autobiography of Che Guevara. In a November 2005 *Esquire* profile titled "The Karl

Marx of the Hardwood," Chuck Klosterman wrote that "Nash is the greatest socialist in contemporary athletics." In May 2006, for an NPR piece, "Steve Nash: Basketball's Selfless Socialist," Nihar Patel brought in University of Chicago economics professor John Huizinga, who thought the characterization "sits pretty well with the way Steve wants to play basketball. He wants everybody to share, and it's the glory of the team that needs to be celebrated."

For Nash, basketball is neither Marxist, socialist, nor communist. "It's more like gambling," he said. "When you gamble, you try to give yourself the best possible odds of success. My goal is to increase the odds of success for each player on the floor, but without negating the odds of success for everyone else in the process." The results of who gives what and who gets what—*from each according to his ability, to each according to his needs*—"sometimes that's tangible, and sometimes that's intangible."

The team and individual results of that 2005–06 season: Nash's Phoenix Suns won the Pacific Division and advanced to the Western Conference finals, where they lost to the Dallas Mavericks. The Suns were the league's highest-scoring team, yet they didn't have a single player among the league's fifteen highest individual scorers. Steve Nash ranked thirty-third in scoring, but first in assists, and went on to earn his second straight league MVP award.

Fifteen years later, another Phoenix Suns point guard, Chris Paul, led his record fourth team to their most wins ever in a regular season: 2007–08: New Orleans Hornets (56-26), 2013–14: Clippers (57-25), 2017–18: Rockets (65-17), 2021–22: Suns (64-18). Three of those four years he led the league in assists—how much he gave the ball to others. Two of those four years he led the league in steals—the work he did to return the ball to his team. In none of those years was he even close to the top ten in scoring. In a 2021 post-playoff-game interview on TNT, Shaquille O'Neal was curious how Paul determines individual-collective balance: "We know you're a traditional point guard but at what time do you say to yourself, 'I'm not looking to get other guys involved, I have to take over this game'?" Paul responded, "I try to feel the game out. I know who I am. I can score. *I can score.* But being in my position, you know you need your teammates. You try to get them involved. But I know *when* it's time, I know what I can do." Just because you can, doesn't mean you should. Knowing when to strike the balance is the key.

While both Nash and Paul are talking about balancing basketball teams, their overriding consciousness of balancing individual and collective interests applies well to correcting rampant societal imbalances like wealth, health, housing, and food security.

Ultimately, like Draymond Green, this balance is about valuing things we didn't used to value. Like Nick Collison and Oklahoma City, it's about recognizing the commitment to achieving the right balance as a highest societal value. And thus, by assigning new values we arrive at new measures, where an economy is not all there is to a society.

When asked about the growth of his invention and his lack of financial equity in it, James Naismith responded without hesitation: "Thousands of times, especially in the last few years, I have been asked whether I ever got anything out of basketball. To answer this question, I can only smile. It would be impossible for me to explain my feelings to a great mass of people who ask this question, as my pay has not been in dollars but in the satisfaction of giving something to the world that is a benefit to masses of people."

PRINCIPLE

3

BALANCE OF FORCE AND SKILL

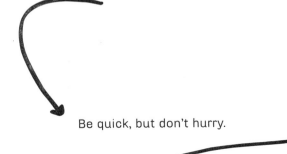

Be quick, but don't hurry.

—John Wooden, the "Wizard of Westwood,"
a record ten-time NCAA championship coach

Naismith wanted to create a game that was less violent and thus less reliant on force. His innovative solution was to rotate the goal horizontally and elevate it. This novel placement required a basketball shot to have an arc, compelling athletes to use a new skill set that highlighted touch and accuracy along with speed and strength. Other popular games with goals—soccer, hockey, rugby, football, baseball—mostly require sheer power or speed to score. If you push the object past or through your opponent's defense, you have successfully achieved your objective: point, goal, strike, out, touchdown. In Naismith's new game, force, strength, and speed still mattered, but you had to balance them with skill and finesse.

Naismith had worked as a lumberjack and knew about physicality. He had also been to divinity school and knew of reason and spirituality. He liked both parts of himself and was drawn to Springfield College Director Luther Gulick's three-sided vision of a Muscular Christianity—mind, body, and spirit—built into the purpose of the YMCA. Naismith not only bought fully into Gulick's triangle of development, but he was especially interested in developing the balance of those elements. After all, the YMCA triangle was equilateral. Mind, body, and spirit were given all the same value.

By taking the "muscular" in Muscular Christianity and balancing it with skill, Naismith forged a new, nuanced sport and made a game for all humanity.

NOBODY ROOTS FOR GOLIATH

Naismith envisioned his game favoring "the tall, agile, graceful and expert athlete . . . rather than the massive muscular man," so he would likely be surprised to see that the modern NBA is packed with a superhuman combination of both. But when Wilt Chamberlain entered the game in the early 1950s, he was seen as an oddity in those quaint angular days. And he was incredibly uncomfortable with how others viewed his size. He stood 7 foot 1 and was also strong, carrying three hundred pounds of proportional, lean muscle. People could not see past his size, however, which bothered him to no end. He hated the nickname "Wilt the Stilt" because it made him sound freakish, preferring the more cuddly "Big Dipper." And because he was so much bigger than the other players, it was easy to root against him. Which made things even worse for Wilt, because he felt misunderstood.

That's not how he saw himself. "Nobody roots for Goliath," Wilt used to say. But hidden inside Wilt's Goliath-like body was a clever, skillful, creative David. He wanted to show people he could balance force and skill. Yet the man had responsibilities. "I thought if I didn't score fifty," Chamberlain said, "I would be letting my team down." That just added to the negative Goliath image, and people called him selfish.

To prove them wrong, he shifted focus for the 1968 season and led the NBA in total assists. No other positional center has ever done that. During that same season, after his coach with the 76ers, Alex Hannum, hinted maybe he couldn't score like he used to, Chamberlain went on to drop sixty-eight, forty-seven, and fifty-three points over his next three games, just to prove that he could.

Throughout his NBA career, he tried to prove his versatility in other ways, setting jaw-dropping records in the process. It took fifty years before Russell Westbrook broke Chamberlain's records of nine consecutive triple-doubles and matched Wilt's 20/20/20 triple-double (twenty-two points, twenty-five rebounds, twenty-one assists).

In college at Kansas, Wilt developed a fadeaway jump shot, simply to show people that a 7-foot-1 player could have finesse. He was well coordinated and would have been an excellent player even if he had been a half-foot shorter. His athletic prowess crossed over into other sports. At Kansas, he shot-putted fifty-six feet, triple-jumped more than fifty feet, and won the Big Eight Conference high-jump championship three straight years. After retirement from the NBA, Wilt was an avid volleyball player and early proponent for a professional league in that sport.

Fearsomely strong and taller than most everyone, he was told that all he had to do was dunk. Yet Wilt sought to prove he possessed a light touch. He became one of the first (if not *the* first) players to execute the dainty finger-roll, rather than bulldozing his way to the rim.

The one thing they say Wilt couldn't do well was shoot free throws. His coach Alex Hannum had a theory that the poor foul shooting was because Wilt was uncomfortable in his own skin and hated standing alone on the foul line. But he couldn't have been that bad, because the night he scored one hundred points, he went twenty-eight for thirty-two from the line.

In the last two regular season games of his career, Wilt sent a message about his ability to do whatever he pleased on the court—particularly to critics who thought his only interest was in points and power. He decided not to score at all. On March 27, 1973, Chamberlain scored *zero* points. He played forty-six minutes without taking a single field goal or free throw. In the Lakers' next game, the last of his regular season career, Wilt scored one point, going one for two from the foul line. It's not that he couldn't score anymore. In the three games prior, Chamberlain produced All-Star numbers. March 21, 1973: nineteen points, twenty rebounds, and seven assists, on eight-for-nine shooting. March 23, 1973: nineteen points, twenty-four rebounds, and seven assists, on eight-for-eight shooting. March 25, 1973: twenty points, twenty rebounds, and three assists, on eight-for-eight shooting.

It's tempting to believe that Wilt scored zero points on purpose. He was so much more talented than everyone else, he'd create statistical milestones to reach just to keep himself amused. Ever sensitive to criticism, he relished showing up those who critiqued his perceived shortcomings. To me, Chamberlain's biblical Goliath characterization would be more accurately described as Hellenic.

One envisions Chamberlain in those days like a Greek god bored with mere mortals—but at the same time envious of them and wishing for their approval. And like a protagonist in a Greek tragedy, he had a *hamartia*—a fatal flaw—which was the frustration of not being seen for who he really was. He was feared instead of revered. He was trapped by his godlike powers and tortured by his human psychology and sensitive ego.

Balance of Force and Skill

It wasn't all in Wilt's head. People really did root against Goliath, and the bias against him was stunning. In the 1961–62 season, Chamberlain averaged a staggering, unfathomable 50.4 points per game—an NBA record that will never be beaten. He also pulled down a mammoth 25.7 rebounds per game. He played in all eighty games, every minute of the season, including overtimes, so he averaged an *over* regulation, all-time record of 48.5 minutes per game. *And yet, he somehow didn't win the MVP.*

And so, when Goliath met David—in the guise of Bill Russell—Chamberlain, like the hero of a Greek tragedy, succumbed to his fatal flaw. Of their eight playoff meetings, Russell's teams won seven.

This, of course, was the outcome Americans wanted. Goliath lost. While Russell was not exactly David—he was 6-foot-9 and weighed 220 pounds—Chamberlain made Russell seem puny. People rooted for Russell. Nobody pulled for Wilt. When Russell's team won, it was a validation for underdogs everywhere. But was Wilt giving the people what they wanted, too? After all, his record fifty-five-rebound game came against the Celtics and Russell in the Boston Garden. . . .

Every mythic story has its lesson. That David can beat Goliath is one lesson. The other lesson is that maybe Goliath is misunderstood. Maybe we didn't see just how far ahead Wilt was. Maybe we didn't appreciate that Wilt's challenge was not about Goliath beating David, but about Goliath displaying the balance of both David *and* Goliath in a narrow-minded world that only saw these two poles of a binary human potential. Wilt Chamberlain embodied the way forward for human and athletic progress, an enlightened management of our talents, abilities, and potential across the spectrum of power and finesse.

On the basketball court, Chamberlain showed a playing style that was unimaginably ahead of his time. He was the predecessor to Nowitzki, Olajuwon, Garnett, Ilgauskas, Embiid. Big men doing it all are everywhere now. In 2021, the doughy, deceptively multifaceted 6-foot-11 Nikola Jokić joined Chamberlain as one of the only two centers to reach fifty career triple-doubles. That year Jokić was awarded league MVP. The following year, Jokić became the first NBA player ever to register 2,000 points, 1,000 rebounds, and 500 assists in a season. He won league MVP again. The modern NBA looks more and more like the old Wilt Chamberlain.

In debates about the greatest basketball player ever, Michael Jordan often gets the vote, but if Wilt had played in the age of nationally televised games, ESPN, and DVR, there would be no contest. Just look at his stats:

Most points, single game: 100

Most rebounds, single game: 55

Highest scoring average, single season: 50.4 (led the NBA seven times)

Highest rebounding average, single season: 27.2 (led the NBA eleven times)

Highest minutes per game, single season: 48.5

First player to shoot over 50 percent from the field, single season

Retired as the NBA's career leader in points and rebounds

He was the total package. As Bernie Lincicome wrote in a *Chicago Tribune* obituary for Chamberlain in October 1999: "If the question is who is the next Jordan, it implies that there will be one. But there shall never be another Wilt." Gods never stay on earth for that long. Wilt Chamberlain ascended back to Olympus, passing away at the young age of sixty-three.

In his day, Chamberlain was something else. He tried to demonstrate the fullest example of the balance of force and skill that the game of basketball requires. There was nobody like him, so it was hard for him to find acceptance. Like in children's fables, Wilt was the classic misunderstood giant, living in a small-minded world of those who were unable to see past his size and strength and appreciate the full range of his gifts.

GOLIATH'S EPILOGUE

Mark Eaton, a 7-foot-4 UCLA basketball player, was thinking he might be facing the end of his career. He tells the story on his YouTube channel: "There I was, standing on the sidelines, huffing and puffing, feeling sorry for myself and thinking, man maybe I just can't play at this level." He was working out with other UCLA players in a Bel Air gym, hoping to make the NBA but failing miserably. He didn't have much besides his height to entice scouts. In his senior year in 1982, Eaton averaged only 1.3 points, two rebounds, and 3.7 minutes per game in just eleven appearances. Those numbers were 50 percent *down* from the year before. Things were moving in the wrong direction. And there he was, at one of the highest-level pick-up games in Los Angeles, chasing faster, more skilled players all over the court. Lunging, missing, getting faked out. He couldn't keep up.

At that moment, bent over, hands tugging at the edges of his shorts, trying to catch his breath, he felt somebody else's hand set down on his shoulder. It was Wilt Chamberlain, now five years in retirement. Goliath to Goliath, Chamberlain told him, "First of all, you are never going to catch that little man. I've been watching you the past few days. You've got size and you've got skills. But you're using it all wrong."

Chamberlain walked Eaton back onto the court and placed him in front of the basket, facing out toward the foul line. Wilt pointed to the rim.

"Your job is to stop players from getting here. Your job is to make them miss, get the rebound, get it to a little guy, watch them score, then jog up to half court and see what else is going on. That's it." And with that, Wilt Chamberlain left the gym.

After retiring from a twelve-year NBA career, Mark Eaton made his living as a motivational speaker. In his talks, he cited that five-minute conversation with Wilt Chamberlain as the turning point in his life. "That was the moment I stopped running around trying to do everything, and instead balanced what I did and what I had to do."

That year, the Utah Jazz drafted Eaton solely because of his height. He was one of the last to get the call—fourth round, seventy-second pick overall. Four years later, the guy who couldn't get off the bench at UCLA, who was now armed with Chamberlain's wisdom, broke the NBA record for most blocked shots in a season. An All-Star in 1989, he was named NBA Defensive Player of the Year twice, led the league in blocked shots for four seasons and still owns the career mark for most blocks per game. The Utah Jazz retired his jersey, number 53, in 1995.

Wilt didn't see a 7-foot-4 giant. He saw a basketball player with a range of potential, relevance, and contribution *if* that range was seen and appreciated. Wilt knew about that. He knew about the range of force and skill in a body perceived as being only capable of one of the two. Wilt helped Mark Eaton see that all he needed was a new way of balancing his force and skill. Eaton simply needed to flip his goal.

Basketball flips the goal. When you flip the goal, you begin to see a wide range of relevant issues and available tools. And then you can balance and rebalance the application of force and skill to solve challenges.

At its inception, basketball was trying to include as many kinds of athletic expression and as many kinds of abilities, assigning all abilities value in the game without making it so that one is more important or more powerful than another. Wilt's legacy is showing what's possible when we open our minds to new ways of creating solutions, to new models of leadership, to wider appreciation for various styles of achievement. We mustn't overvalue one way, one approach, one tool.

As the famous psychologist Abraham Maslow put it, "I suppose it is tempting, if the only tool you have is a hammer, to treat everything as if it were a nail."

NUANCE

The basketball principle of balancing force and skill speaks to the elusive, precious, and vanishing concept in our society of *nuance*.

Nuance is the thread count of cumulative human experience. For every one of us, each moment is different from the one that came before. We constantly face a flood of new information and an incalculable number of facts and circumstances, minute by minute, hour by hour, day by day. Those micro moments, those nuances, mount to a fully composed human experience. The appreciation of nuance is the appreciation of our full humanity, encompassing all of its contradictions, inconsistencies, complexity, and promise. We are complicated, wondrous, ongoing demonstrations of impulse, emotion, and action tempered (sometimes) by control. In other words, we are—at our best—a balance of force and skill. Understanding nuance is where you find that balance.

As Susan Cain's book *Quiet: The Power of Introverts in a World That Can't Stop Talking* so effectively demonstrates, there is a great misconception about what characteristics leadership truly encompasses.

Our corporations, our organizations, our political spheres for too long have rewarded only the brag culture, the loud culture, the look-at-me culture, a value system that Cain calls "the Extrovert Ideal—the omnipresent belief that the ideal self is gregarious, alpha, and comfortable in the spotlight." This misses the power, virtue, and effectiveness of so many people (Cain estimates 33 to 50 percent of us). It filters down to every organizational micro and macro decision and warps the nature of our entire societal output. High-level leadership searches have recently stopped including the words "charisma" or "entrepreneur" in job descriptions because it signals a biased, outdated notion of leadership, eliminating huge swaths of skilled, qualified, and perhaps better-suited candidates. We've been following the old leadership model for millennia.

"We've turned it into an oppressive standard to which most of us feel we must conform," says Cain.

Look around. Has this leadership archetype led the world to a state of more cooperation, harmony, understanding, health, and happiness? Basketball's principle of balancing force and skill is an inclusive human-resource management lens for C-suite recruitment, but it needs to be acculturated at an even earlier stage of talent evaluation.

Debbie Bial saw that traditional college admissions measures and strategies were failing to recognize leadership potential in all kinds of amazing young people. The results of this big miss in admissions were student bodies at top colleges that failed to reflect the diversity of a changing twenty-first-century United States.

In 1989, Bial founded the Posse Foundation, which selects, trains, and sends cohorts of ten students—Posse Scholars—tuition-free to top universities every year. The basic theory is that if the ten carefully but nontraditionally identified high school students attended college together, they could support each other throughout their shared college career, like a posse. The program would increase a student's chance of success at an institution that might be harder to navigate alone. But the ultimate goal of Posse was bigger; the mission focused on developing a diverse group of leaders for the workforce. "Our goal is to change who is sitting at the table," Bial told *The Harvard Crimson,* "to create a new kind of national leadership network in the United States, one that this country has never seen in its entire history." Their results have been phenomenal.

Posse has sent ten thousand students from more than twenty cities to sixty-three highly selective partner colleges and universities.

These partner institutions have awarded over $1.6 billion in scholarships, and 90 percent of Posse Scholars graduate, exceeding the national average for undergraduates. And they don't just graduate. They lead. For example, 80 percent of graduating seniors in 2017 were officers of a college organization. Twenty seniors served as student government or student body president. They also lead their families, as 57 percent are first-generation college students.

In 2007, Bial was awarded a MacArthur "Genius" Grant. In 2010, when President Barack Obama received the Nobel Peace Prize, the Posse Foundation was one of ten organizations with which he chose to split his $1.4 million award. Bial has received a slew of other prestigious distinctions, including honorary degrees from a number of universities and recognition by countless leaders in policy, government, education, and social justice.

How does Bial make such good choices when selecting her Posse Scholars? How does she find people who not only are missed by the traditional measures but also outperform those who are typically chosen by them?

She developed a unique strategy to evaluate student potential, which doesn't rely on standardized tests like the SAT or ACT. It's called the Dynamic Assessment Process (DAP) and has been used to serve thousands of students looking to show top colleges and universities what they're made of. DAP takes place over a period of three months and involves large group interviews with up to one hundred participating nominees, individual interviews, and small group interviews. It puts nominated students into small group activities that allow trained evaluators to observe traits and characteristics that don't show up in a paper application or on a written test. Observers benefit from this holistic process and can look for leadership, communication skills, and the ability to work well on a team. They look for problem solving and critical thinking skills as students lead group discussions or complete dynamic tasks. Each year approximately seventeen thousand students are nominated by college counselors, principals, and community organizations. Only eight hundred are selected. The program is highly selective, but what DAP has achieved is unusual in that it finds smart, capable, ambitious young people who might have been missed in the traditional college application process.

Debbie and I became friends in college and have stayed connected ever since. Shortly after she won the MacArthur Fellowship, she invited me to become an evaluator. It was a transformative learning experience. Over a two-week period I observed hundreds of high school students. The value of being able to observe up close and reflect with fellow observers on the uniqueness of each candidate—and the many shades of human contributive ability on display—cannot be overstated. We were constructing more fully dimensionalized profiles of actual people than a faceless, standardized exam or GPA ever could. All the things I see now as a professor in a college classroom, the qualities I value in students, the telltale signs of success, I saw and valued as an observer. I couldn't help but think I wished colleges had seen me in high school as fully and carefully as this process does. I pray that there's a process that really sees my daughter and her high school classmates when they're trying to be fully, truly seen.

Some of the trend data is encouraging. Eighty percent of undergraduate institutions in the United States didn't require applicants to submit ACT or SAT scores for fall 2022 admissions, according to the advocacy organization FairTest. That's up from 43 percent five years prior.

It's time to get the balance right.

Numeric, blunt-force standardized tests and GPAs are convenient for college admissions machines to churn out expedient—but not accurate—evaluations. Nuanced, balanced, basketball-istic DAP is much more accurate but requires a lot more effort. Aren't we worth it?

JOY HANGS IN THE BALANCE

Bodies can do both: force and skill. And because they can do both, we should be interested in the full capabilities of both. Basketball recognizes and appreciates that ability range and prizes the balance. By virtue of its physical goal—the horizontal, elevated basket—the game insists on that balance. The sheer, natural simplicity of the game's physical movements is brought into visual focus by the lack of equipment. The game's participants expose the full flower of human athletic ability. That's why basketball is so pleasing to watch.

The arc of a shot can only go so fast. The limp-wristed follow-through, the finger roll, the touch pass, the alley-oop. And yes, the slam dunk. At 6 foot 9, 250 pounds, the powerfully built LeBron James glides balletically between defenders. The slender and diminutive Steph Curry can influence the outcome of a game just as much as the massive Shaquille O'Neal did. Think of Jason Kidd—built like a linebacker, running the break like an Einstein—

able to perfectly time and deliver a pass or dribble past opponents. Or Charles Barkley at 6 foot 6 (barely), out-rebounding an entire league, 60 percent of whom were taller than he. George Gervin, the Iceman, who was 6 foot 7 and thin as a rake, playing like a small man, inventing a hundred different ways to score, every night. Allen Iverson, listed at six feet tall—if even—and weighing only 165 pounds, imposing himself in a league of giants and physically dominating them. Nikola Jokić, 6 foot 11, looks like he would lose a foot race to just about everyone and has a vertical leap of "not so much," but his quickness, vision, touch, timing, guile, and gravity elevate him to a class of performance unto himself. He's really strong, too. And Jimmy Butler, who exhibits the full spectrum of both force and skill, but does so in a manner that pushes him to exhaustion. Competitively, epically, he finds the skill he needs when the force has left his body; he musters the force required when his skills are slipping.

For an original, unmatched array of both force and skill, look no further than Julius Erving. Dr. J, who redefined both the slam dunk and the finger roll, and reinvented the game's stylistic possibilities through his ability not only to jump higher but to stay up longer, extending his limbs like an elongated Lladró figurine, found spaces in the air that others didn't even know existed. No one put more new colors on the basketball palette.

The naked canvas of the basketball court is also quick to expose glaring imbalances between teammates, especially when two star players aren't able to figure out how to equal the scales. Sam Anderson vividly explained in *Boom Town* how Durant and Westbrook's two ends of force and skill were not able to find balance:

"Durant and Westbrook were a mighty but imperfect fit. They clashed and blended, amplified and diminished each other, in ways that were hard to parse. KD was civilization; Russ was chaos. KD was the metronome; Russ was the thrashing guitar solo. KD was the scenic cliff, Russ the waterfall raging primally over the top of it. It was tempting to call them a yin and yang, but in a yin-yang, the oppositions are perfectly balanced. KD and Russ were more like a yorn-yarng, or a bling-blornk-blarnxttthhh; some kind of oblong, asymmetrical shape in which clashing colors bleed into one another and you can never figure out which way is supposed to be up. Together, they were the embodiment of life's ineluctable disharmony. True equilibrium seemed impossible."

Westbrook and Durant, force and skill, could not find their balance, and ultimately success together eluded them.

Sam Hinkie, the Philadelphia 76ers general manager from 2013 to 2016, insisted that players, fans, and owners "trust the process." Hinkie's iconoclastic approach to building a basketball team resembled an investment-banking approach to acquiring, gutting, and rebuilding an underperforming business. In a lengthy resignation letter, Hinkie called it "a culture of finding new, better ways to solve repeating problems." "To do this," Hinkie insisted, "requires you to divorce process from outcome. You can be right for the wrong reasons." Hinkie concluded that "it is worth noting that over the long term, basketball team building is about one primary thing—the players."

The right players matter, but so does the right balance. Since 2013, during and after Hinkie, the comings and goings of so many players—including Joel Embiid, Jahlil Okafor, Nerlens Noel, JJ Reddick, Ben Simmons, Jimmy Butler, Michael Carter-Williams,

JaVale McGee, Nik Stauskas, Markelle Fultz, Al Horford, James Harden, and Dwight Howard—have failed to get the Sixers past the Eastern Conference semifinals.

It's worth noting that Jrue Holiday, drafted by the 76ers in 2009 and dealt away by Hinkie in 2013, was the key ingredient to balancing Giannis Antetokounmpo—whom Hinkie passed on in the 2013 draft—and to Milwaukee's 2021 NBA championship win. Go figure.

In basketball, the greater the mastery of that balance of force and skill, the greater the success. So much comes back to Bill Russell. The blocked shot in basketball can be one of the most intimidating shows of force. After a foreboding block, Dikembe Mutombo would wag his finger to indicate authority and domination, admonishing the shooter to never do that again. Highlight videos surface nightly of a defender swatting a shot attempt into the stands, followed by a glimpse of the victim's humiliation. The thing is, a shot taker and his team retain possession after the block, no matter how far back into the stands the ball is sent. Russell said a block is not much good if you can't control the ball and possess it. For Russell, the block should create a turnover. He took the shot block to a higher level.

Level one blocked shot: stop a potential basket and perhaps deter future offensive aggression of the same kind. Level two blocked shot: achieve the aforementioned benefits, but also win possession. Russell, he of the unmatched eleven NBA titles, saw true basketball greatness as the ability to master a balancing of the two, making the blocked shot the highest form of balance between force and skill. In *Second Wind,* the elegant memoir he penned with Taylor Branch, Russell described moments of such exquisite balance that they elevated him, in the heat of competition, to a place of transcendent personal peace. "There'd be a natural ebb and flow that reminded you of how rhythmic the game is supposed to be. I'd find myself thinking 'This is it. I want this to keep going.' . . . I literally did not care who had won. I'd still be free and high as a sky hawk."

PRINCIPLE
4

POSITIONLESS-NESS

Studying just one school of thought every day—whether it's Confucianism, Buddhism, Taoism or Jeff VanGundyism—can limit your imagination. If everybody thinks the same way, where do new ideas come from?

—Yao Ming, *Yao: A Life in Two Worlds*

I n 1898, as interest in basketball
was growing nationally, James Naismith accepted a position at
the University of Kansas to be director of both the chapel and
physical education. That same year he formed the university's first
basketball team. And over the next forty years there, he mentored
two coaches who went on to represent the two competing disciplines of the modern game: Forrest "Phog" Allen and John McLendon.

Naismith met Phog Allen the same year he arrived in Kansas.
Allen had discovered the game at the Kansas City Athletic Club
and was a local legend. He and his brothers took to organizing
packed-house AAU tournaments, becoming quite the basketball
impresarios in the process. His biographer Blair Kerkhoff states
Allen "had created a basketball event, promoted it, won it, then
cashed in on it." Naismith took notice of Allen and encouraged
him to enroll at the University of Kansas.

After he had played just one season for Kansas, officials at Baker
University in Baldwin City, Kansas, approached Allen with an
offer to coach their team. Naismith tried to discourage him from
leaving, and famously said to Allen, "You can't coach a game like
basketball. You play it." Allen disagreed. He had come to believe

there was a "correct" way to play basketball—assigned player positions on the court and strict, coach-dictated plays—and he insisted it be adhered to rigidly. Allen's coaching success over the next four decades, including replacing Naismith in 1919 as athletic director and leading Kansas to a record of 590 wins and 219 losses, led to his fixed-position style being adopted by coaches at all levels of the sport, even today.

Allen's Hall of Fame adherents include Adolph Rupp, Dean Smith, and Ralph Miller. Phog Allen was about coaching and control. Rigidity of play and position. Coach centered, not player centered. Player assignments were fixed and defined. His teams were also rigid in racial composition. He never fielded a team that wasn't whites only.

Naismith, somewhat marginalized after Allen took over, stayed on as faculty in the Kansas physical education department. In 1933, at age seventy-two, he met his final disciple, John McLendon. On his first day at the University of Kansas, John McLendon walked into Naismith's office and informed him that he was Naismith's new advisee. Naismith asked who had decided that. McLendon said, "My father." Naismith replied, "Fathers are always right."

McLendon was the first African American admitted to the Kansas physical education program; already, he signaled an altering of position. In a *New York Times* excerpt of his unpublished autobiography, McLendon wrote that Naismith "deplored any form of discrimination, segregation or prejudice, and helped me to surmount glaring institutional discriminatory practices during my junior and senior years."

It was not only a racially prejudiced society that Naismith deplored. Though he and Phog Allen publicly showed no disrespect for each other, Naismith never, in all those years they shared at Kansas, came around to Allen's vision of basketball as a fixed-position game. And in McLendon, Naismith finally found an equal-minded advocate to move the game and his positionless ideal forward. "Naismith didn't draw any plays. He talked about the essence of the game," McLendon said. "I used to go over to his house at night to talk about basketball and life."

One day, Naismith and McLendon were out at a park watching kids eight to ten years old playing ball. "There wasn't an adult present, and he [Naismith] said stop and watch this game and see what you can see," recalled McLendon. "He was watching the movement of the ball and I said, 'All the players chase the ball wherever it goes.'" Naismith said, "*That's* the way the game is supposed to be played."

McLendon asked for more. Naismith explained, "When you have the ball, from that point you attack the basket. When the other team has the ball, from that point you attack them."

"I patterned my whole game after that philosophy," McLendon said.

Landing his first head coaching job at the all-Black North Carolina College in 1940, a year after Naismith died, McLendon expanded on Naismith's idea—attack on offense *and* on defense—by designing a system based on constant movement. McLendon's game was played baseline to baseline, requiring full-court aggressive defense and pushing the ball up-court on offense. The plan was for a shot to be taken once every eight seconds. What McLendon invented—fluid, positionless, relentless, end-to-end, motion-based basketball—was the fast break.

John McLendon and the fast break ceded control to players.

This was a pure manifestation of what Naismith would soon identify in *Basketball: Its Origin and Development* as one of the fundamental "unchanging factors" of the sport: "No Man on either team shall be restricted from getting the ball at any time that it is in play." Coaches didn't create the positions, the situation did—the facts and circumstances on the court did. Players were not locked into roles or silos.

McLendon placed decision-making and self-determination in their hands. He coached at historically Black colleges and universities for twenty years until breaking the color barrier as a professional head coach in 1959.

McLendon's fast break was an expression of movement that was free, unstructured, unassigned, and self-determined. It was not undisciplined; rather, it was the demonstration of principled, studied preparation to create opportunity and execute in the moment while in motion.

In McLendon's vision, basketball is the language of freedom—the freedom to be who you are and to create in the space you're in without someone else, without society, assigning permission or prescriptive roles to you. This was the essence of the game; the essence of freedom, of the healthiest mind, body, and spirit. If Naismith passed a baton to anyone, it was to McLendon.

"He taught me everything I know about basketball and physical education," McLendon said of Naismith in 1996. "Everything I did when I was coaching, I can trace back to learning from him."

"Their relationship was one of the amazing things," said University of Kansas film and media studies professor Kevin Willmott, who directed the PBS documentary *Fast Break: The Legendary John McLendon*. "Through McLendon you get to know this other side of James Naismith that I don't think people talk enough about. He sees basketball as a way to better society and make better men."

Toward that end, Naismith was trying to develop the valuable human quality of "initiative," which he described as "the ability to meet new conditions with efficiency." "In basketball," he wrote, "a player must react to conditions without time for deliberation." Or, as Bill Russell put it in "The Psych . . . and My Other Tricks" in *Sports Illustrated* in 1965: "There is no time in basketball to think: 'This has happened; this is what I must do next.' In the amount of time it takes to think through that semicolon, it is already too late." For that, said Naismith, a player "cannot depend on the coach for the next move but must face the emergency himself."

The fast break, like life, is sprawling, unfolding, ever new, and ever changing. It is immediate. What is the best way to manage oneself in a constantly new and changing world? Understand how to run the break, like McLendon taught? Or, like Allen maintained, hope that things slow down so you can set up and resume your position, even though that position under the circumstances might be irrelevant or obsolete?

Both Phog Allen and John McLendon were inducted into the Naismith Basketball Hall of Fame. But as time has passed, it is McLendon who has become the enduring expression of what Naismith intended: In life and in basketball, none of us are just one thing.

BEHOLD THE UNICORN

Naismith knew better than most that none of us are just one thing. He himself changed career paths several times, going from woodsman and athlete to divinity student, physical education teacher, and medical doctor. He understood that it makes no sense to be forced into a single position. And the superstars of today are leading the way when it comes to reimagining roles on the court. No longer does the forward do x and the guard y, or the center just stand under the basket and wait for the pass or rebound. Instead, it's a league of unicorns. Giants who do it all.

Seven-footers like Giannis Antetokounmpo and Kevin Durant can do everything—handle the ball and run point, create shots and shoot threes, make the key pass and distribute scoring opportunities. And they can still dominate inside, rebounding, blocking shots, scoring over and around defenders on the block with classic "big man" footwork. And oh yes, they dunk on people.

In its 2019–20 NBA preview, *The Ringer* declared it was the "Year of the Unicorn." "The 'Unicorn Era,'" wrote Danny Chau, "is ultimately a reimagining of what's possible for all players (and not just in the NBA)—a renewed sense of creativity in a sport that suddenly feels boundless."

In basketball's new era, what was once seemingly impossible is now true on every play. Bigger, taller players like LeBron James and Karl-Anthony Towns are often their team's primary ball handlers. Seven-foot-plus players were once assigned only to play "inside," but Anthony Davis and Joel Embiid regularly pull up and nail threes from long range.

In the 2020–21 season, 6-foot-11 Nikola Jokić became only the second center ever to reach fifty career triple-doubles. The first was Wilt Chamberlain, who had seventy-eight. Does the word center even apply anymore? Jokić is also just the ninth player in history to record fifty triple-doubles; only Magic Johnson and

Oscar Robertson got there faster than he did. Jokić is one of three players in NBA history to lead his team in points, rebounds, and assists at least twenty-one times in a season (2020–21); the other two are Russell Westbrook (2016–17) and Giannis Antetokounmpo (2018–19). The two-time, do-it-all MVP is the *first* NBA player to rack up 2,000 points, 1,000 rebounds, and 500 assists in a season (2021–22).

In today's game, labels like guard, forward, and center are practically obsolete. Instead, it's become a multi-position league with the most valuable players operating as "point forwards." A paragon of the latter-day point forward is Luka Dončić—a player who fits the physical description of a classic power forward, but who is also responsible for classic guard duties; bringing the ball up the court and being the primary facilitator on offense. So many offenses now run through the point forward, who creates new opportunities because of their complete basketball repertoire, plus a host of expanded opportunities by seeing over or shooting over the defense. Other good examples are LeBron James, Kevin Durant, and Jayson Tatum.

Observing Dončić during the 2022 playoffs, former eighteen-year NBA player and 2007 NBA Coach of the Year Sam Mitchell told Brian Geltzeiler of Sirius XM NBA Radio, "Luka is doing things offensively we haven't seen since Michael Jordan. . . . He's unique in that it's his style of play at his size." At six foot eight and 230 pounds, Mitchell sees in Dončić an unprecedented basketball Hydra: "Luka is built more like Karl Malone, plays like Magic, but has the touch and finesse of Larry Bird. He is something that we've never seen before and, quite frankly, with his size and skill set, we may never see again."

A generation ago, a player as big as Dončić never would have played point guard or guarded the perimeter; instead, they'd be relegated to the low post, buried in the paint, where their full skill set would be hidden. A tall player like Dončić would have been automatically assigned to the front court, seen only as "a big"—in other words, he would have been limited. The modern coach sees more. The modern coach sees unicorns.

In his first week after being named the new Brooklyn Nets head coach, Steven Nash, a two-time NBA MVP, announced in a press conference that 7-footer Kevin Durant would play all five positions. Because, why wouldn't he? As Shakespeare wrote:

All the world's a stage,
And all the men and women merely players;
They have their exits and their entrances;
And one man in his time plays many parts.

Basketball understands. The game is the premier stage for demonstrating a Shakespearean world where none of us are just one thing. Naismith would say basketball has always believed in unicorns, that the game was built for them.

Positionless-ness is inherent in the game of basketball, but also a principle that has become an inescapable and broad societal truth. Positionless-ness reflects and refracts the human condition of the twenty-first century. It is the future of work, of personal and professional development. In 2017, a Deloitte Human Capital survey found that college graduates are changing and will change careers every four to five years for a total of twelve to sixteen different jobs in their lifetime. According to a February 2022 LinkedIn study, Gen Z was changing jobs at a 134 percent higher rate than they were in 2019. Positionless-ness is not only the current, ideal state of basketball—it is the necessary state of our present day.

POSITIONING OURSELVES FOR THE TWENTY-FIRST CENTURY

We know that the future of work is moving toward positionless-ness. However, one of the most stifling social problems today is the narrow siloing of people based on old ways of academic preparation. In this model, the hyperspecialized skills students learn are misaligned with the needs of the workforce, which results in fewer professional opportunities down the line and limited career growth. In his bestselling book *Range,* David Epstein argues that today's professional and educational obsession with specialization inherently denies potential and closes possibility. It makes us a less capable society.

"The drive to specialize," writes Epstein, "infects not just individuals, but entire systems, as each specialized group sees a smaller and smaller part of a larger puzzle." Specialization creates a system of "parallel trenches" where "everyone is digging deep in their own trench, rarely standing up to look over at the next trench, even though the solution to their problem resides there." He argues that "our greatest strength is the exact opposite of narrow specialization. It is the ability to integrate broadly." The best way to solve complex problems in any field is to learn multiple ways of solving problems from multiple arenas, then bring all those perspectives to bear when you go deep in a single arena. Those are the thinkers who are awarded Nobel Prizes, receive MacArthur Grants, and discover cures.

The future of AI technology and fifty other warp-speed technological advances practically ensures that many of today's jobs—as well as entire industries—may become obsolete. We know right now that young people will change not just jobs but careers at least four to five times in their lives.

We've got to move the future of higher education toward training people for what work is actually going to be like. Epstein argues that right now, higher education departments are too narrow. They're not giving students tools to analyze the modern world—not giving them the "habits of mind to dance across disciplines." It is the multidisciplinary learners, says Epstein, who are solving the world's most pressing and difficult problems. The world needs unicorns.

Prominent educator and innovator Cathy Davidson also believes that higher education is broken. In her 2017 book, *The New Education,* she indicts a system that is antiquated and nearly irrelevant. Her somewhat mocking title refers to an 1869 concept for higher education of the same name, proposed by Harvard professor Charles Eliot and designed to produce long-term professional managers in single industry fields. His "revolutionary" academic design, now over 150 years old, is still largely in place today: specialized learning silos called majors. That "new" education was "designed to train and measure specialized knowledge production in order to pigeonhole people into old hierarchical corporate structures."

A thirty-year career at one company, in one field—even a thirty-year span in an entire industry vertical—is no longer a reality. Davidson implores that in preparing our young people, we desperately need to "go beyond the inherited disciplines, departments and silos." We need to offer them educational challenges that promote success after graduation "when all the educational testing has stopped."

"No road map shows what lies ahead after college"—no more grades, requirements, answer keys, professors, advisers. Instead, Davidson says the real world—minus syllabi and scaffolding—will feel more like "*Here be dragons.*"

The way to equip students to better face and fix problems in our rapidly changing real world, a world in perpetual flux, is a new kind of teaching that focuses not on highly specialized, rapidly inapplicable degree programs but, Davidson insists, on educational modalities that are multidisciplinary, experiential, and student centered. We need curriculums that teach "learning how to learn— the single most important skill anyone can master."

"What should we be teaching?" asks philosopher-historian Yuval Noah Harari in his *21 Lessons for the 21st Century.* "Most important of all will be the ability to deal with change, learn new things, and preserve your mental balance in unfamiliar situations. In order to keep up with the world of 2050, you need not merely to invent new ideas and products, but above all reinvent yourself again and again."

We find ourselves in a once-in-a-century moment of resetting and reimagining for so many of our institutions. Now is a time of reinventing and rethinking old, vexing, neglected issues. Who do we want figuring these things out? Do we want the same old people from the same old positions? Or is it now time for position-*less* people to meet this moment, a moment of historical, never-before newness and change? Who is most ready to run a full-court planetary fast break?

MAJORING IN POSITIONLESS-NESS

Zeynep Tufekci, a professor at the University of North Carolina at Chapel Hill and frequent contributor to *The New York Times,* was right about everything. For the past decade, Tufekci has been publishing anti-conventional data-soaked theories on major public interest issues in popular media, from *The Atlantic* and *Scientific American* to TED Talks, Twitter, and a 2017 book with Yale University Press, *Twitter and Tear Gas.*

In March 2020, when the CDC recommended that only healthcare workers wear masks, she was the first in the United States to publicly speak out and say no, everyone should wear a mask. When cities closed beaches and parks to prevent gatherings, she said no, those are the safest gathering places. She wrote about aerosol transmission and the importance of keeping windows and doors open for better ventilation. She was right every time. And because of it, the CDC changed their guidelines. Let's be clear—she saved lives.

"I've just been struck by how right she has been," Julia Marcus, an infectious disease epidemiologist at Harvard Medical School, told Ben Smith of *The New York Times.*

When the pandemic hit, Tufekci could see that we were in both a health emergency and a communications emergency. At the University of North Carolina, Tufekci had long been using pandemics as a vehicle to teach students in her introduction to sociology classes about globalization, exponential growth, and how connected people are. As an interdisciplinary scholar with expert communication skills, she was well equipped to bridge the gap between scientific research and people's everyday lives. "Somebody needed to read those papers and say to the general public here's what it means for you," Tufekci said. The whole world was in fast-break mode, and Tufekci knew how to run full-court.

As she drew more attention during the pandemic, an August 2020 *New York Times* profile by Ben Smith, "How Zeynep Tufekci Keeps Getting the Big Things Right," revealed a remarkable history of Tufekci being quietly ahead of the curve on huge societal issues: debunking a prevailing notion that Twitter was a primary driver of major social upheaval (2011), warning media outlets that their coverage of school shootings creates more of the same (2012), lecturing an Obama operative that social media microtargeting in political campaigns would dangerously incubate social division (2012), explaining how disinformation propagated on Facebook could fuel ethnic cleansing and authoritarianism (2013), and showing how YouTube's recommendation algorithm could be used as a tool of radicalization (2017).

How does a former computer programmer turned sociologist, now an associate professor at the University of North Carolina School of Information and Library Science, get big things right in her noncredentialed areas of epidemiology, public health, government, and politics?

Tufekci chalks it up to three basic characteristics: (1) a global perspective, gained during a back-and-forth childhood spent between Turkey and Belgium and an adulthood working in the United States; (2) actively accumulated, varied, multidisciplinary knowledge; and (3) a broad, inclusive systems-based thinking approach, as she told Ezra Klein in February 2021 on his podcast, "The problems in the world don't come in a single discipline."

Tufekci engages with life and her own intellectual development in the same way a basketball player finds herself on the basketball court. She never saw herself confined to a specific spatial or functional position; rather, she sought to locate the truth of her present and evolving situation. She sought to solve the challenge of her facts and circumstances. She went wherever she needed to go to figure it out.

To cope with a difficult childhood she voraciously read science fiction, imagining better worlds than hers where technology might hold the key. She embraced a then-nascent internet culture and took a job as a computer programmer at IBM while still in her teens. There, she joined global online discussion groups inhaling discourse on global issues. She became fascinated by one especially multifaceted online community, the Zapatista Solidarity Network, which supported militarized indigenous activists in southern Mexico protesting against neoliberalism and land privatization imposed by the North American Free Trade Agreement. The group was aided and abetted by sophisticated digital community organizing. To understand it all, Tufekci traveled to Chiapas, Mexico, to see the Zapatistas for herself. That's how you learn—multidisciplinary, experiential, student-centered active learning. Tufekci's early formative quests for knowledge are reminiscent of the way another young scholar, Bill Bradley, played basketball at Princeton.

Positionless-ness

In his 1965 *New Yorker* profile, John McPhee recalled student-athlete Bradley on the court, innately positionless, constantly looking for a new creation of self: "He goes in and swims around in the vicinity of the basket, back and forth, moving for motion's sake, making plans and abandoning them, and always watching the distant movement of the ball out of the corner of his eye." That positionless consciousness would have an intellectually restless Bradley later reflect that as a professional basketball player he often felt "like an artist in the wrong medium." This from a basketball player whose multidisciplinary résumé includes Rhodes Scholar, US senator, author, and presidential candidate. He's also in the Naismith Basketball Hall of Fame.

Once a consciousness of positionless-ness becomes ingrained as a habit of mind, it multiplies. The inclination to learn more about more things and integrate across disciplines becomes not just motivating but second nature, perhaps even first nature. NBA superstar Kevin Durant credits playing basketball as the first experience that showed him just how limitless his pursuits could be.

"I started to crave more and more of those life experiences and I realized they were tied to the game," Durant told a special NYU-student session of *The Boardroom*. "I understood basketball was a way for me to learn more, see more and have more friends. Once I played the game for that small reason, the world started to open up for me. I'm just craving more and more experiences, more and more perspectives." Durant is one of the most successful off-the-court athletes, with a varied portfolio of tech and entrepreneurial investments, media projects (including helping produce *Two Distant Strangers,* winner of the 2021 Oscar for Best Short Film), and an active charitable foundation. Durant has the means, sure, but he also has the "range": the multidisciplinary drive to do, create, and solve—all successfully.

Boston Celtics standout Jaylen Brown has also been using the off-seasons to continue to learn and grow. "Many times we see this as something separate: education, technology, sports, music. . . . And many times we forget to build bridges and connections," he explained to Claire Miller of *Fast Company* in July 2019. That's what drew Brown to get involved with the nearby MIT Media Lab, which coined the term *anti-disciplinary* as the stubbornly nameless, silo-less academic approach they take to solving real-world problems.

When Zeynep Tufekci speaks of her complex systems–thinking approach, it sounds an awful lot like the MIT Media Lab's anti-disciplinary approach. "When I say systems thinking," Tufekci told Ezra Klein, "I'm saying look at the whole and its interactions as much as possible to understand both each part of it, but also how it all comes together."

Like anti-disciplinarity, Tufekci's systems thinking defies recognition from traditional academic silos. "There's no academic departments about it," she said. "I learned a lot, for example, from ecology and biology. I get the concepts from across many fields. I try to get my students to think about complex systems distributed across many fields. It's almost like the scientific method kind of thing, I think, but for the entire world."

The arc and pattern of Tufekci's positionless, silo-less search for knowledge mirrors Jaylen Brown's. Brown learned Spanish on his own. He plays the piano. He did internships at Base Ventures, a California venture capital firm, and was offered another at NASA. He is learning Arabic and Indonesian, which he got into while visiting the island nation. He taught himself guitar, but now takes classes.

"I am the intersection of everything," said Brown. "I represent the Celtics, the University of California, Berkeley, my family, myself. . . . When I go out, I am part of all that, and there are bridges—between basketball and technology, between technology and education. The key is to look at them as a whole, not as separate entities."

The MIT Media Lab has been equally impressed with Brown, and in 2019 named the then-twenty-two-year-old as one of its 2019 Director's Fellows. When asked what anti-disciplinary learning means to him, Brown responded that it's not just a way of learning, it's an existential human purpose: "It's basically learning different things and combining them," said Brown. "That's why we're here."

POSITIONLESS-NESS IS PROLOGUE

In 1944, John McLendon arranged a "secret game" (which remained unknown until 1996): North Carolina College versus an all-white team of former Duke players. In the North Carolina College gym, while most people were in church, McLendon's fast-break style demolished the Duke team 88–44. Proof of concept established. As John Thompson pointedly observed in Dan Klores's film *Basketball: A Love Story,* McLendon's fast break "was considered to be undisciplined—until white coaches started doing it."

A player on five Boston Celtics championship teams in the 1960s and '70s, Don Nelson mused to *Sports Illustrated*'s Chris Ballard in May 2019: "I had spent my whole life asking 'Why are point guards expected to only pass, why are small forwards expected to only score and why are centers expected to only post up?'" In the early '90s and early 2000s as Golden State's head coach, he broke convention by competing with 6-foot-7-and-smaller positionless lineups with the Run TMC Warriors and later the We Believe Warriors. Pushing the positionless paradigm further, he stationed 7-foot-7 Manute Bol on the perimeter to shoot threes. "Hell, what if a big operated more in open space, and could shoot the lights out, make great passes, be playmaker and ballhandler?"

"Well, why not?" purred Phoenix Sun coach Mike D'Antoni, who in 2003 looked around in resignation at an NBA dominated by classic big men: Shaquille O' Neal, Tim Duncan, and Kevin Garnett. "You're not going to beat Shaq if you rolled out a conventional center—he's going to destroy him," D'Antoni told Dan Peterson in the popular Serbian basketball journal *Kos Magazin*. "You're just playing for second place, basically. We had Nash and Stoudemire and we thought, 'Let's try this.'" *This* was what came to be known as an offense constructed with no classic center determined to score in "seven seconds or less," believing the more space they created on offense the less guardable they were. Space was the new height, and positions—guard, center, forward—no longer mattered.

Today, Milwaukee Bucks coach Mike Budenholzer employs a philosophy *Sports Illustrated*'s Chris Ballard described in April 2019 as "positionless motion. No bigs or wings or guards. Just five players, all interchangeable, creating a glorious 'randomness.'" This NBA title–winning stratagem maximizes the special omni-capable gifts of 6-foot-11 superstar Giannis Antetokounmpo, but ties directly to Navajo Rez Ball culture—a distinctly positionless, nonstop running, seamless offense-to-defense style of play. Budenholzer himself played high school basketball in Holbrook, Arizona, where his father coached and he was exposed to the Rez Ball style of play.

Positionless-ness is basketball's beating heart. Positionless-ness has been a fundamental principle of the game since its inception. In basketball, every player can play every position, and any player may find themselves at any place on the court at any time. The best teams today speak often and only about playing positionless basketball. It's now the accepted, ultimate state of play. Positionless-ness means not just that tall players can play any role, but that any player can, will, and must play any role. That's basketball reality. Old ways of playing defined positions—center, guard, forward—limited what each player was taught and the potential for what each player could really do.

In the ideal state of basketball, there are no silos, but rather human flexibility and interchangeability. At any given moment on the court, you might find yourself in an entirely new situation—new facts, new circumstances—that you need to solve. To say *That's not my job, that's not my position* is insufficient. You need to be and do whatever is required in that new time and place. There's no manual or answer key. There's just a unique challenge that you and your teammates have to solve together. The solution? You need to be *it,* whatever *it* is. Adopting a position of positionless-ness is the best preparation for whatever comes your way.

Positionless-ness as a societal proposition, expressed through basketball, was ahead of its time; now, however, it's right on time.

Positionless-ness is both a practical way to approach twenty-first-century problems as well as a new twenty-first-century consciousness.

Life is a fast break, positionless and rarely the same. It's a constant state of readiness to learn more, go elsewhere, and innovate. If you look at it this way, then you'll be prepared to solve for wherever the ball goes—hunger, disease, infrastructure, personal career change. We are not just one thing and neither is our world.

In 1980, rookie Magic Johnson (already breaking the positional mold as a 6-foot-9 point guard) was asked to jump center in place of the injured Kareem Abdul-Jabbar in Game 6 of the NBA finals versus the Philadelphia 76ers. Johnson responded by playing all five positions that night, recording forty-two points, fifteen rebounds, and seven assists, and leading the Los Angeles Lakers to their first championship in ten years.

"Who would have thought we could win in Philadelphia without Kareem and with Magic playing center?" Lakers head coach Paul Westhead told *The New York Times*. "Everybody thought the guy who thought that was some demented coach, the kind who reads too many books. But the move to center really wasn't as strange as it seemed."

Not if he read the book on Naismith or McLendon. No, not strange at all.

PRINCIPLE
5

HUMAN ALCHEMY

Having sat through scores of high school and college games, I recognized a good player when I saw one, and Barack quickly passed the test. He played an athletic, artful form of basketball, his lanky body moving quickly, showing power I hadn't before noticed. He was swift and graceful, even in his Hawaiian footwear. I stood there pretending to listen to what someone's perfectly nice wife was saying to me, but my eyes stayed fixed on Barack. I was struck for the first time by the spectacle of him—this strange mix-of-everything man.

—Michelle Obama, *Becoming*

When Dr. Luther Gulick first asked the faculty to come up with a new game at Springfield College, he wasn't hoping for a daring new vision. Instead Gulick framed the discussion by declaring, "There is nothing new under the sun. All so-called new games are simply recombinations of the factors of things that are now in existence." Gulick believed the solution would be, like a chemistry experiment, "the recombining of existing elements to make a new chemical substance."

Intuitively, Naismith felt that wasn't right. He wrote in *Basketball: Its Origin and Development,* "I realized that any attempt to change known games would necessarily result in failure. . . . It was evident that a new principle was necessary." It wasn't chemistry that was needed. It was *alchemy.*

Alchemy transforms essential matter from its original form to a different, superior form; the original element disappears and becomes something else.

Sports book after sports book talks about "team chemistry," but basketball was always meant to be team alchemy. It is often said that the hallmark of a great basketball player is that she makes her teammates better. On the best basketball teams, the best teammates make each other better because they make each other *different—*

someone else they could never be but for the effect on each other. They alchemize. Successful basketball teammates are no longer what they once were. Success on the basketball court comes from precisely that alchemical identity transformation.

Chuck Klosterman in 2005 wrote about Steve Nash, Phoenix's former All-Star guard, "The reason Nash destroys people is that he transmogrifies the Suns' offense." The game's form and function, when played well, has that change effect on those who play it.

For Naismith, the bliss state of basketball was when the game itself transmuted into a human alchemy lab. "When the individual was permitted to move about anywhere, so long as he did not have the ball, the game became spirited and kaleidoscopic."

Exactly like a kaleidoscope. Fully spectral, yes, but more than that—other-colored, other-shaped—the original color fragments alchemized from meeting other fragments through the refracted light of the world. The results are more beautiful, more fascinating, and totally different from the individual specks of color.

Analogies between basketball and jazz have come in great supply from venerable sources like Stanley Crouch, Nelson George, and Wynton Marsalis. It's interesting to note that the American musical form began to spread in the late nineteenth and early twentieth century, contemporaneous with the rise of basketball. In May 2009, explaining the similarity between the game and the music, Marsalis told reporter Bill Rhoden that both are about where "improvisation meets form in the context of a particular groove and rhythm." Like the five players together on a basketball court, the jazz ensemble arrives at its best performance through the fusion of spontaneous joint discovery and decision-making.

The jazz performer interprets a tune in individual ways, never playing the same composition twice. Depending on the performer's mood, experience, and interaction with band members or audience members, they may change melodies, harmonies, and time signatures. Done well, all players in the ensemble transmute, creating something and *being* something none could be without the others. It's an aspirational state of performance Marsalis calls "virtuosity."

Naismith understood the powerful effect humans in close concert could have on one another. One hundred twenty years later, neuroscience validated his beliefs.

In 2008, Daniel Goleman and Richard Boyatzis published "Social Intelligence and the Biology of Leadership" in *Harvard Business Review.* It could have just as easily been published in *SLAM,* because they're describing how a basketball team works. *Social* intelligence, an extension of emotional intelligence, is a "set of interpersonal competencies built on specific neural circuits" that kicks in when a co-worker interacts with others and inspires them to be more effective. The study explained how the brain's "mirror neurons" enable individuals to reproduce the emotions they detect in others and, thereby, have an instant sense of shared experience. Mirror neurons subtly ping-pong feelings, good and bad, between people. When your teammate is socially intelligent, you're feeling her feelings and that feels good, which sends your good feelings back to her, and everyone is positively synced up, on board and part of a mutual, neurally networked cooperative. Goleman and Boyatzis documented that great teammates engage in daily socially intelligent behaviors that "powerfully leverage this complex system of brain interconnectedness."

I asked Dr. Rosemarie Perry, a research scientist at NYU's Neuroscience and Education Lab and the founder and executive director of an applied social neuroscience nonprofit called Social Creatures, about how much Goleman and Boyatzis's work still resonates today. "This article pretty much encapsulates my entire philosophy around performance as a social resource," she said. "Except now we have twelve more years of updated neuroscience research findings to back it up." Perry also works as a consultant for an NBA team, assessing social intelligence in player personnel and conducting performance assessments on prospective players through interviews and psychological evaluations, which are distilled into recommendations to the front office for the purposes of making good draft picks. She continues to track these social intelligence assessments of the entire team throughout the season.

What she does is different from Athletic IQ (AIQ), which measures a specific kind of cognition valuable for athletes in performing specific actions in different sports. For example, AIQ measures certain intellectual abilities that relate directly to hitting a baseball better, being a better pass rusher, or shooting threes more consistently. Perry is instead trying to measure cognition on a more fluid scale. "We are collecting cognitive measures, but how *we* use cognitive data derives from a very different philosophy (from AIQ) that acknowledges that cognition is not truly innate/fixed but rather incredibly malleable to stress/environment/culture and *especially* social contexts." She insists that cognition develops primarily through social interactions.

"What ultimately matters is cognitive performance within the actual social context that a player will be performing in, which is something that is not specific to the sport of basketball, but rather specific to a team's culture and relationships. So my philosophy is more about understanding cognition as something that can be nurtured and is highly sensitive to day-to-day circumstances/situations/relationships."

But might it be fair to wonder, I asked, whether basketball, because of the design and structure of its play form—a smaller play space, bodily proximity, no fixed positions, only five on a side, nearly continuous neural interactions, spontaneous decision-making, and essential interdependence—creates a social context that is more influential on cognitive performance than other sports? That basketball's human alchemy is an advanced concept much like the brain's neuroplasticity? When, like basketball, we are thrown together with the right people and meet the right circumstances and conditions, everyone becomes new and better selves?

"Yeah, I don't disagree," she replied. "I would love to start more intentionally exploring the intrinsic contributions of basketball to development and performance."

FEAR AND LOATHING AND THEN A CHAMPIONSHIP

In the summer of 1974, Clifford Ray was sent from Chicago to Golden State in a trade for the Warriors' beloved legend, leading scorer, and eventual Hall of Famer Nate Thurmond. Prior to the beginning of the season the Warriors also lost Cazzie Russell (second-leading scorer) and Clyde Lee (starter); Jeff Mullins, a starter and the third-leading scorer, was injured. It was a rebuilding year. The best prediction was for the Warriors to finish in fourth place in their division.

How Basketball Can Save the World

It seemed so certain that the team would not make it to the postseason that their home arena, the Oakland–Alameda County Coliseum, booked the Ice Capades during that time. If the Warriors did make it to the playoffs, they would have to play in the nearby Cow Palace in Daly City.

Ray had been in the league a few years and thus far had had a largely undistinguished career. But when he landed in Oakland, he was on a mission to win a championship. And he felt he knew how to do it—by changing the perception of the league's most hated player, Rick Barry.

Barry was well known for two things: his subversive, iconoclastic, underhanded free throw; and being the most arrogant, impossible SOB ever to play the game of basketball. Nobody got along with the guy. Even in his oddly premature autobiography, *Confessions of a Basketball Gypsy* (which, when it was released in 1972, was expected to be a semi-apology for his behavior), Barry admitted that he'd once punched a nun. In the same book, his own mother called him greedy.

In Barry's second NBA season (1966–67), he scored 40.8 points per game in a losing effort in the finals (Michael Jordan was only two-tenths of a point better with a finals average of 41.0 points per game in 1992–93) and observers sniffed dismissively, calling Barry a ball hog. Despite his consistently high assist totals, fans derided Barry, as Ron Reid wrote in *Sports Illustrated* in 1974, as someone who "would sooner give blood than give the ball to a teammate." An unflattering 1983 *Sports Illustrated* profile by Tony Kornheiser later cemented his poor reputation, featuring a string of stinging quotes from former teammates and associates: "He had a bad attitude. He was always looking down at you" (Robert Parish). "He lacks diplomacy. If they sent him to the UN, he'd end up starting World War III" (Mike Dunleavy). "You'll never find a bunch of players sitting around talking about the good old days with Rick. His teammates and opponents generally and thoroughly detested him" (former Warriors executive Ken Macker).

And then there's the Bill Russell "watermelon grin" incident, which is discussed at length in Bill Simmons's sublime *The Book of Basketball.* During the second half of Game 5 of the 1981 NBA finals, CBS play-by-play man Gary Bender drew attention to a 1956 Olympic team photograph, one in which Russell, the African American basketball legend, was smiling ear to ear. Barry, working alongside Russell as an on-air analyst, commented jokingly, "It looks like some fool over there with that, um, that big watermelon grin." Amazingly, CBS chose to cut to the announcing table after the exchange, focusing in as Russell physically turned his back on Bender. I defy you to find a more awkward sequence in television history.

There is nothing that can be said to defend Barry's attitude and terrible takes, but as far as his being a ball hog, Clifford Ray had some other thoughts on the matter, which he relayed years later, in 2014, to Peter Hartlaub at NBA.com.

"So I called a meeting with the guys on the team, had Rick leave and all the coaches leave. I asked them how many guys think they could score forty points per game. Nobody raised their hand, so I said if Rick plays forty-eight minutes a night, we can depend on him at least putting in thirty points. I said, 'How can you have any kind of jealously or resentment toward someone who is going to give and commit to that much every single night? What we should do is try to do everything we can to collectively bring everything that's needed for us to be competitive and see what happens.' Everybody agreed and from that day on, we started doing things like having breakfast at each other's house. Whenever we did things, we did them together. When you have that much trust, it's only going to create a positive thing. I know people say to me that I did this and I did that, but we all did it collectively."

What they *did* was win it all, alchemizing to pull off arguably the biggest upset in NBA Finals history. The Warriors had a 48–34 regular season record. Their finals opponent, the Washington Bullets, had a regular season record of 60–22. Only once has the disparity in regular season victories between the two teams in the NBA finals been greater, and only by one game: in 2016, Cleveland versus Golden State. To get to the finals, the Bullets defeated the NBA defending champion, the Boston Celtics, in the Eastern Conference finals—a team that also had a 60–22 regular season record. The Bullets were overwhelming favorites in the media (many called the Bullets-Celtics series "the real Finals"), but in the best-of-seven series the Warriors swept the Bullets in four games straight. Not seven, not six, not five. Four straight.

The dramatic fashion in which the Warriors won games made their success even more stunning. The Warriors came from behind in nine of their twelve playoff wins and three of their four finals wins. The three finals comebacks overcame deficits of thirteen points or more. The comeback was the trademark of this team all season long. To heighten the drama, the Warriors' wins almost always seemed to come in close games. The average margin of victory in the 1975 finals was four points, *still the lowest in NBA history,* with two of the four games decided by one point.

As hard as it was to imagine before it happened, it was even harder to accept that it really did happen. After the Warriors won the 1975 finals, the sports world was in a state of shock and denial, which may account for the otherwise inexplicable lack of coverage and recognition for what was a truly miraculous accomplishment. They are the only NBA champions in the modern era—Trump anomaly aside—not to meet the president or make the cover of *Sports Illustrated.*

In the case of the 1975 Warriors, the team transmuted into something that was more than the sum of their parts. Yet the human alchemy of that team was not its greatest alchemical transmutation. The ultimate alchemy: Rick Barry transformed (momentarily) into a likeable person.

This single team created a unique relationship with Rick Barry. Though Barry, a "Top 75" all-time NBA star, was undoubtedly the best player on every team he ever played on—high school, college, and pro—his teammates and coaches never once voted him captain. Except for 1974–75. Now that's truly the transformative power of human alchemy.

That's our capacity to affect one another in ways that, as Gandhi wrote, get us to "be the change you wish to see in the world," by becoming someone neither you nor anyone else knew you could be.

In the case of the 1974–75 Warriors, the first catalyst to transform Barry and his teammates was Clifford Ray. But it wasn't just Ray. It was Ray meets Barry meets the rest of the team, plus all the other surrounding macro and micro world conditions. The 1974–75 Golden State Warriors experienced a remarkable confluence of internal and external factors contributing to their powerful alchemy.

The Warriors were the first franchise in a major American professional sports league to have a full-time Black head coach, Alvin Attles. Attles, with his owner's blessing in 1975, broke the unwritten league rule for how many Black players could be on a team and how many would start at home games. Attles, ahead of his time, innovatively emphasized player interchangeability throughout the entire roster. He knew that giving players nearly equal playing time (most NBA teams of that era relied on their starters with minimal substitution) would motivate them as far as career advancement; in turn, he would get greater overall production from the sum of those parts.

Strikingly, racial barriers were being broken by the Warriors during a time when Madison Avenue, and concomitantly network television, feared that the NBA might be "too Black" (too much fighting, too many drugs, and overpaid players) for white fans. This fear-based perception was fed more by the popularity of what was considered an even Blacker league, the rival ABA, with whom the NBA seemed destined to merge. Rick Barry, by the way, should be properly credited as *the* pioneer of modern sports free agency for legally challenging the reserve clause in 1967 *two years before Curt Flood* did with Major League Baseball. As the first NBA player (and a superstar, no less) to jump to the rival ABA, Barry started a salary war between the leagues, increasing player salaries by 500 percent over an eight-year period.

The world around that Warriors team was changing. That

summer Hank Aaron incited Southern white anger by eclipsing Babe Ruth's home-run record, and Muhammad Ali stoked Black nationalism by beating George Foreman in Zaire. That August saw the resignation of President Nixon, the dawn of free agency in Major League Baseball, and the end of US involvement in Vietnam. Progressive politician Jerry Brown became governor of California while dating Mexican American music star Linda Ronstadt. The 1974–75 Warriors were in line with the zeitgeist of the changing nation and the Bay Area.

Who we become and what the world becomes are inextricably linked. The principle of human alchemy is how we combine with each other and the truth of the present world, transforming into what we need to be in order to make the world what it needs to be.

THE GREAT RESET

Maybe now, more than ever, the world needs human alchemy. *Time* magazine calls it "the Great Reset." In a special issue in partnership with the World Economic Forum, the magazine stated, "The Covid-19 pandemic has provided a unique opportunity to think about the kind of future we want," and asked "leading thinkers to share ideas for how to transform the way we live and work." McKinsey & Company set up a special section on their website called "Return, Reimagine, Reinvent" that offers "a regularly updated collection of articles" for leaders to "rethink" ways of working, providing expertise on postpandemic "reentry" to help organizations lead the "recovery."

Right at the start of the pandemic, Nick Cave, songwriter and creative force sui generis, beautifully wrote in the March 2020 edition of his monthly newsletter, *The Red Hand Files:*

> Together we have stepped into history and are now living inside an event unprecedented in our lifetime. We are forced to isolate—to be vigilant, to be quiet, to watch and contemplate the possible implosion of our civilisation in real time. When we eventually step clear of this moment we will have discovered things about our leaders, our societal systems, our friends, our enemies and most of all, ourselves. . . . As an artist, it is a time to take a backseat and use this opportunity to reflect on exactly what our function is—what we, as artists, are *for.* Perhaps, we will see the world through different eyes, with an awakened reverence for the wondrous thing that it is. This could, indeed, be the truest creative work of all.

Everything is on the table. Do we rethink capitalism? How might we redirect Hollywood? So many office buildings to repurpose, for what purpose? Should we reimagine schools? Reform or deform the police? Restructure the Supreme Court?

We are not talking about creating new relationships among old institutions (chemistry). We are talking about new institutions interdependently creating a new, different, better world (alchemy). Transformation of fundamental societal institutions necessarily changes us. It will change our relationships to each other, to those institutions, and, significantly, to our conception of self in this world.

We will need models of human alchemy that respond to new

needs, new behaviors and life rhythms, new global value systems. Is basketball's human alchemy the model for the kind of interpersonal effect we want?

What we do know is that at the onset of the Great Reset, it was basketball players who were the most immediately and visibly alchemical.

SHUT UP AND ALCHEMIZE

In the United States, one of the purportedly great alchemizing events that takes place every four years is a national presidential election. In 2020, both political parties stated loudly and unambiguously that this election was not just about the candidates. Our entire democracy was on the line. Voting had never been more important.

But the pandemic complicated things. Typical voting locations were the kind of prohibited indoor venues where you could likely catch Covid. That made it harder to vote in person. And while the option for mail-in voting was perfectly legal, the president ordered the postmaster general to remove post office boxes across the country, while also falsely warning of imminent voter fraud through mail-in balloting. That made it harder to vote by mail.

Though LeBron James was quite busy that summer, sequestered in the NBA bubble and working hard to win a fourth NBA championship, he saw the forces of voter suppression and knew full well what was at stake for the country, for his family, and for the world. He had to do more. He had to be more than just an NBA champion.

On June 23, James launched the nonprofit More Than a Vote,

an organization with a single-minded focus on getting more people to the polls. This was James alchemizing into a national voting rights advocate. The alchemizing didn't stop there. In order to achieve his mission, James concluded that the mechanism for voting itself had to be different. He calculated that there needed to be a big-idea solution to help with people's fear of being in close quarters during the pandemic, plus the intimidation of in-person voting, plus the diminishing accessibility of mail-in voting. His idea, which he manifested, was to transform sports stadiums and arenas into mass public voting booths.

By Tuesday, November 3—Election Day—over fifty stadiums and arenas from every kind of sports league were open for voting. And through More Than a Vote, James signed up over ten thousand volunteer poll workers.

The basketball player who alchemized into a voting advocate, who alchemized stadiums into polling centers, which alchemized American voting, inspired other alchemical transformations. Chef José Andrés, founder of the World Central Kitchen, no longer sees a stadium but "one gigantic kitchen" to feed the hungry. Around the world, stadiums and arenas were converted to mass vaccination sites. What next, what else? That's the right alchemical mindset that started with LeBron James, a basketball player.

In the summer of 2020, entire professional basketball leagues alchemized into social justice organizations. In the midst of a national racial reckoning, the NBA and WNBA became clear, active, and intentional global platforms for Black Lives Matter. The WNBA players, however, took their societal platform to a whole new level.

The WNBA teams in their summer bubble, like the NBA, wore shirts and displayed other messages of support to nationwide protests for justice sparked by the murders of George Floyd, Breonna Taylor, and many others before them. But when Senator Kelly Loeffler (R-Ga.), an Atlanta Dream co-owner, spoke out publicly against the Blacks Lives Matter and the Say Her Name movements, the role of the WNBA players alchemized into something more focused.

Players and fans pressured Loeffler to sell her shares of the team. She refused. Then, in August, after a meeting of the WNBPA executive board that included WNBPA Board of Advocates member Stacey Abrams, WNBA players from the Dream—as well as players from Chicago, Seattle, and Phoenix—started wearing "Vote Warnock" shirts during televised warmups before games. Warnock was Reverend Raphael Warnock, Loeffler's registered Democratic opponent for the 2020 Georgia Senate race, who at the time was polling at about 9 percent. The WNBA promotion and accompanying publicity immediately raised Warnock's profile, lifted his finances, and contributed mightily to the efforts of voting rights activist Stacey Abrams and her organization Fair Fight.

After the closest senatorial election in Georgia history, both Georgia Senate seats flipped from Republican to Democrat following a runoff. That happened. And it happened when basketball players mixed themselves with the social and political instability of an entire nation and together made themselves and the country something else.

As an interesting sidenote, in February 2021, after Kelly Loeffler had left the Senate, she sold her shares in the Atlanta Dream to a consortium that included Renee Montgomery, the first former player to be part of a WNBA ownership group. Alchemy begets alchemy.

WHO'S GOT NEXT? ALL OF US

Maya Moore was at the pinnacle of her basketball career. But she just couldn't be that anymore. The world would not let her. And she would not let herself. What was required was another way of being, which meant being something else, entirely.

In February 2019, when she was perhaps the best women's basketball player in the world, Moore walked away from playing the game to commit herself completely to the fight for criminal justice reform. "I'm sure this year will be hard in ways that I don't even know yet," Moore said to the *Minnesota Star Tribune*. "But it will also be rewarding in ways I've yet to see, too."

Moore focused on one case: the wrongful conviction of Jonathan Irons in 1998. Her great uncle had told her about Irons, a sixteen-year-old from Missouri who had been convicted by an all-white jury of first-degree assault, first-degree burglary, and armed criminal action resulting in a fifty-year sentence. No blood, footprints, or fingerprints tied Irons to the crime.

She went on to befriend Irons, visiting him in prison and attending his hearing. Eventually her work culminated in March 2020 with a judge overturning Irons's conviction. And he left prison a free man—and also in a relationship with Moore. "There is life we want to live, things we want to do, things we feel called to do together to help make our world a better place," Moore told

Kurt Streeter of *The New York Times* in May 2021. "This sense of freedom is huge for both of us now."

Moore has yet to return to playing basketball. According to an article by Chris Herring and Neil Paine on the analytics website *FiveThirtyEight,* Moore may have sacrificed more for a social justice cause than any other athlete. Not only was her résumé "worthy of GOAT consideration"—six WNBA Finals appearances and four titles, a league MVP award, two NCAA championships, and two Olympic gold medals—but in leaving the game at age twenty-nine, the years she has since missed were statistically the most productive remaining in her career. This is especially true for Moore, who plays a pro sport that pays much less than others, requiring her to play overseas just to make up the difference. Unlike male pro athletes of similar prowess, Moore did not have the chance to create a tremendous reservoir of financial security. She also knew the WNBA collective bargaining agreement would be negotiated in 2019, likely resulting in a substantial salary increase for her had she chosen to continue playing.

She let all that go. She was already someone else doing something else. Maya Moore heroically alchemized.

In the heat of the 2020 summer of protest and social unrest, Natasha Cloud opted out of the WNBA season to devote herself entirely to social justice activism. Like Maya Moore she felt compelled to answer a different and higher calling. She accepted that she'd forfeit her salary, but was happily surprised that Converse would honor its shoe deal with her. In a bit of alchemy of their own, the shoe company announced they'd cover her 2020 salary, donated $25,000 to Cloud's Philadelphia social justice organization, and voiced future plans to produce a documentary featuring Cloud.

Alchemy begets alchemy.

First basketball players, then big business, then . . . commercial real estate? Education? Public health? Who's next?

Our world is changing in seismic, fundamental ways at light speed. Each of us must answer the call of this world. We can no longer be who we were.

Positive transformation of a society requires more than just improvement; it requires alchemy. Every person and institution must engage openly with the changing world and mix in bravely with it, not to become better but to become different—and thus better—because that alchemy is right for what is needed now.

To put it bluntly, we cannot stay the same and then expect things to be different. When we find new ways to approach each other with our differences, when we include new voices in our conversations, then our conflicts, our problems, and our selves— *this world*—will be the alchemical change we wish to see.

Maya Moore looked around at her world just as Naismith did at his, and both arrived at the same conclusion: "It was evident that a new principle was necessary."

MAKE IT GLOBAL

You can go anywhere in the world and there's really only a few things we all share. You can talk about food, talk about God, music, sex or love. And you can talk about basketball. Basketball is a global common denominator.

—Dan Klores, Peabody Award-winning filmmaker and basketball laureate

B asketball was global at concep-
tion. After all, here was a man from one country, Canada,
whose parents originated from another country, Scotland,
inventing a game in another country, the United States. Putting
aside the YMCA mission of promoting Muscular Christianity, it's
unlikely the border-crossing James Naismith ever thought to himself, "Even though I'm from another country, this game I'm creating is really only good for the country I'm standing in." No, the
globality of basketball was in the DNA of its inventor, and it was
also in the world around him.

Naismith stood in a United States still traumatized by the
death of hundreds of thousands in the American Civil War, a country whose government continued to pursue the massacre of its
indigenous Native Americans. On the other side of the world,
China was bleeding internally following the Boxer Rebellion. The
Anglo-Zulu War had ravaged South Africa in the previous decade.
Czarist Russia was pillaging its weakest and poorest across Eastern
Europe. Skittish Western European nations began making secret
alliances. Global mass migration was on the rise, as the world began
sleepwalking toward its first great all-consuming conflagration of
mechanized global armed conflict.

This was the planetary vibration that surrounded Naismith

when he invented his game. Consciously or unconsciously he, like a prism, refracted the brokenness of the world and his own personal history to create a microcosmic solution to its ills. Other men of his time also saw sports as a way to improve the world and the people in it. President Teddy Roosevelt declared sports a proper stage to demonstrate national preparedness for war. French aristocrat Pierre de Coubertin created the modern international Olympic movement, believing the spectacle of world amateur games could inspire peace among nations. Naismith was neither Roosevelt nor de Coubertin. He created a single game that was stateless—meant for any people, anywhere, anytime—with basic principles that fostered cooperation, ease of play, spatial intimacy, self-governance, and even a kind of freedom.

It was meant to be global from the start.

Immediately, basketball became culturally ingrained through YMCA outposts in France, Australia, Brazil, and China. China in particular connected to the game almost instantly, and by 1895, just three and a half years after its invention, Naismith's disciples were teaching basketball on every continent.

Word of the game spread fast. Reports came to Naismith of the game catching on in India, Persia, and Alaska. In South America the game was played in Uruguay and Argentina. In Japan and England, only girls played until 1913, when the boys caught on. The Philippines took to it right away. So did Jamaica, Haiti, and Puerto Rico in the West Indies. Canada knew the game—not just because of Naismith, but because four of the original ten basketball players at Springfield College were Canadian. By 1914, the game was in full swing in Russia, Belgium, Spain, and Italy.

Then came the war, which greatly accelerated global spread of the game. The YMCA served as a World War I rehabilitation, conditioning, and leisure organizer for troops in Europe. Quickly, basketball became the primary health and wellness activity for soldiers of every Allied nation. Naismith himself, overseeing the YMCA basketball program abroad, was stationed in France for *nineteen months,* preaching and promoting the game to combatants and civilians as he traveled through Europe. French soldiers sent to Madagascar actively played basketball while stationed there, which introduced the game to neighboring Constantinople, Cairo, and Beirut.

After the war, basketball became so organized and popular in Europe that Prague, Portugal, Switzerland, Latvia, Italy, Greece, Hungary, Bulgaria, and Romania founded an "International Federation of Basketball" (forerunner to FIBA) in 1932. Amazingly, in a sign of how universal basketball had become in 1936, the game was invited to be an official Olympic sport at the highly anticipated Berlin games, giving it tremendous global attention.

Much has been made of the Dream Team of 1992, when NBA players were first permitted to participate in the Summer Olympics in Barcelona, as the moment when the whole world truly began to embrace basketball. But that moment came not with the Dream Team of 1992 but with Naismith's dream of 1892. The sensation of the Dream Team in Barcelona was the payoff from the intentional hundred-year global grassroots campaign preceding it.

Before Naismith's death in 1939, the rules of basketball had been translated into almost fifty languages and dialects. One of the last things he wrote in *Basketball: Its Origin and Development* was how his global vision for basketball had so powerfully manifested at that point: "I am sure that no man can derive more pleasure from money or power than I do from seeing a pair of basketball goals in some out of the way place." Not in his wildest dreams, however, could Naismith have imagined how the global scope and influence of his game would continue to phenomenally expand.

IT'S EVERYWHERE, IN EVERYTHING, LIKE NOTHING ELSE IS

How global is basketball? There are two ways to measure it: ubiquity and influence. On the global stage the biggest world sports are cricket, soccer, and basketball.

Cricket remains incredibly popular in previously English colonized territories like India, but it's far from popular or even present everywhere in the world the way basketball is. Nor does it yet have a powerful mass youth culture like basketball that fuels the game's continuing global growth.

Soccer is undeniably everywhere—and for good reason. It's a joy to play and requires no equipment besides a ball and any two objects thrown down to fashion a goal. There's no question that in terms of sheer total fandom and participation, soccer is ahead of basketball. But even with titanically world-famous players like Messi and Ronaldo, soccer still cannot match basketball in terms of global trends and cultural influence. And that influence is only growing.

First, the fandom and participation gap between the two sports is closing. Taking professional sports league market value as an indicator, in the past decade, the average NBA franchise valuation has risen 476 percent, about twice as much as average top European soccer league teams. A July 2021 collection of data by *The Boardroom* shows a significant social media gap favoring the NBA over the Premier League; this gap applies to Instagram followers (NBA 57.1 million, Premier League 46.7 million), Twitter followers (NBA 37.7 million, Premier League 27 million) and YouTube subscriptions (NBA 16.8 million, Premier League 1.7 million) alike. Since 2015, basketball world participation rates have increased 18 percent to soccer's 13 percent.

When it comes to forecasting trends and investments, reports by major consulting firms from Deloitte, PwC, McKinsey, and KPMG all predict basketball will dictate what the sports business future looks like. All of these firms identify basketball as the top Gen Z sport, or at least in the top three, along with soccer and Esports.

It goes beyond the commercial influence of pro sports leagues. Basketball sneakers dominate the sneaker industry, which has come to dominate all footwear. The bestselling sneaker of all time is the first signature basketball shoe, Chuck Taylor Converse All-Stars. The most valuable sneaker in the world: Nike's Air Jordan. Air Jordan redefined sneakers as high fashion and, incredibly, transformed them into investment vehicles. The sneaker resale market is now a multibillion-dollar marketplace. On a given month, some iteration of Air Jordan will claim the top five or six slots in the StockX ranking of the top ten highest-selling sneakers. Typically, only one or two other brands will even crack the top ten. It is mind-boggling to acknowledge the influence of basketball on footwear in that the Jordan Brand, emanating off the singular talent of the basketball player Michael Jordan, who was the most marketable human being on the planet from the early 1980s through the early 2000s, continues to dominate the global sneaker market. Even more remarkable is that top global soccer teams like Paris Saint-Germain, in an effort to create more market relevance for their brand, are collaborating with the Jordan Brand on their uniforms, spikes, and gear. To sell more soccer apparel they need Jordan's basketball silhouette.

The international character of today's NBA is significant and increasingly disproportionate in its overachievements. While an impressive 30 percent of the league is made up of non-American players from forty-one different countries, an even more impressive 40 percent of league MVPs since 2001–02 have come from outside the United States. The NBA is now influenced as much by the rest of the world as it is a global influencer. The league's cognoscenti, considered the most forward thinking in pro sports, open-mindedly look outside its borders for new ideas.

And countries all over the world that are *not* basketball's country of origin have developed deep emotional, cultural, and even political ownership claims to the game. The oldest basketball court in the world is not in the United States, but in a YMCA in the ninth arrondissement of Paris, France, that was built in 1893 and today is cherished and revered as a communal treasure.

Due to a number of converging demographic and cultural factors, basketball is now the number one sport among young people in Canada, surpassing ice hockey, and the country will forever claim ownership of the game's originator.

No country loves basketball more than the Philippines. The nation has more courts per capita than any other country in the world, and they're used in every conceivable way, even for funerals. As a result of being strapped for cash to deliver social services, major government debates center around the appropriation of public money to create and maintain basketball courts, equating courts with any other essential public need. Played in flip-flops from the countryside to back alleys, the game is everywhere in the Philippines. The Philippine national NBA fan awareness rate measures at a world-beating 98 percent, and during the NBA pandemic bubble, the country had the highest viewing percentage in the world.

Israel's defeat of the Soviet Union (which refused to recognize Israel's legitimacy) on its way to winning the 1976 EuroLeague basketball championship became a global visibility turning point for the young nation's defense of statehood when its star player, Tal Brody, announced in a postgame interview that the tiny country was now "on the map"—the words resonating in Israel and around the world.

If there's any question as to how much national pride Russia ties to basketball, note that the Russian film *Three Seconds* (aka *Going Vertical*), a 2018 drama about the USSR's controversial victory over the USA to win basketball gold in the 1972 Munich Olympics, is the highest-grossing domestic film ever in Russia.

And there is no question that the 1992 USA Olympic Dream Team (Michael Jordan, Magic Johnson, Larry Bird, Charles Barkley, et al.) set off a global basketball fever, accelerating the game's popularity and growth all over the world and putting basketball at the top of Olympic viewership.

Also in 1992, on the same stage that the Dream Team played, the Lithuanian national basketball team brought desperately needed global attention to Lithuania's fight for independence from the former Soviet Union. The "Other Dream Team" with two Hall of Famers—Arvydas Sabonis and Šarūnas Marčiulionis— even attracted financial support from the Grateful Dead, who subsidized the tie-dyed uniforms.

Today the game is everywhere. Indigenous Mayan communities in Guatemala play at the foot of a volcano, perhaps where the game has its ancient roots. In Native American communities, the game serves as a singular galvanizing force on reservations across the United States.

Africa now has a league of its own, the Basketball Africa League. Barack Obama got involved at an early stage, believing the venture could change Africa "because for a rising continent, this can be about a lot more than what happens on the court." A new basketball league in Africa may create fresh cultural traction away from the colonial importation of soccer toward something Africans can claim as theirs, connected to a cultural form so important to African Americans. It is the first professional league outside of North America officially involving the NBA. Maybe it's the case that with fourteen Africans in the NBA, Africa is changing the league and not the other way around.

The Coppa Italia—an annual, in-season, March Madness–style Italian Basketball League tournament that grips the nation—has already been adopted by the WNBA (as the Commissioner's Cup), and the NBA will likely be next.

Basketball is so global that the so-called Euro step—where an offensive player driving to the basket is stopped by a defensive player, picks up their dribble, then takes a long, seemingly illegal (but not really) gallop step, successfully getting around the defender—may not even come from Europe.

The game's advanced-level power move may have been created by Cuban leader Fidel Castro, as shown through declassified documents assembled by the writer Micah Wimmer. Basketball, not baseball, was Fidel's first love. Relatively tall at 6 foot 3, Castro played religiously wherever and whenever he could on state visits and back home, organizing heated pick-up games among his staff. "Obviously everyone played *for* Fidel," recalled his bodyguard. "It was out of the question for him to lose a game."

Castro often remarked that basketball skills of speed, dexterity, cunning, fast reactions, and anticipation were the ideal training for young revolutionaries. Che Guevara's journal entry on December 12, 1962, suggests, however, that Castro's flaunting of the Euro step may have taken it a step too far: "In his frequent basketball matches, Fidel has started using a new move he simply calls 'The Step.' It is undeniably effective, yet is its goodness equally undeniable? As revolutionaries we must not merely pay attention to ends, but to means. I worry that this flash and pomp is not befitting of the revolutionary leader. It serves to separate him too much from those caught in the chains of a maudlin life, marred by oppression and economic strife. Yes, it leads to a basket, but at what cost to the communal spirit?"

Basketball has the power to open doors to closed societies where nothing else or no one else could. North Korea, a notoriously reclusive and secretive nation, invited former NBA player Dennis Rodman to visit in 2013; he has returned multiple times since, often accompanied by a group of other former NBAers to play exhibition games. While North Korean leader Kim Jung-un remains an enigma, he is known to be an avid basketball fan who grew up watching the 1990s Bulls dynasty.

The cultural effect of basketball runs through the entire Korean Peninsula. In the late 1980s in South Korea, a powerful force of influencers known as the Oppa Army emerged. These influencers were a group of female fans obsessed with tall, handsome male basketball players, and they actively bolstered the Nonggu Dejanchi (Grand Basketball Festival), a newly created national Pro-Am basketball tournament. Throughout the '90s, the Oppa Army redefined female fandom in South Korea, evolving into the hyperactive fan engine of the megapopular music genre, K-pop, that today dominates on a global scale.

Perhaps no cultural phenomenon did more to spread the popularity of basketball to young people throughout South Korea, Vietnam, China, and the entire Pacific Rim than *Slam Dunk,* the Japanese manga (comic) by Takehiko Inoue. Written in thirty-one volumes from 1990 to 1996, *Slam Dunk* has sold 157 million copies worldwide. It is the eighth-bestselling manga of all time. *Slam Dunk* has been adapted as a Game Boy video game, is the basis for four feature films, and was adapted into an acclaimed anime television series that aired from 1993 to 1996 across Asian countries and continues to be broadcast worldwide. In 1994, *Slam Dunk* received the prestigious fortieth Shogakukan Manga Award for the shōnen category. Shōnen manga are typically aimed at teenage boys, but the emotional content of *Slam Dunk*—the trials of a high school boy trying through basketball to understand himself and win over the affections of a female classmate—resonated powerfully with an entire generation of young people. It appealed (and still appeals) to male and female readers in Europe and the United States, and especially across Asia, where it popularized basketball in a personal way that raised the sport's shared meaning and importance—6,700 miles away and one hundred years after its creation in Springfield, Massachusetts.

Yet no stronger statement can be made about the global influence of basketball than its status as the most popular sport in the world's most populous nation: China. It didn't start with Yao Ming. China was one of the first countries to receive the sport, and it was the first to embrace it like no other. It's a remarkable history of a special relationship between China and basketball that must be understood.

In the midst of what China refers to as the century of humiliation (1839–1949), a period marked by Western and Japanese imperialism, natural disasters, and civil war, basketball arrived almost as quickly as boats could travel. The first stop was the port city of Tianjin in 1894, with YMCA basketball missionaries preaching an attractive philosophy of building a strong nation through strong bodies. During the Long March of 1934–35—a military retreat undertaken by Mao Zedong's Red Army to evade the Chinese Nationalists—communist soldiers frequently played basketball to create cohesion and boost their spirits. By the mid-1930s basketball was voted the co-national sport of China alongside soccer.

When Mao Zedong came to power in 1949, he expelled everything that was foreign, except for one thing: *basketball*. Without bourgeoisie affectations like classical music, popular novels, movies, and other sources of cultural enrichment, children and young adults set up backboards and hoops in courtyards and alleyways, pouring time and energy into the accessible game of basketball.

The People's Liberation Army (the successor to the Red Army) adopted basketball as its central camaraderie-building activity. From 1949 into the 1980s, all of China's best players were from the military. Basketball was unbelievably important to Mao. The first time he opened China to the West was for basketball: a diplomatic competition with France's Les Tricolores team, which visited the People's Republic of China in 1966. Mao's rare gesture of openness was a symbol of change, both internationally and domestically. Basketball was not only his chosen vehicle to establish the first bilateral relation with a Western nation, but also a signal of change to his own people.

Under Maoist China, basketball developed for two generations in complete isolation—so much so that the Chinese thought it was theirs. As historian Helen Gao noted in *The Atlantic,* "Until the NBA arrived in the late 1980s, basketball had come to feel so intrinsically Chinese, most people did not even associate it with America."

After Mao's death in 1976, China slowly reopened to the world, and the arrival of free NBA broadcast rights in 1987 took a country already enamored with the game to astronomically high levels of engagement. Yao Ming's arrival in the NBA in 2002, and his subsequent superstardom, cemented basketball's place in Chinese national pride.

Studies across twenty contemporary Asian markets by the research firm Ampere Analysis showed that among Chinese sports fans, the NBA is the favorite pro sports league (ahead of the Champions League), and basketball is the favorite sport. Those studies also show Chinese sports fans are younger than the national average age, which bodes quite well for the continued favorable future of basketball in China. It's hard to overstate what this means in terms of scale.

Compare basketball's importance in China to its popularity in the United States. Some 640 million Chinese citizens consume NBA programming and products. That means there are more NBA fans in China than there are people, total, in the United States. The NBA has two hundred stores spread throughout China, while it struggles to keep one NBA store open in New York City. China has opened NBA Play Zones in Beijing, Shanghai, and Chengdu—huge spaces where there are tons of basketball-related activities for kids and families to participate in. The Jr. NBA has official curricula embedded in close to fifty thousand Chinese schools. No other private, non-Chinese entity has such a relationship with the Chinese state-run schooling system.

After decades of a one-child policy, which began in the 1980s and coincided with the NBA's ascent in the Chinese national zeitgeist, the game of basketball has become the perfect way for kids to connect with one another. Young Chinese professionals today meet for pick-up basketball after work in the way that Americans meet for happy hour.

Writ large, the shared, deeply rooted love of basketball—both past and present—may be a common ground for China on a number of fronts. Hong Kong has 1,500 outdoor courts. Taiwan was the first to play pro basketball during the pandemic. Tibet loves basketball and always has; in 1946, *Seven Years in Tibet* author Heinrich Harrer found no games of any kind on the rocky terrain there except "a small ground for basketball."

In a country so populous, geographically vast, and ethnically diverse (comprising fifty-five different ethnic minorities), basketball is a shared love. It is truly remarkable how a cultural form that originated in the West can be the common denominator amid peoples as diverse as China's. The right international motif for China may not be the yellow star or the "Belt and Road" but a ball and a hoop.

Which is why the China-NBA rupture was such a missed opportunity. When Daryl Morey, then general manager for the Houston Rockets, tweeted support for Hong Kong protesters in October 2019, he enraged the Chinese government. They canceled lucrative media contracts and harshly condemned the NBA, creating an international tremor. Chinese citizens took to social media and the streets to demonize and boycott the league. The highly public outburst that ensued involved a boiling pot of issues including free speech, democracy, sovereignty, Chinese history, and a web of international commercial entanglements between the CCTV, Tencent, the NBA, and multinational sneaker companies. Adam Silver, Joe Tsai, LeBron James, and Yao Ming all found themselves managing awkward public stances on a daily basis.

There were great differences among all involved, but there was also fundamental commonality. It was the obvious thing: basketball. Why not start there? It's not just that they love the NBA in China. It's that they love the game. Was this about the Rockets (Yao Ming's former team) and the NBA? Was this about Hong Kong and China? It was about all those things. Yet when individuals from other Western entities—businesses, a soccer player—tweeted similar objections to Chinese government actions, there was not nearly the same level of backlash. Nothing got nearly the kind of reaction that Morey got. Why?

Because it wasn't about the NBA, it was about basketball, the most popular sport in the most populous nation. Basketball existed in China before the NBA. It's one of the national pastimes. Yet no one recognized the opening to say, Okay, what can we all agree upon? *The game.* That was the basic starting point, a 130-year through line for Xi Jinping, the people of China, Hong Kong, the United States, and the NBA.

Basketball captures and fascinates like few other things, maybe no other things, in the world. Few cultural forms have grown so consistently, even as the world has changed so much. Basketball transcends point of origin and conflicts between people, corporations, governments. In the years since the creation of basketball, governments have risen and fallen, people have passed on, corporations have grown or dissolved, borders have been redrawn, nations have formed and re-formed, the names of countries have changed, trends have come and gone, ideologies have been proven and disproven—but basketball has grown in places big and small, near and far. The influence and global momentum of basketball has only increased and continues to grow every day, everywhere.

WHAT IN THE WORLD DO WE HAVE IN COMMON?

In a world of nation-states, there are so many challenges that require stateless solutions: climate, disease, hunger, human trafficking, water, cyber security, digital currency, space exploration.

These things affect everyone, everywhere. They interrelate all nations, all peoples.

But how can we even get to that when so much time is spent on ongoing international struggles over power and resources—as well as endless internecine and seemingly unsolvable conflicts between neighbors about borders?

How Basketball Can Save the World

Albert Camus likened World War II to a plague. He asserted that this "disease" knows no borders. It is planetary, and as such we must change our global operation. His question was simple: After this shared global horror, where do we—the world—go from here? "The Human Crisis" ("La Crise de l'homme") was a lecture delivered by the Nobel Prize–winning author on March 28, 1946, to a full house at the McMillin Academic Theatre at Columbia University. He called for the people of the world to build global collective consciousness by forming "communities of thought outside parties and governments to launch a dialogue across national boundaries; the members of these communities will affirm by their lives and their words that this world must cease to be the world of police, soldiers and money, and become the world of men and women, of fruitful work and thoughtful play."

Almost a century later, the metaphor became reality. There was a global plague, but no global response, no ability to come together to see that we are all the same now. The whole world failed.

How do we avoid this recurring human crisis? Then, as now, we emerged from the crisis, but not without great loss. Will we repeat intergenerational global failure? The besieged Ukrainian president, Volodymyr Zelenskyy, directly implored the United Nations on April 5, 2022: "How we will reform the world security system? How we will really guarantee the inviolability of universally recognized borders and the integrity of states? How we will ensure the rule of international law? . . . There can be no more exceptions, privileges. Everyone must be equal." The nation-state structure is not working so well. Looking around the world today, it seems ever more like the edgy, pre–World War I global construct of Naismith's time and the post–World War II global dilemma observed by Camus.

"This crisis," said Camus, "is also based on the impossibility of persuasion. People can only really live if they believe they have something in common, something that brings them together."

But there's so little we agree on. Where do we begin? Can we find one thing in the world we're all okay with? What on earth is there that will literally unite the nations?

WORLD BASKETBALL DAY

The world's most official consensual global body, the United Nations, establishes "International Days." These days purport to serve as "occasions to educate the general public on issues of concern, to mobilize political will and resources to address global problems, and to celebrate and reinforce achievements of humanity." The hope is that each day becomes "a springboard for awareness-raising actions." The way an international day gets on the calendar is by resolution from the UN General Assembly—made up of 193 countries, that is, most of the states of the world—briefly laying out the substance of what and why for each day.

To date, the United Nations has designated 184 different international days, including popular days like the International Day of Human Rights, International Women's Day, World Water Day, and the International Day of Peace—as well as some less well-known days like World Radio Day, World Tuna Day, Asteroid Day, World Migratory Bird Day, and World Toilet Day. It is interesting to note that in just the last decade, we now have an International Day of Sport for Development and Peace (2013), an International Day of Yoga (2015), and a World Chess Day (2019).

These days, like many other actions taken by the United

Nations, are in service of the admirable "Transforming Our World: The 2030 Agenda for Sustainable Development, "adopted by all UN member states in 2015, which the United Nations refers to as "a shared blueprint for peace and prosperity for people and the planet, now and into the future." The essence of that blueprint is "an urgent call for action by all countries—developed and developing—in a global partnership" recognizing an integrated, all-in global agreement "that ending poverty and other deprivations must go hand-in-hand with strategies that improve health and education, reduce inequality, and spur economic growth—all while tackling climate change and working to preserve our oceans and forests." The United Nations understands that "in order to make the 2030 Agenda a reality, broad ownership of the SDGs (Sustainable Development Goals) must translate into a strong commitment by all stakeholders to implement the global goals."

Goals are end points. In order to reach goals, we must have a place to begin.

Why not start with a global common denominator: something that's everywhere, influencing everyone—especially young people—in ways that matter on so many societal levels? Let's start with just one day that recognizes not what we lack but what we have and what we share. A day that identifies a common space and celebrates a consciousness of sameness, openness, statelessness; a sense of ownerless, barrierless, cooperative oneness; a global common denominator of global common joy. A space where all are free to join. The year 2030 is almost here. Agreed-upon goals need an agreed-upon place to begin. The following is my proposed resolution to begin with a World Basketball Day.

United Nations

General Assembly

XX Session
Agenda item XX

Resolution adopted by the General Assembly on 21 December 2023
<DRAFT PROPOSAL>

World Basketball Day

The General Assembly,

Recalling that the goals of establishing International Days in the first place is to create special time and space everywhere, all over the world " to educate the general public on issues of concern, to mobilize political will and resources to address global problems, and to celebrate and reinforce achievements of humanity."

Affirming the designation of such awareness raising days like International Day of Happiness, World Health Day, World Mental Health Day, International Day of Sport for Development and Peace, World Philosophy Day, International Day of Living Together in Peace, International Day of Yoga, World Chess Day, International Day for the Eradication of Poverty, International Day of Human Rights, International Women's Day, World Water Day and International Day of Peace

Especially affirming the International Day of Human Solidarity; "The concept of solidarity has defined the work of the United Nations since the birth of the Organization"

Guided by The 2030 Agenda for Sustainable Development, our "shared blueprint for peace and prosperity for people and the planet, now and into the future"

Animated by the 17 Sustainable Development Goals, our " urgent call for action by all countries - developed and developing - in a global partnership"

Acknowledging Basketball's global ubiquity

Recognizing Basketball's low barrier to access across material wealth and erasure of barriers to race and nationality

Recognizing Basketball's omni-influential operation and impact in and across global spheres of commerce, peoplehood, gender inclusion, peace and diplomacy

133

How Basketball Can Save the World

Recognizing that Basketball creates a unique space of cooperation, spatial intimacy, physical movement and an interdependence that allows participants to see each other as human beings first and foremost

Understanding that beyond participation, the game itself presents a worldview of 13 Principles, remarkably consistent with and in service of the 17 Sustainable Development Goals

Understanding furthers that to reach the globally agreed upon end point of the 2030 Agenda for Sustainable Development and the 17 Sustainable Development Goals, the world needs a globally agreed upon starting point of shared one-ness; a global common denominator

Empowered by the global impact of designated International Days as a "springboard for awareness-raising actions"

1. *Decides* to proclaim 21 December as **World Basketball Day**

2. *Invites* all Member States, organizations of the United Nations system, other international and regional organizations, the private sector and civil society, including non-governmental organizations, individuals and other relevant stakeholders, to observe World Basketball Day in an appropriate manner and in accordance with national priorities, and to disseminate the advantages of basketball, including through educational and public awareness-raising activities;

3. *Encourages* everyone everywhere to play, watch, read, discuss or otherwise connect to the game, which will be a connection to each other everywhere affirming our global common one-ness which maybe, just maybe, can push us toward the idea of one world instead of many nations, united, to do the things only one world can do, starting with Basketball, one thing we all do.

4. *Stresses* that the cost of all activities that may arise from the implementation of the present resolution should be met from voluntary contributions; but any person or organization that has made a dime off this free 130-year old gift to the world ought to consider contributing accordingly

5. *Notes* that this World Basketball Day comes one day after International Human Solidarity Day; the former being an intentional first concrete united global expression of the latter

6. *Requests* the Secretary-General to bring the present resolution to the attention of all Member States, the organizations of the United Nations system and other relevant stakeholders for appropriate observance.

MAKE IT GLOBAL

MoreFree is a Chinese pick-up basketball legend. In China, he's the gospel preacher of playground basketball culture, its values and virtues. He travels and plays all over his diverse, mammoth nation. He has won numerous playground competitions all over China, and he organizes the largest pick-up basketball tournament in the world's largest nation: Sunset Dongdan, held annually in Beijing. "People, nowadays, are relying too much on languages; on words; on basic vocal communication," MoreFree told our students. "Instead we should go back to the roots of ourselves—communicate in an even better way. I chose basketball. It's a very good way."

MoreFree has played in pick-up games in almost every country, on every continent—from Compton to Cameroon—in communities each far different from any he's previously experienced and from each other. MoreFree calls basketball "my real passport—it gives entry to everywhere in the world." The game is his country—geographically borderless, open, and nationless. With basketball, MoreFree maintains a citizenship that is global and transferable.

Bill Bamberger, a renowned, award-winning photographer and professor at Duke University, would wholeheartedly agree with MoreFree's sentiment that on the basketball court, the idea of nation-states is an old idea. Basketball is its own country, its own language, no matter the place.

Bamberger's acclaimed photo books and one-person exhibitions have explored large cultural and social issues of our time: the demise of the American factory, housing in America, and adolescents coming of age in an inner-city high school. His 2019 project

Hoops is the first and only collection he's ever shot where the photographs have no people, just basketball courts.

"Sometimes it's not even the court that's the point," said Bamberger to our NYU class. "It's the architecture. It's the place. It's what that says about bringing this game into all kinds of places; how similar and how different. It's the fact that basketball happens everywhere."

Over fifteen years, Bamberger has photographed twenty-two thousand courts, in forty-two American cities and fifteen different countries spread across six continents. Bamberger says that an empty court—whether on the side of a barn, in a church, back alley, or dry dirt plain—tells him as much about the people there as it does about people everywhere else. He is passionately convinced that any basketball court is the universal prism through which we can understand both a particular community and our shared humanity.

"Think about it this way," he explains. "A basketball backboard is six feet wide, forty-two inches tall, the hoop as you know is ten feet off the ground, eighteen inches in diameter. It's a pretty simple design premise, right? And think about how different all the backboards are, all of the courts are. Think of how diverse we are as citizens of this country and of the world, and yet also, powerfully, the commonality."

We are not so different. We already have a shared language, an Esperanto-plus-plus. It's basketball. We have a shared common platform, a common global forum, a shared global instrument with which individual peoples and nations can say here is a place where we can all be together. Where we can begin to solve many things that affect us all.

This is not to say that a plan cannot be just right for a local situation. Of course it can. Bamberger simply means that we must carry a global consciousness, not an isolationist one. We must not think of ourselves as fundamentally different from one another merely because we are separated by geography through the accident of birth. As we move the planet forward, what are the things we will build that are for all of us? What things will speak to all of us, in a language that is not trapped in the past with its old prejudices, preconceptions, and limited mindsets? We made the borders, and we can unmake them.

James Naismith was operating in a borderless, global mindset, standing in one country though he came from a different one. His view was global. How could it be anything else? The game itself has become ubiquitous and influential because its intentional core principle for a *shared* global construct is the pathway to the only truly sustainable global future. Like Naismith imagining a new model for a new game, we have the power to break through to new models of global existential progress. If when we conceive of those models, like Naismith, we make them global.

PRINCIPLE
7

GENDER
INCLUSIVE

I said to my team something that I truly felt and I know they felt, and it just appeared different on TV, but I'm not apologizing for it because I don't feel like I need to apologize. It's what I honestly felt with my team at the moment. I wouldn't take it back. We've gone to war together. We believe in each other. So I'm in those moments, and that's how I am, so I don't apologize for doing that. I'm just me, and I have to just be me.

—Adia Barnes, University of Arizona women's basketball coach, caught on camera after a 2021 NCAA tournament semifinal victory coloring her enthusiasm with a four-letter word

J ust a week into the advent of basketball in the Springfield College gym, a group of women teachers from nearby Buckingham Grade School began to spend their lunchtime watching the new game. Soon after, they approached Naismith and asked whether they could play. He didn't flinch. "I saw no reason why they should not," he wrote in *Basketball: Its Origin and Development*. There was no hesitation, no "let me check with the head of school." That was it. The game wasn't even a month old, and women were playing it, every day.

No other competitive team sport included women at its origin.

The nearly immediate inclusion of women in anything in 1891, let alone team sports, was a wildly progressive development. Women were living in a gender-unequal society under restrictive gender norms, still thirty years away from getting the right to vote. The belief was widely held that female participation in competitive team sports might lead to un-womanly qualities like muscles, scowling faces, and competitive natures that would turn off potential fathers with whom to bear children.

Nevertheless, they persisted.

While the women were playing lunchtime pick-up in the Springfield College gym, twenty-three-year-old physical education professor Senda Berenson, down the road at Smith College in Northampton, read Naismith's 13 rules, published on January 15, 1892. She thought basketball would be the perfect game for her female students. She also knew she had to modify the game to mollify her administration. Senda made a few changes, the most significant of which was to divide the court into three sections, limiting where players could go to avoid the appearance of excessive female exertion. The only male allowed to attend the first game in 1893 was the Smith College president, because only he was a man of sufficient dignity and self-control, able to handle the sight of women moving athletically. But now the genie was out of the bottle.

By 1895, hundreds of women's leagues had formed in YMCAs and colleges around the country. On April 4, 1895, Berkeley played Stanford in the first women's intercollegiate game. In November 1909, an illustration titled *Woman with Basketball* graced the cover of *The Saturday Evening Post*. Women and basketball had reached mainstream America.

Interestingly in those early years, when basketball arrived in England, Japan, and parts of South America, it began as a sport for girls only—for the inane reason that because girls played it, boys refused to do the same. Women taking to his new game delighted Naismith to no end. He totally understood that basketball was "really the first chance women have to participate in an active sport."

One cannot help but note that Naismith married one of the first female basketball players, Smith College star Maude Sherman. Naismith wrote fondly of how Maude stayed "actively interested in the game and often commented on the progress the game had made." There's an iconic photo of a grinning Naismith holding a peach basket a couple of feet away from a woman poised to toss a ball at him. That's Maude. This athletic woman was his partner in life and thought. Naismith had zero issue looking at women as athletes—or as anything but a normal, equal partner in all pursuits, especially in the ideal he created.

By the beginning of the twentieth century, basketball was a lingua franca in the American women's movement. In an essay titled "The Value of Girls Basketball" in the 1909 Kokomo (Indiana) High School yearbook, *The Kokomo Kamera*, a female student had the temerity to write: "In this age of women's movements, few people have realized yet that the movement which is doing the most for womankind is centered in our High Schools. A new type of girl has sprung up in our country. A girl more perfect mentally, morally and physically, than the girl of twenty years ago. This is the basketball girl. Many are her detractors, numerous are her critics, but her champions and supporters see in her the future greatness of American womanhood.... From the High School basketball girl is being developed that strong self-reliant woman, the woman who is cool and keen in her judgement, quick and sure in her action, calm and unselfish in her dealings. Altogether, the perfectly developed woman."

Witnessing how women had taken to basketball, an emboldened Naismith wrote with great satisfaction that the "gentle arts"—sports formerly relegated to women like badminton and cycling—were from then on "doomed to be displaced."

If only the world had followed the principle of gender

inclusion, fundamental to basketball *from the beginning*. Basketball was a future-forward sport that found itself colliding over and over with patriarchal gender norms of the present. Even those who governed the organized game did not fully equalize the rules of men's and women's basketball until 1971.

Yet the spirit of basketball as a vehicle for gender inclusion lives on, unvanquished. Stubbornly, the game moves the world forward toward long-overdue gender inclusion by producing people who demonstrate that principle through their powerful examples.

GOT TO SEE IT TO BE IT, BUT SOMEBODY'S GOT TO BE IT FIRST

Dawn Staley had to be included. She grew up playing on the courts near the Raymond Rosen housing project in North Philadelphia. Boys regularly told her to go home, jump rope, and bake cookies. Not only was she small, she was the only girl there. But she stayed out all day and even some nights. Dawn got in the game. She came home with bruises and cuts. Her mother worried. Her baby was the youngest of five, with three older brothers and a sister.

Dawn felt at home on the court. She felt alive. She felt present. She played all by herself, sometimes, alone when it was dark out, shooting at a milk crate that had been nailed to a lamppost.

"As a kid," she told Maggie Mertens from *Cosmopolitan* in a 2017 interview, "I played not just basketball but baseball, softball, tackle football—anything the guys were playing, I wanted to play.

Some of my earliest lessons in perseverance were being turned away from the basketball court by the guys in the neighborhood when all I wanted to do was play. With persistence, I found I could wear them down and get out on the court."

She had to be included. Which meant she had to work harder. Winter afternoons she went to Moylan Recreation Center with her own ball. That was smart, because boys asked to use the ball. She would agree, but only on the condition that she be allowed to play, too. They rolled their eyes, until the best player there, Hank Gathers, included her.

Dawn got in the game. She worked even harder. And that got her a full ride to the University of Virginia. Her coach, Debbie Ryan, knew she was something else. "Dawn is special to the game," Ryan told *Sports Illustrated* in 1990. "God decided to make only one of her."

Dawn graduated in 1992. With no US pro league for women, she played overseas for three years, in Spain, France, Italy, and Brazil. The United States Olympic Committee decided they wanted to create a 1996 Atlanta Olympics women's Dream Team like they'd done with the men at the 1992 Barcelona games. Dawn made the team, which demolished every other country, beginning a still unbroken streak of successive gold medals with dominant margins of victory, unrivaled in Olympic team sports history.

Dawn and her 1996 teammates provided the excitement and strategic impetus to start two women's professional leagues—the ABL and then the WNBA. Big steps for gender inclusion, to be sure, but there was one more coming.

Nike sponsored a major public art project that summer: one-hundred-foot, building-size murals of nine athletes in eight cities. There was Charles Oakley in New York, Michael Jordan and Scottie Pippen in Chicago, Barry Sanders in Detroit, Jerry Rice in San Francisco, Cal Ripken in Baltimore, Mike Piazza in Los Angeles, and Mookie Blaylock in Atlanta. And at 8th and Market in Center City Philadelphia: Dawn Staley.

As recounted in Sara Corbett's *Venus to the Hoop*, Dawn's mother welled up with tears upon seeing the mural, saying, "That's my baby." For Dawn, now all grown up, the work was just beginning. Now she had to be included to make sure others got included.

She played pro ball, in the ABL from 1996 to 1998, then transferred to the new WNBA in 1998. But playing wasn't enough. In 2000, she accepted the head coaching job for Temple University women's basketball. For six years, she coached at Temple, a Division I program, *and* played in the WNBA. Who does that? No one but Dawn Staley. For two of those seasons—2000 and 2004—Dawn Staley played WNBA *and* coached Temple *and* won the gold with the Olympic team. Who does all that? Women do.

"We are masters at mastering more than one thing at a time," she wrote in 2021 in "A Message from Dawn Staley," a *USA Today* editorial. "Women are built for anything and everything. No offense to men, but we have a strength that men don't, because we bear the children. We need women to remember that, and lean on that strength."

Dawn had more to show us: about women, about herself, about who and what basketball can include in its meaning. In 2008, she took the head coaching job for the women's program at the University of South Carolina. This was the SEC, the conference of legendary coach Pat Summit. South Carolina had no real history of women's basketball achievement. But Dawn had history there. Her mother was from South Carolina; she came north as part of the Great Migration looking for a better life.

Dawn Staley went to work, just like when she was a kid in North Philly, building a program from scratch, in her own image. "When she came to the program [in 2008], you could pick wherever you wanted to sit in the arena," said a local newscaster. "Now tickets to her program are the hottest ticket in the state."

That's because in 2017, Dawn Staley's South Carolina women's basketball team won the national title. She did it with an all-Black roster, in a state where the Stars and Bars still flew over the State House just two weeks earlier.

She now has three gold medals as a player and two NCAA national titles (another in 2022) and a gold medal as a coach. She was inducted into the Naismith Memorial Basketball Hall of Fame (2013) and the Women's Basketball Hall of Fame (2012).

In January 2021, a giant statue of A'ja Wilson, a Black female basketball player from the 2017 championship team, was erected on the University of South Carolina campus in front of Colonial Life Arena, where the men and women play. This was an incredible juxtaposition and demonstration of inclusiveness on a state campus that also has a wellness and fitness center named after segregationist politician Strom Thurmond. This was the same campus on whose grounds A'ja Wilson said her grandmother was not permitted to walk.

Twenty-five years after her Nike mural in Philadelphia, Dawn Staley had to look at that statue and think to herself, "That's my baby." And now at the intersection in North Philly where she used to shoot jumpers into that milk crate on a lamppost, there is a sign that reads "Dawn Staley Lane."

"People look in from the outside and don't understand," Staley told William Rhoden at *The New York Times* in 1996. "That's the way of the world. These are my roots. This is all I know: Stand tall, walk the walk and live the life." Living by that code, Dawn Staley has broken the mold. She has shown what is possible.

Eric Boynton reported Staley's answer when she was asked at an April 2021 press conference about her interest in coaching in the NBA or WNBA: "No ounce of me really wants to coach outside of college."

And what's her biggest accomplishment? "Just being a dream merchant for the players I coach." If they dream it, she wants them to be it. And to be it, she knows they've got to see it—and not just on a basketball court.

"If all the players I've coached, if they've always seen the WNBA in their lives, if they've always known the WNBA to exist, they have something to reach for. Now that Kamala Harris is our vice president, some political science major, Black students, if they want to stay in that field, they have something to reach for," Staley told Caitlin Yilek of CBS News in March 2021. "Representation matters. It does."

What's at stake for daughters, sisters, mothers, and grandmothers everywhere—on campuses, in legislatures, in C-suites, in sports, in houses of worship—is including their dreams in the world's reality. Basketball and Dawn Staley have set forth a game plan for every aspect of gender inclusion.

HER, HIM, THEY: EVERYBODY, EVERYWHERE

In the twenty-first century, we find ourselves at once experiencing a long overdue reckoning in gender relations and a distressing undoing of progress in gender equity. The powerful #MeToo movement has called out long-standing sexual harassment in Hollywood, the cultural arts, and every kind of workplace. Australian women claim the most unsafe place to work is among their lawmakers in parliament. In Great Britain women took to the streets to protest the murder of a female marketing executive, Sarah Everard, who was innocently walking home one early evening. It was said "she did all the right things." As if it's "right" to live in a society where all women must walk this earth hyper-vigilant of male attack. Mieko Kawakami's novel *Breasts and Eggs,* recently translated into English, brought global attention to Japan's oppressive, patriarchal gender mores and prompted a backlash in Japanese society, which was further magnified by embarrassingly clueless sexist comments by top Tokyo 2020 Olympic Committee officials.

The 2020 Japanese Olympic Committee reminds us that systemic gender inequity and disempowerment leads to systemic abuse, like in the case of Larry Nassar and Team USA gymnastics. That even with fifty years of Title IX, we see a steady, alarming decline in female head coaches and a shocking separate and unequal treatment of men and women at March Madness. We also see disproportionate political and legislative energy put toward the exclusion of transgender athletes. In the summer of 2022, after the Supreme Court of the United States took away a woman's constitutional right to choose, the WNBPA, in an official statement, asked rhetorically, "Are we in a democracy where guns have more rights than women?"

To address and combat inequity there must be empowerment. But there can be no empowerment if there is absence. That absence has reached a crisis point. The pandemic erased decades of women's workplace progress. In February 2020, women in the American workforce outnumbered men. After Covid, millions of women left the workforce permanently. The World Economic Forum's *Global Gender Gap Report 2021* projects it will take women in North America 61.5 years to achieve economic parity with men, and 136 years worldwide.

We can't wait that long. At its inception basketball made a unique statement for gender inclusion. Look at the world, and how little progress has been made since.

MOGADISHU, SOMALIA

Over the decades, women's and girls' basketball in Somalia has become a forum for women's rights in that war-torn country. Specifically, basketball in Somalia has become a powerful statement of the importance of women's rights in the twenty-first-century Islamic world. In Somalia, girls play basketball in defiance of death threats from the militant Islamic extremist group al-Shabaab, who do not believe in basic rights for women. The girls play anyway. The game has become the flashpoint for where and whether Somalia, a country trying to reclaim itself, becomes a safe, gender-equitable society or not.

Somalia's first women's national basketball team was formed in 1970 and participated in African and regional competitions over the years. During the collapse of Somalia's central military government in 1991 and the decades of civil war and clan rivalry that followed, the Somalia sports infrastructure collapsed along with it. Women and girls had to self-organize their own basketball games.

In 2006, the Islamic Courts Union, which controlled Mogadishu and large swathes of the country, prohibited women from playing sports, specifically targeting basketball as a "satanic act" against the principles of Islam. Al-Shabaab announced brutal plans for punishing "un-Islamic" female basketball playing by sawing off players' right hands and left feet.

The national team captain, Suweys Ali Jama, received regular telephone calls from al-Shabaab, threatening to kill her if she didn't stop playing basketball. The day before her wedding they called her to say they knew where the wedding party would be held and that if she did not publicly declare that she would quit basketball, they would bomb the reception. Suweys postponed the wedding.

Al-Shabaab's influence is a powerful deterrent. Most boys tell the girls they'll never marry a woman who plays basketball. Neighbors and family members tell girls to stay home and not play. The girls, in turn, do not trust intimate friends and relatives, and won't say they're going to play basketball. So they walk out of the house, covered in traditional religious clothing, veiling their faces to show piety and to keep from being recognized, carrying a bag full of basketball clothes. They surreptitiously head to an enclosed compound, walled off by bullet-ridden cement walls, where no one can see them play.

Each day they play, they feel empowered. "It made me stronger," Amaal, a young player, told *The New Yorker*'s Alexis Okeowo in 2017. "I used to be at the house doing nothing—I never had any friends. Basketball lets me know more about myself. I'm around women who are passionate, who are my friends."

Another woman, Aisha, defied her grandmother's warning to stay inside, away from the men with guns. But the pull of basketball was too important, Aisha said. "We need to go after our dreams and what we want for ourselves."

They get that from just doing the thing they love: basketball. They love it because it lets them love themselves. Which means they're here, on earth, included. It ties directly to the special power of the game to be an expression of inclusion and equity for women.

The death threats, however, never stop. In 2011, women's basketball became something of a high-profile national showdown. The Somali women's team arranged a national tournament in the village of Garowe. But just days before, a group of influential Islamic clerics issued an official statement, a *fatwa*, urging those who truly practice Islam to go to the tourney and cut the players' throats. The women played anyway. For these women, in their practice of Islam, basketball has become an article of faith.

"I will only die when my life runs out—no one can kill me but Allah," Suweys Ali Jama told Shafi'I Mohyaddin Abokar of the Inter Press Service news agency.

"I am a human being and I fear, but I know that only Allah can kill me," stated twenty-one-year-old Mohamed, inspired by her team captain Ali Jama's sentiments.

Aisha saw theological inconsistency in it all. The "Islamic" ban of women's basketball clashed with her understanding of Islam. It didn't make sense to her that God would care about a girl playing basketball if on a daily basis a girl tried to be faithful and good. She considered herself devoted to Islam. She had memorized the Quran. She had read most of her uncle's library of Islamic books. "Praying and reading the Quran and going through these books gives me the feeling of being connected to God. It gives me the feeling that, on Judgment Day, I will not be judged because I missed my prayer or anything else," she explained. *Anything else,* like basketball. If anything, she felt playing basketball was instrumental—not detrimental—to her Islamic faith.

After decades of a life-threatening ban, living in a country in shambles from violence, drought, and famine—what motivates these women to commit to basketball, putting their lives at risk daily?

"It's not for me. It's for the girls who are watching. Because I know it can change their lives, just like it did for me." That's peace activist Ilwad Elman, daughter of the late peace activist Elman Ali Ahmed, who was known as the Somali Father of Peace. Ilwad, a Nobel Peace Prize candidate in 2019 and 2020, heads the Elman Peace foundation fighting for fundamental human rights, gender justice, peace, security, and social entrepreneurship. She knows the women of Somalia must have a place to go to feel free, to have a voice. At the Elman Peace Centre in Mogadishu, she focuses on helping survivors of gender-based sexual violence and women suffering from the overwhelming gender inequality. Her main, not-secret weapon: basketball.

In the summer of 2019, five hundred girls showed up to a basketball day clinic held at the Elman Peace and Human Rights Centre in partnership with Giants of Africa, an organization that empowers African youth through basketball, cofounded by continental hero Masai Ujiri. He is the first and only African-born president and general manager of a professional sports franchise in North America, the NBA's Toronto Raptors.

Masai Ujiri tells the girls in his opening talk: "There's nothing wrong with Mogadishu!" His message and the message of that clinic: There's nothing wrong with *you*. There is nothing wrong with being a woman. No matter what the world tells you. Basketball will tell you different.

Amid rubble, oppression, and the threat of death, basketball is a wellspring for Somalian women and for Somalia itself—and beyond Somalia, it has been rippling out as a wellspring across continents for young Islamic girls, wherever they are.

What's at stake with basketball's principle of gender inclusion is not only the future of Somalia and the future of Islam. It is nothing less than the progress of all of us. That progress—or lack of progress—is, for all of us, like in Somalia, a matter of life and death. The life or death of us, our societies, our world, our daughters, sisters, mothers, and grandmothers. The "future is female" means the future is inclusion. That future is urgent.

We get there, to that future, by understanding how high the stakes are. We get there by seeing gender inequity is an unsustainable course for humanity. We get there by insisting on full gender inclusion from the beginning, at the core, in everything we do. However we get there, we must get there, *now*.

NO MORE WHAT IF, ONLY WHAT NOW

As a diminutive teenager in the 1970s, Nancy Lieberman rode the subway two hours from Rockaway Beach to Harlem, where she was told by the men at Rucker Park to turn around and go home.

The future Hall of Famer and women's basketball pioneer shot back: "Is your name Rucker? No? Then it ain't your park. I got next."

Period, end of story. It's never been said better.

We are a planet of regions. Every region has different tribal, racial, and ethnic divisions. But all places on the earth—regardless of tribe, race, or ethnicity—have gender. Basketball says what is created is created to be used, enjoyed, and benefited from by every human gender. And the world can no longer tolerate any other way.

It's not just Somalia. Look who was on the front lines protesting brutal autocracy in Belarus. It's all women. Look at the woman Stacey Abrams, who bravely led the voter rights movement in Georgia, which became the flickering candle of free and fair US elections. Look at Canan Kaftancioğlu, called the "Stacey Abrams of Turkey," facing years of imprisonment for publicly challenging President Recep Tayyip Erdoğan's rule. Look at the coalition of successful women in Lagos, known as the Avengers, risking their lives opposing police brutality, leading one of the largest social protests in Nigerian history. Or the women in Myanmar, openly resisting the crushing military leaders who ousted the civilian female leader. Or Frances McDormand, Oscar in hand, demanding an "inclusion rider" in actor contracts to stop repulsive Hollywood abuse and inequity. Take the Scottish Parliament, which voted unanimously to require menstrual products be provided to its citizens for free. Scotland is the first country in the world to address "period poverty"—removing financial barriers that can prevent those who need pads and tampons from obtaining them. Consider New Zealand female prime minister Jacinda Adern rewriting her nation's labor laws and forcing a society-wide reckoning on the value of "women's work," which requires a national unlearning of decades-old bias about gender and labor.

When it is said "the future is female," what is meant is that the future is gender inclusive. "Does that mean," a student in our class asked five-time Olympian and Naismith Hall of Famer Teresa Edwards, "you think, at all levels, men should compete with women?" Her answer, shaking her head, "*That* doesn't matter." In other words, it's the wrong question. When it comes to basketball and gender, the starting point is inclusion, for everyone, across the entire spectrum of gender identity. "How do we *all* get included?" is what we need to ask. Inclusion means inclusion. Limited gender-binary thinking excludes a lot of people.

Teresa Edwards understands that basketball gender inclusion is about re-creating a new consciousness around the notion of inclusion. It's not about opening doors. It's about why have doors at all.

Whatever solution, plan, policy, or law you have for whatever problem or need, if it's not gender inclusive, across the full spectrum of gender identity, then it will fail the world going forward.

Whenever you start something new, it must be at its inception and core, culturally, operationally, structurally, gender—all gender—inclusive.

WHAT IF

In Michigan, there's a historic initiative currently taking place: the Task Force on Women in Sports. It's a bold *what if* project that begins with important basic questions. What if we could have a do-over when it comes to creating a gender-equitable sports ecosystem? What would it look like? Not a subleague, no *W* in front of its name but, like Naismith himself, redefining inclusion from the outset. Like Naismith, reject the old notions and begin with a radical notion of full gender inclusion. Explode the gender paradigm. The project is led by Secretary of State Jocelyn Benson, who is already making history in Michigan, where for the first time in the state, the governor, attorney general, chief justice of the Michigan Supreme Court, and secretary of state are all women. "Liberate Michigan," indeed.

It's an exciting initiative. By the time this book is published, the governor should have the task force's final recommendations on her desk. *What if?* What if like Naismith we look at gender inclusion afresh? What if we create a game or system that redefines the values of gender in the system? What if the system were gender inclusive, like basketball was from the beginning? For gender, we have to think like we have not thought before. For gender inclusion, basketball was never a *what if.* For gender inclusion, it was a *what now.*

PRINCIPLE
8

NO BARRIER
TO ACCESS

For those who know the Playground, that playground is you.

You can play high school or college for four years.

You can play Pro for a decade.

You can play playground basketball for life.

It is the only constant in a true ballplayer's heart, the highest truth in ball, period. For those who know, they know this well.

—Bobbito Garcia, from "For Those Who Know...
The Playground" included in photographer
Larry Racioppo's *B-Ball NYC*

N ecessity was the mother of Naismith's invention. His new game had to be played indoors, on a hard floor, in a restricted space. Now we need even less. Just a ball and a hoop. Basketball can be played by yourself. Try that with any other team sport. It simply doesn't work. You shoot, get the ball back, shoot again. It's easy. That is why you can find a basketball hoop nearly everywhere today—housing projects and cornfields, urban playgrounds and suburban driveways, courtyards and barnyards, the Tibetan peaks and African plains. Anyone can play it anywhere, right now.

That was the intent and reasoning. "The game we sought would be played by many," recalled Naismith in *Basketball: Its Origin and Source*, "therefore it must be easy to learn." Easy to learn meant easy to play. That had a lot to do with the choice of ball. Sports with small balls usually needed a stick—baseball, lacrosse, hockey, cricket, golf, tennis, squash. "In each of these games," said Naismith, "the use of intermediate equipment made the game more difficult to learn." Better to create a sport with a large ball that "could be easily handled and which almost anyone could catch and throw with little practice."

Just as the game itself was easy to play, the playing area had to be easy to create to make the game as accessible as it could be. In his introduction to *Rules for Basket Ball* (1892), the first published book of basketball rules, Naismith explicitly stressed accessibility as the first precondition of basketball play: "It should be such as could be played on any kind of ground—in a gymnasium, a large room, a small lot, a large field, whether these had [an] uneven or smooth surface, so that no special preparation would be necessary."

He then emphasized, "This is especially necessary in large cities where in order to get a good-sized field you must go to a considerable distance, thus rendering it inaccessible to many." And finally, "Basketball may be played on any grounds and on any kind of a surface."

It's true that like basketball hoops set up in driveways and on the sides of barns, other sports lend themselves to smaller, mini-versions of play adapted to limited spaces—touch football in the street, makeshift *futsal* in the favelas, pond hockey. But in their fullest, official versions, field sports require a 330-foot-long pitch, while basketball requires only ninety feet from end to end.

Barriers to access would have been a salient notion for James Naismith in 1891. During the Gilded Age, the ruling economic model was the monopoly, definitionally shutting out access and opportunity for social mobility to poor whites. They had it better than racial and ethnic subclasses who, as Gilded Age historian Richard Wright wrote, "became the targets of horrendous violence and repression."

The United States, in the moment of Naismith's invention, socially and legislatively barred access through the Chinese Exclusion Act, Jim Crow laws, the federal subjugation of Native Americans, and overwhelming widespread anti-immigrant sentiment. Economically, politically, legally, and socially, the United States was a country primarily operating on a principle of access: who had it (the elite) and who didn't (the masses).

So what did Naismith do? He created a sport with no barrier to access. That was why he left theological study and came to the YMCA, believing "that there might be other effective ways of doing good besides preaching." What good would any idea, program, or solution do if no one could get to it? Necessity for Naismith was both situational and societal.

The idea of no barrier to access—that everyone gets to play, that it's easy to enter the game—is a basic principle of the human condition. We all want that basic permission, for ourselves and for our children. That's what made basketball so popular, so fast, and why it continues to grow in popularity today. *It's so accessible.* How many things in the world is that true for in structure, in intent, and in reality?

THE PLAYGROUND IS OPEN

Playground basketball is the last, best, true communal experience on earth. It's free, it's open almost all the time, and it requires no ID, no proof of residency or citizenship, no dues, no membership, no dress code, no test score, no credit check. Presence equals admission. The only requirement is you have to share and participate with others, if others are there. The space is intimate. The experience is physical. It is meritocratic (winner stays on) and collaborative. It is unsupervised, self-governed, self-organized, voluntary, bound only by a social contract assented to by those who are present. There are no coaches, no referees, no commissioner, no official governing body. No gatekeepers.

Great books have been written and films made about this very special world. Authors and filmmakers have waxed rhapsodic, anthropologic, and mythologic about the custom, lore, and legend of what is distinctly (though certainly not exclusively) an urban phenomenon. To name a few: *The City Game* by Pete Axthelm, *Heaven Is a Playground* by Rick Telander, *Asphalt Gods* by Vincent Mallozzi, *Hoops Nation* by Chris Ballard, and *Soul in the Hole* directed by Danielle Gardner.

The best among them, *Doin' It in the Park,* is an independent 2012 documentary directed by Bobbito Garcia and Kevin Couliau. The filmmakers visited 175 courts in eighty days exploring the definition, culture, and social impact of New York's summer basketball scene. Garcia narrates the film, giving it an ultimate authority and grounding. His vocal imprimatur is no less than God narrating the Bible. That's because Garcia is a New York City native who has put an indelible footprint atop multiple urban movements, principally basketball, hip-hop, and sneakers.

Garcia is one-half of "Stretch and Bobbito" on WKCR, the legendary 1990s radio program that introduced the world to an unsigned Nas, Biggie, and Wu-Tang, as well as an unknown Jay-Z, Eminem, and the Fugees. In 1998 *Source Magazine* voted them the best hip-hop radio show of all time. As the progenitor of sneaker journalism, Garcia penned his landmark *Source* article "Confessions of a Sneaker Addict" in 1990, then in 2003 became the critically acclaimed author of *Where'd You Get Those?* In 2005, ESPN's *It's the Shoes* series, hosted by Bobbito, became the first show on the subject in broadcasting history. A former professional basketball player in Puerto Rico, Garcia also performed in the ground-breaking Nike "Freestyle" commercial. In 2007, the brand released seven co-designed Air Force 1 sneakers bearing his name.

Garcia explained to our NYU students what access to playground basketball means to him: "Well, it's a social space that is for many a safe space; I know it's been mine for decades. And so we can talk about it, in lofty terms, as like a sanctuary. Or when I was writing the script for the film, I wrote 'Basketball is religion, the park is my church.' . . . I think for many it provides a meeting point that is open."

Openness is where it begins, Bobbito says. It's the very issue of who can play that's so important: "It's like I have to sneak into a gym or I have to be a member of the New York Athletic Club . . . but the park is open. Once they unlock the gate, it's from 6 a.m. until 1 a.m. and a lot of parks of course don't even have gates. So, it is a space that doesn't take membership; that doesn't take registration."

It is not that other recreational spaces are not accessible or open. One can go to a park and do any number of other activities—walk, hike, fish, mountain climb, bike, or run. There are, however, simply more public basketball courts because they don't take up as much space, and they're not hard to get to. This is especially true in urban environments where vast green public spaces are typically not as close as the nearest basketball court. Sure, one could go to the public library. But not only are there more basketball courts in cities than public libraries, but libraries and their services are staffed, run, and supervised by others. The urban basketball court is run by us, whoever we are, when we get there.

Wes Moore, a Rhodes Scholar, decorated US Army combat veteran, and CEO of a top poverty-fighting nonprofit called the

Robin Hood Foundation, in his bestselling book *The Other Wes Moore* described life-edge decisions forced upon inner-city youth, and he explained why a pick-up basketball court in a difficult section of the Bronx melded together "high school phenoms running around overweight has-been guys . . . drug dealers . . . scrubs talking smack a mile a minute . . . church boys who didn't even bother changing out of their pointy shoes and button up shirts . . . freelance thugs . . . 'A' students . . . the dude sweating through his post office uniform when he should have been delivering mail, and the brother who'd just come back from doing a bid in jail." In the playground pick-up game, identity-irrelevance elevates everyone who enters the space. "We were all enclosed by the same fence, bumping into one another, fighting, celebrating. Showing one another our best and worst, revealing ourselves—even our cruelty and crimes—as if that fence had created a circle of trust. A brotherhood." The playground game's shedding of social status is transformational; it enables a different kind of sense of self, a new feeling of what you can be, which makes you want to return and have that feeling again.

Or as Pete Axthelm wrote in his seminal *The City Game,* about Black New York City neighborhoods in 1970, the summer after the Knicks won the NBA championship: "Basketball is the city game. Its battlegrounds are strips of asphalt between tattered wired fences or crumbling buildings; its rhythms grow from the uneven thump of a ball against hard surfaces. It demands no open spaces or lush backyards or elaborate equipment. It doesn't even require a specified number of players; a one-on-one confrontation in a playground can be as memorable as a full-scale organized game. Basketball is a game for young athletes without cars or allowances—the game whose drama and action are intensified by its confined spaces and chaotic surroundings."

Moore and Axthlem reflect what so many others have come to see. That urban American playground basketball, because there's no barrier to access, had become an oxygen tent for African Americans. As scholar Onaje X. O. Woodbine observed in his 2016 study *Black Gods of the Asphalt,* the last several generations of Black basketball players grew up in a time when street basketball had become their primary, often sole forum for social resistance in the face of "unprecedented street violence and the collapse of black social institutional buffers (church, school, family and so on)." Basketball courts became a natural environment for the most disenfranchised to exercise empowerment. Having found the one space where there were no gatekeepers—no coaches, no NCAA—their own voices could develop.

Woodbine says, "The playground became a new locus for the convergence of black expressive culture in hip-hop, with rap music, break dancing, and 'go hard or go home' style of basketball often performed simultaneously on the court." The association of hip-hop, the modern poetry of social protest, with its basketball accoutrements—long baggy shorts, low black socks, shirts under the jersey, sneaker identity—became a new language on all these fronts arising out of playground basketball and asserting itself in the broader commercial marketplace.

On the court, a distinct kind of playing style emerged. Nelson George, in the insightful *Elevating the Game,* called it "the black aesthetic," reflecting how after four hundred years of living in another America, a different style of basketball would evolve from a drastically different lived experience.

The playground and its Black aesthetic became so influential in the evolution of basketball and its compelling larger cultural impact, that the gatekeepers came in to limit access again and again. From 1967 to 1976, in high school and college basketball, the dunk was outlawed. This was not only an obvious measure to curb the particular gifts of a generational talent from New York City playgrounds named Lew Alcindor (Kareem Abdul-Jabbar), but it was aimed generally at removing a weapon commonly employed on the urban playground. In Black America, it was understood to be a coded rule to blunt an act of perceived Black masculinity and aggression.

In the 1980s, a fandom choice between Magic Johnson (Black) or Larry Bird (white), according to USC professor Todd Boyd ("Notorious Ph.D."), was really about who *you* were. The choice wasn't solely about basketball but about race, he told *The Ringer's* Michael Weinreb. And race, in turn, meant style of play, which meant speaking coded language about the "right way" (white) to play, about the perceived contrast between "athletic talent" (Black) and "intelligence" and "hustle" (white), about street (Black) versus old school (white). *Black Planet* by David Shields chronicled in detail the cultural milieu of the Seattle Supersonics for the entire 1994–95 season, depicting star guard Gary Payton as the embodiment of a league in racial conflict—a troubling world where perspectives of the nearly 100 percent white owners, reporters, play-by-play announcers, referees, head coaches, and the commissioner were divergent and disconnected from nearly 80 percent of Black players. What was "real basketball" versus who was "keeping it real," and who decided? And what was being meant when either was said? All the racially coded language around professional, commercialized basketball was aimed at invalidating the playground, the last bastion of African American access and all the expressions of Black ownership that flowed therefrom.

Toward the end of the twentieth century, basketball had become the talisman for America's discussion around race. The playground was the birth of that discussion. The playground game, its ethos and creativity, flowing from a rare place of ungated African American access, had burst into mainstream commercial consciousness.

In his classic 1993 analysis "Be like Mike? Michael Jordan and the Pedagogy of Desire," Michael Eric Dyson explained with clear-eyed straight talk that Jordan's Black aesthetic on the court was "indissolubly linked to the culture of consumption and commodification of black culture" but without Black consent, capitalizing to the tune of billions of dollars on "black juvenile imagination at the site of the sneaker." Yes, Dyson said, the street was powerfully influencing the broader American cultural landscape, but not necessarily to the benefit of urban Black youth. Rather, this phenomenon was "expanding inner-city juvenocracy, where young black men rule over black urban space in the culture of crack and illicit criminal activity, fed by desires to 'live large' and to reproduce capitalism's excesses on their own terrain."

Still, Dyson concluded that "basketball is the metaphoric center of black juvenile culture, a major means by which even temporary forms of cultural and personal transcendence of personal limits are experienced." And while he was distrustful of what Jordan's commercial appeal represented—"the black athletic body deified, reified, and rearticulated within the narrow meanings of capital and commodity"—Dyson conceded it is "nevertheless a remarkable achievement in contemporary American culture." Look where the playground had taken us.

How Basketball Can Save the World

When the gatekeepers try to limit or encroach on the limitless sense of self that playground basketball critically develops, they corrupt that experience, distorting the principle of no barriers to access into a damaging illusion.

Darcy Frey, author of the enduring journalistic achievement *The Last Shot,* spent two years chronicling Coney Island playground stars attending Lincoln High School in hopes of landing a Division I scholarship, leading to the NBA dream. On the last page of the book he explains his arrival at that disillusionment: "Which makes this process of playing for scholarship not the black version of the American Dream, as I had thought eight months earlier, but a cruel parody of it. In the classic parable you begin with nothing and slowly accrue your riches through hard work in a system designed to help those who help themselves. *Here,* at seventeen years of age, you begin with nothing but one narrow treacherous path and then run a gauntlet of obstacles that merely reminds you of how little you have; recruiters pass themselves off as father figures, standardized tests humiliate you and reveal the wretchedness of your education, the promise of lucrative NBA contracts reminds you of what it feels like to have nothing in this world."

Bobbito Garcia is ever mindful that with so many gatekeepers, creating more and more gated spaces—"elite" levels of basketball play—it's critical that non-elite basketball players always be able to know the barrier-free experience of playground ball. So he created even more access, a global tournament called Full Court 21, "where there's no teams, there's no teammates, no coaches, no tryouts, no subs. Anyone can register, 14 and up; ... boys and girls, non-binary as well, gender nonconforming. And you come, and you play, and you participate, and you get a t-shirt; I'm on a mic ...

you get that authentic New York playground experience. It's not 3-on-3, it's not Club, it's not 5-on-5; it's like anybody can play. It's the most inclusive idea that's available right now—I think it's going to become an Olympic Sport. I truly believe that. You know, the Olympics just made outdoor 3-on-3 an Olympic sport for 2024, officially! I think my tournament is next."

Bobbito treats playground basketball as an area of scholarship. He ties it back to Naismith at the beginning and end of his film, referencing the inventor's express desire to "change lives by providing a physical and spiritual outlet that will positively affect society as a whole." How could there be a gate to that? For all the basketball purists, what could be purer than what the inventor intended? He envisioned the playground.

Understood lyrically and never better than in *Hoop Roots* by Jon Edgar Wideman, the centrality of the playground creates an *Elsewhere*. Essentially and vitally it is "this sphere where you can be larger than who you are, belongs to nobody....Yet you can go there. It's in your hands. White people nor nobody else owns it. It's waiting for you to claim it."

THE BLACK TAX

Systemic racism remains America's unreconciled original sin. Its cruelty and complexity have been compounded over four hundred years of slavery, Jim Crow, conscious and unconscious bias, police violence, and incarceration. Even in a "free" American society, racial barriers to access are formidable, in that they are societal and institutional, visible and invisible. Generationally, this amounts to a deficit.

It is an appreciable "Black tax" that stifles Black economic mobility. From racial covenants to redlining to high mortgage denial rates, if you're Black there are barriers to owning a home. In neighborhoods where there is Black home ownership, it's harder to keep that home as "urban renewal" results in gentrification demolishing black communities, including homes and Black owned businesses, which decreased by 41 percent in 2020 alone.

It's harder to get a business loan when you're Black. It's harder to get a job interview, which makes it harder to elevate Blacks to the C-suite. And without corporate Black leadership there are higher turnover and attrition rates among Black employees, resulting in entrenched, layered structural inequality that becomes harder and harder to deconstruct.

Voter suppression laws throw up barriers to Black political representation. Because of the racial wealth gap, there are lower overall political donations from African Americans to support Black interests. Laws don't change. Blacks suffer from a disproportionate healthcare disadvantage, leading to worse health and less education, which perpetuates the cycle of disadvantage. All these barriers make it nearly impossible to create or sustain African American generational wealth.

It's not a gap but a chasm of privilege, another world of access—or more accurately, lack of access—experienced by Blacks in America. Denial of access is necessarily the denial of ownership. And has not the issue of *ownership* been central to the African American experience: ownership of the body, ownership of civil rights, ownership of economic self-determination?

In the realm of basketball, we see the African American assertion of ownership in ways not seen much elsewhere, defying systemic racism. The premise of basketball was and is systemic access. To remedy the racial ownership gap, we must fundamentally equalize access, removing barriers that are cumulative, generational, and inherently structural.

CALLING BANK

In the United States, one of the main obstacles to wealth creation for poor people, who are predominantly people of color, are the cost-prohibitive barriers to obtaining a bank account. There are an estimated 70 million people who have no bank account, which mires them in perilously insecure, inescapable poverty.

But what if the no-barrier-to-access model of playground basketball was applied to breaking the cycle of the poverty suffered by the unbanked? Make banking *accessible*—allowing anyone to walk in off the street and set up an account, for free, no matter how much money they have. Like playgrounds, these banks would be everywhere. And we wouldn't have to build one single new building.

This is the brilliant idea of Mehrsa Baradaran, a law professor at the University of California, Irvine, and an expert on financial inclusion, inequality, and the racial wealth gap. In her book *How the Other Half Banks,* she proposes returning the historic public banking function to local US post offices.

Baradaran says systemic barriers to access prevent the poor from banking; this keeps them poor and often sends them into uncorrectable bankruptcy. Deregulated for decades, commercial banks stopped serving the poor because, while it costs the same amount to service big and little depositors, banks make more money on big depositors. So banks discourage low-level depositors with crushing fees—overdraft and checking fees—while those capable of establishing and maintaining a minimum balance, unattainable for initial low depositors, receive overdraft protection and free checking. This sends poor people into the clutches of payday lenders and check cashers who charge them even higher fees to turn paychecks into cash, pay monthly bills, or send money to a spouse. Borrowing for emergencies at these places triggers the highest interest rates. The unbanked spend 10 percent of their income on simple financial services—*more than they spend on food*—amounting to an $89-billion-a-year predatory industry.

"The fact that so much money is being spent by the poor to pay for simple financial services that the nonpoor get for free is a tragedy," says Baradaran. She sees it as a moral failure of government. Banks get loans from the federal government on favorable terms in order to give low-interest loans to citizens. Yet deregulated banks are simply not interested in extending credit beyond preferred customers. Even after the taxpaying public funded an epic bailout in 2008 for the irresponsible actions of the banking industry, the banks still abandoned the poor. "The social contract has been breached," Baradaran wrote.

The issue for Baradaran is not about saving post offices (though that's a positive net result), it's about serving democracy, by giving systemic access for people to build a path toward ownership of a home, a business, and a fair and future stake in America. It's about dismantling systemic racism.

Like the playground basketball court, everyone—no matter who you are—needs a place to begin to feel what it's like to exercise self-determination—creative, economic, physical. Like Wes Moore in a playground game in the Bronx, the shedding of social status once you walk onto the court is the same as when you walk into a post office. Because very little stops you from entering the space and playing. The post office does not demand ID, citizenship status, or minimum income levels to do business there. It's ideally set up to also be the place you bank.

Postal banking is not far-fetched. Historically, the post office served that function, and its original central mission was equality of access. The Post Office Act of 1792 created accessible local postal services as a means of creating a healthier democracy; they gave everyone, everywhere, the facility of nationwide communication and knowledge sharing. Decentralized governmental post offices became community go-to spaces for all kinds of commercial interactions. A century later in 1892, in Naismith's time, the post office became a place that the working poor trusted more than banks. They were convenient, because they were open during the hours that fit the life-schedules of the working poor. What better place for the poor to do their banking? In 1910 the United States Postal Saving System (UPSS) was formed—a formalized postal banking system that sustained the American poor through the Great Depression. By 1966, with poverty at historic lows, President Lyndon Johnson cut government costs by abolishing UPSS. Up went the barriers.

According to Onaje X. O. Woodbine, this was right around the time "opportunities for poor and working class blacks actually declined," and "'the streets'—an alternative set of role models, institutions, and values arose out of this vacuum." Playground basketball, omnipresent and accessible, began to take up the mantle of the urban community forum for the robust exercise of Black ownership and Black self-determination.

Think of postal banking as playground basketball for Black economic mobility. Baradaran says the post office is uniquely positioned to bank the unbanked because it's already barrier-free. "There have never been barriers to entry at post offices, and their services have been available to all, regardless of income." Structural and systemic access are hallmarks of the post office. The post office is everywhere, like the playground, and it already performs so many functions for the unbanked community. Post offices never left the regions forsaken by banks and other businesses. The poor and marginalized would rather do business in the post office because they just don't feel comfortable inside a bank. That's because, says Baradaran, the "cultural and class barriers" that keep people away from mainstream banks do not exist at local post offices. Both inner-city and rural post offices are often manned by people of that community.

In October 2021, the US Postal Service announced it would pilot offering no-cost or low-cost banking services including check cashing, bill paying, ATM access, expanded money orders, and wire transfers at select locations in Washington, D.C.; Falls Church, Virginia; Baltimore; and the Bronx, New York. It's a start.

As Naismith said, "The game we sought would be played by many." The game was basketball, and by extension, according to Baradaran, it is democracy. Both share the same principle: easy to access. Like Baradaran, Naismith primarily had the urban poor in mind when he said, "This is especially necessary in large cities where in order to get a good sized field you must go to a considerable distance, thus rendering it inaccessible to many."

And as Bobbito said of the playground, at the post office, you don't need a membership or registration card. It's open. It's public. Getting there is all that's required.

Baradaran proposes an innovative, implementable model of access to restructure the structural inequality. Reparations, truth and reconciliation, educational reform, police reform—all these things must come into play in addressing four hundred years of systemic racism. And also, we must include the most marginalized by removing the margins. We must give franchise to the most disenfranchised. We must remove barriers to access. It's a basketball principle.

Post offices, like playgrounds, offer barrier-less access and can—channeling Bobbito channeling Naismith—"change lives by providing a physical and spiritual *and financial* outlet that will positively affect society as a whole." Now add *political, educational, medical, judicial.* Go to those spaces and remove the barriers to access. See what happens.

IN ACCESS WE TRUST

On July 8, 2010, LeBron James set off the age of athlete empowerment with "the Decision" that he, not team owners, would decide where he played. His precedent inspired others such as Kawhi Leonard, Anthony Davis, and Kevin Durant to take charge of the ways and means of their professional lives. Both Durant and James have built complex, diverse, and consequential ownership portfolios outside of their on-court playing. They invest like owners because they *are* owners—owners both of substantial financial concerns and of themselves. And their personal ownership quests have paradigmatic impact beyond the financial realm.

Several times in the past few years, Draymond Green insisted that NBA owners no longer use the term *owner* because it is racially insensitive. Green said to ESPN's Nick Friedell, "When you look at the word 'owner,' it really dates back to slavery. Let's stop using the word owner and maybe use the word Chairman." The NBA assented and teams began using new terms such as *chair, CEO, governor.* "To be owned by someone just sets a bad precedent to start," Green explained. "It sets the wrong tone. It gives one the wrong mindset."

Green has the mindset of access, which is the mindset of Naismith, which is the mindset of the playground, which is why the claiming of ownership and the rejection of being owned is coming from basketball, from the ethos of the playground. And when the playground senses a barrier going up or a gate being built, that's where the pushback comes from.

That's why Jalen Rose is suspicious of basketball analytics. He points to the racial imbalance between NBA management and players, keeping blacks (80 percent of the players in the league) out of organizational power positions because they never learned analytics. Rose told *The New Yorker's* Isaac Chotiner in 2019 that the trend toward overvaluing basketball analytics represents "an opportunity to funnel jobs to people who don't have the lived basketball experience by saying that, 'I am smarter than you because the numbers back up what I say, and I am more well-read. I study more. I am able to take these numbers and manipulate my point.'" This use of analytics is about control of performance, not advancement of performance. "They didn't play at most levels," Rose points out, "but [analytics knowledge] suffices as their 'experience' and validates their opportunity for power."

Resistance to gatekeepers is in the blood of basketball, and that resistance is never disentangled from issues of race. *High Flying Bird,* a razor sharp 2018 film conceived by André Holland, acts out a striking hypothetical scenario: What if during an NBA lockout the players started to organize and play games on their own? The film takes issues of basketball ownership and race head on. One of the sage characters in the film, a Holcomb Rucker figure, states outright, "There's a reason why the NBA started integrating as the Harlem Globetrotters exhibitions started going international. Control. They wanted control of a game that we played, and we played better." Ownership and control are what Holland and the film refer to as "the game on top of the game." Which is not the game of basketball but the sophisticated layering of barriers to access.

Basketball's thesis is about removing barriers to access. Ask Naismith who owns basketball and he'd say, "no one and everyone." Efforts to own what was meant to be ownerless cannot sustain. There will be no "shut up and dribble."

As Draymond Green stated, "Very rarely do we take the time to rethink something and say, 'Maybe that's not the way.'"

The rethinking has begun. Barriers are slowly being questioned, recognized, removed.

When you see the *Los Angeles Times* and *Kansas City Star* publicly apologize for historic neglect of Black voices and perspectives, the barrier of denial is being removed. When major news organizations like ABC and MSNBC hire African American women to head them—Kimberly Godwin and Rashida Jones, respectively—barriers to leadership are being removed. When local and federal governments, public and private institutions remove monuments commemorating racial injustice, they eliminate societal barriers that communicate Blacks are not really entitled to access here. But when the justice system still disproportionately incarcerates and murders so many African Americans, requiring Black parents to have "the talk" with their children, barriers to access for possessing a baseline sense of existential security remain. When African Americans feel that they cannot talk freely and openly around white Americans, resorting to an alternative language of "code switching" spoken only out of white hearing, that's a barrier to access between all of us.

We can meet systemic racism with systemic access. Basketball is one such systemic model. It is no accident that in the United States, where race is a core issue, the most alienated group—African Americans—flock to basketball. Basketball, from the start, envisioned a simple yet powerfully effective concept of inclusion: no barrier to access. It's a model with a proven and distinguished record of successful economic self-determination and ownership: James, Durant, Curry, Carmelo, KG, Draymond, D Wade, Shaq, Charles Barkley, Kobe, Michael Jordan, Magic Johnson, Junior Bridgeman.

"LeBron and Michael stand out because they're exceptions, but the fact ownership is on someone's mind tells us that things have changed. My generation, guys were talking about opening up barbershops and car washes, maybe nightclubs, and that was applauded, that was like, 'Oh, cool.' That's what was considered possible," USC professor and media commentator Todd Boyd told CNN. "We have to appreciate what has happened to make someone dream differently."

Access happened. It begins there. It must be perceived and real and everywhere: YOU have access. The medium (basketball) is the message (access). That principle must guide our work now and ahead.

PRINCIPLE
9

FOR THE OUTSIDER, THE OTHER, AND THE MASSES

To the next generation of Asian American ballers—man, I so wish I could have done more on the NBA court to break more barriers—esp now—but you guys got next. When you get your shot, do NOT hesitate. Don't worry whether any-one else thinks you belong. The world never will. If there's any chance to doubt, they will. But when you get your foot in the door, KICK THAT DOOR DOWN. And then bring others up with you. I didn't get it done, but I have no regrets. I gave my ALL and hold my head high.

—Jeremy Lin, Twitter, May 18, 2021

J ames Naismith was keenly aware that immigration was a loaded issue. He was an immigrant himself, new to America when it was experiencing its largest influx of immigrants up to that point. Sure, Naismith was from Canada, so he looked and sounded much like the majority: white Anglo Americans who feared and resented the masses pouring in from Eastern and Southern Europe and China. Perhaps being both at once—outsider and insider—imbued him with a special empathy.

Nonetheless, Naismith had problems to solve. On a micro-level he needed to come up with an engaging game played in a confined indoor space during winter for Springfield phys-ed students. On a macro-level he was, in devising this new game, serving the greater YMCA mission to elevate the mind, body, and spirit of the urban American laborer. He was thinking of all the people living and working in cramped, small spaces, in tenement apartments and overcrowded factories.

And while the Young Men's Christian Association spread the game to its denominational membership from city to city, it was the millions of ethnic newcomers who found the game's barrier-free accessibility an ideal way to demonstrate their citizenship and belonging. Primarily these were Eastern European Jews and Southern European Catholics. They felt the hate, the othering. They couldn't afford travel or entry to green spaces; if they could, most of the time they weren't allowed to step foot on them. They didn't feel that welcome at the YMCA either and often were excluded there. But what was in reach was basketball.

For the next half-century, basketball became the animating force for new and first-generation urban Americans to Americanize—to prove they belonged. In a country where the burning issue was how to deal with immigrants, Naismith's micro-macro solution worked on a socio-street level like nothing else.

Jews pioneered organized basketball in the United States. Hundreds of thousands fled persecution in Eastern Europe, finding their way to cities like Boston, Cleveland, Seattle, Chicago, and Philadelphia. By 1920, half the Jews living in the United States were in New York City. But even here, they were met with crude, institutional anti-Semitism. The New York City police commissioner declared half the city's criminals were Jews. Harvard president Charles Eliot chimed in and stated that Jews were overly intellectual, crafty, physically inferior, and should not be permitted to intermarry. Excluded by cost and discrimination from accessing field sports, the Jewish community built parallel indoor athletic facilities at community centers such as the Young Men's Hebrew Associations and settlement houses. University Settlement House, chief among them, created a "basketball faculty" led by Harry Braun. Braun's innovation elevated the sport entirely. Borrowing from lacrosse, he created the fundamentals of up-tempo play: quick short passes, moving without the ball, keeping your head up and always looking for an open teammate, the backdoor cut, the look-away pass, and man-to-man defense including switching to help. His figure-eight style of constant movement came to be called "Jew Ball," which still serves as the basis for successful modern motion offenses of NBA champions like the Knicks in the '70s, the Lakers in the '80s, the Bulls in the '90s, the Spurs in the 2000s, and the Warriors in the 2010s. The settlement-house basketball teams, particularly the University Settlement team, had become some of the best in New York City. University Settlement won the Inter-Settlement League championship in 1903, 1904, and 1905; in 1907, it swept the Senior and Junior Division championship titles in both the Inter-Settlement League *and* the AAU. The earliest professional leagues (Blacks were not allowed) were dominated by Jews, including Hall of Famers Dolph Schayes, Barney Sedran, Harry Brill, and Nat Holman.

Similarly, Catholics coming from Ireland, Italy, Poland, and Croatia were labeled as criminals, anarchists, and socialists who would ruin the United States. Demagogic politicians said the way to beat the Catholicism out of them and put proper America in them was through the public school system. To preserve their religion and culture, the Catholic community created a separate parallel education system of Catholic schools. As poor as the communities they served, but eager to step on a level playing field and prove they belonged, these schools needed a sport that required little equipment and no grass. They focused on basketball. It was through this system that an innovative first-year coach—Ray Meyer at DePaul University in Chicago in 1942—pegged a gawky, bespectacled 6-foot-10 George Mikan as the future of the game, training the big man to move like a little man, which revolutionized the game. Mikan ushered in the birth of the NBA, and

Catholic school basketball became an American treasure; its high schools and colleges became perennial twentieth- and twenty-first-century powerhouses. From the legends of the Big East—Villanova, St. Johns, Georgetown, Providence, Seton Hall, and Marquette—to Loyola Chicago, Sister Dolores Schmidt, Loyola Marymount, and Gonzaga.

Like the Notorious B.I.G. observed of dire urban conditions: "the streets is a short stop / either you're slingin, crack rock or you got a wicked jump shot." True then and now, options were fraught and limited for urban ethnic minorities in the early twentieth century. Basketball became the most positive available expression of assimilation. The combination of ethnic identity and basketball seemed to get the best response from their own communities and others outside of them.

The earliest barnstorming teams fronted ethnic labels. There were Jewish teams from New York like House of David and Chinese teams from San Francisco like Hong Wah Kues. The New York Celtics were made up of Irish, Dutch, and German immigrants. And though still legally and socially segregated, the most marginalized group—Blacks—had formed successful teams known as the Black Fives, like the Harlem Rens. These ethnicity-based team brands appealed to in-group fans but also gave the marginalized newcomers public platforms of pride and cultural assimilation.

The game came to represent a formidable tool for national cohesion. UC Berkeley ethnic historian Ted Vincent wrote, "Basketball was the game of Franklin Roosevelt's New Deal coalition of Jews, Catholics, and Blacks."

Forty years into his invention, and through two generations of the United States' most robust and socially fractious period of immigration, Naismith's basketball had become a primary tool to redefine America by redefining who was American.

GIANNIS

Giannis Sina Ugo Antetokounmpo was born in Athens, Greece, to Nigerian immigrants. But despite having lived in Athens his whole life, he was undocumented. Like millions of undocumented immigrants around the world, neither he nor his parents had any official status at all. Nevertheless, Giannis was eligible for the NBA draft. On June 26, 2013, at the age of eighteen, the Greek prime minister granted him an immediate exception for official Greek citizenship. The next day he traveled to New York for the NBA draft, with a valid Greek passport. From then on, he became known as the Greek Freak.

Since then, the two-time league MVP and NBA champion has become both a source of immense national pride and pointed national debate. Mainly, who is Greek? As one Greek-born daughter of African-born parents put it to Peter Goodman of *The New York Times* in 2019, "The same person cheering Giannis could swear at me on the road."

Giannis and Greece present a tremendous case study, emblematic of our modern immigration moment. It started in the early '90s after the fall of the Soviet Union, when immigration to Greece skyrocketed. From there, Greece became known as somewhat of a global immigration sieve. *The New York Times* reported in 2012: "The 126-mile border between Turkey, which is not in the European Union, and Greece, which is, has become the back door to the European Union, making member countries ever more resentful as a tide of immigrants from the Middle East, South Asia and Africa continues to grow." Combined with the national economic collapse of Greece—the "debt crisis," which lasted from 2008 to 2018—the country, gripped by fear and austerity, was ripe for the rise of Golden Dawn, a nationalist, xenophobic, neo-Nazi, racist, Holocaust-denying white supremacist political movement that identified the scapegoats for all Greece's troubles: immigrants.

The debt crisis, which destroyed the country's economy, left many Greeks destitute and angry. Golden Dawn tapped into that anger, rising from the fringes and winning eighteen seats in parliament in 2012.

Right after the NBA Draft, Golden Dawn party leader Nikolaos Michaloliakos publicly challenged the citizenship of Giannis, in the crudest of terms: "In the zoo if you give a chimpanzee a banana and a flag he'll be 'Greek' too?"

Giannis knew Golden Dawn well. They were the ones he feared as a kid, walking the streets of the Sepolia neighborhood in Athens, looking for food, selling DVDs and sunglasses to support his family, sharing one pair of shoes with his three brothers, and living an invisible existence on the fringes of Greek society. Later, as a teenager, when he began training to play basketball for a local team, practicing until midnight, he slept on a mat in the gym because he was afraid to walk home in the dark.

Today, that basketball court in Sepolia has been lionized with a giant mural likeness of Giannis covering the entire playing surface. Giannis Tsiggas, a café owner who used to give the Antetokounmpo brothers snacks, says perceptions are changing. "It's wonderful for Greece," he told Peter Goodman. "We are all proud of Giannis. We all say he is our kid, even the people who didn't like him back when they said, 'He's just a black boy.'"

From the moment he was drafted, Giannis has inspired young people across Greece. As Nikos Papaioannou, an NBA journalist in Greece, reported, "The underprivileged kids, the ones born here from parents from Africa, they say that he is the beacon for all the kids to see where you can go."

TIRED, POOR, HUDDLED MASSES

Who is a citizen? Who has the right to vote, to work, to get an education, to share equal rights? Who belongs here? Who gets to play? These are questions that every society must strive to answer. And as the ideological divide between democracy and autocracy grows ever more acute, the issue of who belongs has come increasingly to the forefront—from Germany and Hungary to Marseille, Malmö, and Minneapolis.

Every day, massive protests rock cities around the world. Like a pressure cooker exploding, fed-up, frightened people are taking to the streets. And when countries explode, people run. They run from drug lords, gangs, sexual violence. From torture. From war. Because climate change has brought drought and famine and fires. Because they're starving. Because they love their children. For so many reasons, they run to find a better life.

Today, immigrants and refugees are flooding international borders in record numbers. But a fair, efficient process to decide who gets to cross those borders? That's broken. The very concept and validity of nation-states—who is a citizen, what does being a citizen mean—is up for grabs.

The simple truth: The history of most of us started somewhere else. Yet we fear outsiders—fear they will change who *we* are by being *them*; fear they will change the "character" and "values" of our nation.

We look for policies and political candidates to fix "the border problem." But it's really inside the border that's the problem. Even when someone comes from somewhere else, when do they get to say they are from the new place in which they find themselves standing? When are *they* one of *us*? How long do they remain *them*?

We can build walls. We can cage children. Or we can find a way to understand and accept that people move about this earth. Then we can find a model that engathers, gives access, and bestows citizenship without othering. Is there a way they can arrive as the other, then become one of us—and still get to be who they are?

Maybe basketball was a good tool a hundred years ago for creating belonging in a time of mass immigration, but will it still work the same way in today's world?

THE TORONTO MODEL

What's the number one sport in Canada? Hockey, of course. When you think of Canada, you think hockey. Well, yes and no. Hockey is old Canada. Basketball is new Canada—or, more accurately, *new Canadians.*

Canada absorbs more immigrants than any other country in the world. They have what anyone would call a liberal immigration policy. Their immigrants first came from China, the Philippines, and South Korea, then Africa, Eastern Europe, the Caribbean, the Middle East, South Asia, and a dozen other countries.

What sport do these new Canadians take to? Not hockey. It's expensive—you need skates, sticks, pads, pucks, ice. It's a strange sport to most of them. Basketball, with its low barrier to access, requiring very little from people who often come with very little, makes more sense. A 2017 landmark study from Solutions Research Group confirmed that among these newcomers to Canada, basketball is overwhelmingly the preferred sport, beating out both soccer and hockey.

Currently, one in five Canadians are immigrants. Two in five Canadians are from somewhere else or have at least one parent who is from somewhere else.

This is an intentional, desired result. Legislation in the 1960s and 1970s embraced multiculturalism and laid the groundwork for the immigrant population of Canada today. On October 8, 1971, Prime Minister Pierre Trudeau introduced the multiculturalism policy in the House of Commons. It was the first of its kind in the world. In 1976 that policy explicitly codified Canada's commitment to refugees, mandated federal and provincial officials to develop immigration targets together, and cast immigration as a tool for meeting the country's cultural, economic, and social objectives. In 1977, the Citizenship Act was changed, making it easier for foreigners to naturalize and have rights as Canadian citizens. In 1978, Canada's Immigration Act outlined a new policy making eligibility for immigrants transparent and eliminating discrimination from the process.

In 2018, Canada overtook the United States as the world's top refugee resettler. And in 2019 Canada welcomed roughly 340,000 new permanent residents—the highest number in more than a century. They overwhelmingly love basketball, and in Toronto, the city that takes in more new Canadians than anywhere else in Canada, they especially love the Raptors.

In 1995, the NBA awarded Canada two franchises: the Toronto Raptors and the Vancouver Grizzlies. The Grizzlies left for Memphis after five years. The Raptors doubled down. One particularly exciting player on the team, Vince Carter, and his legendary dunk-contest appearance in 2000, positively influenced a lot of Toronto youth. A growing population of Canadian immigrants in those years became dedicated NBA fans, and then they started to reproduce. The floodgates opened.

Canadian immigrant offspring like Jamal Magliore (Trinidad), Cory Joseph (Trinidad-Tobago), Dylan Ennis (Jamaica), Tristan Thompson (Jamaica), and Kelly Olynyk (Ukraine; second generation) started populating NCAA Division I teams and then got drafted first-round by NBA teams. *Two years in a row*—2013 and 2014—the number one picks in the NBA draft were first-generation Canadians from the Toronto basketball scene: Anthony Bennet (Jamaica) and Andrew Wiggins (Barbados). The latest crop of NBA picks from Canada continue the trend: Jamal Murray (Syria/Jamaica), Nik Stauskas (Lithuania), Thon Maker (Sudan), Melvin Ejim (Nigeria), Trey Lyles (United States), RJ Barrett (Jamaica), Shai Gilgeous Alexander (Antigua/Barbuda), and Iggy Brazdeikis (Lithuania). Today, the only country that has more players in the NBA than Canada is the United States. The same goes for women, like Kia Nurse, Bridget Carleton, Natalie Achonwa, and Laeticia Amihere. Toronto has become the global hotbed of premier basketball talent. If you're a rising young basketball prospect with NBA aspirations, you are just as or more likely to choose a Toronto-based program like Orangeville Prep instead of a well-known US-based program. The BioSteel All-Canadian Basketball Game, a showcase that's now nearly a decade old, has come to rival the McDonald's All-American Game when it comes to the sheer talent on display. The players are among the best high school juniors and seniors in Canada, which these days is to say they are among the best high school basketball players in North America—or anywhere in the world.

That is serious, undisputed global basketball street cred. And it's transformed the Canadian street. The dreams of young new Ontarians are no longer being born in the rural ice ponds of Thunder Bay, but on the downtown Toronto asphalt at the corner of Jane and Finch.

Those dreams were validated in a moment of singular national unity—transcending the patriotic fervor of any World Cup or Olympics—when the Toronto Raptors won the NBA championship in the summer of 2019. The team itself was a mix of Canadians, Africans, Europeans, and Americans, led by a Nigerian-born general manager, Masaji Ujiri, and fronted by the official team ambassador, Drake, a hip-hop megastar born to an African American Catholic father and a white Canadian Jewish mother.

Toronto and the entire country were sent into a euphoric national celebration. The culmination of the NBA championship and overt multiculturalism as a source of national pride and national unity flowed through the streets, the media, and the government.

That pride and unity found a human emblem in the turban-wearing, Indian-Canadian Sikh superfan Nav Bhatia, who had attended every single Raptors game since the very first in 1995. Nav is a classic immigrant success story. He came to a new country with nothing. Went to the toughest neighborhood where no one else would go. Sold more cars than any other salesman. Bought his own dealership, which turned into more dealerships. He'd made it in Canada, and all along he connected his Canadian identity to the Raptors. Before the 2019 NBA Finals, the heartwarming story of the unlikely Canadian superfan in the front row had been noticed. But with the whole world focusing on Toronto at the end of May 2019, ABC News correspondent and anchor Muhammad Lila illuminated the meaning of Nav in a series of tweets the night before the Finals began:

"When you're an immigrant, nothing feels more Canadian than waving a Canadian flag while cheering your team. Sports is the great equalizer. . . . In any other city, a guy like Nav might stand out. But not in Toronto. We're a place where immigration works. Multiculturalism works. Ask anyone who's been to a Raps game and they'll tell you it's the most diverse place in the world. . . . You'll hear a dozen languages, see black guys in dreads hanging out with Korean guys eating poutine. In other cities that would be weird. In Toronto it's perfectly normal. It's how the 6ix rolls. . . . So when you see a guy like Nav, you're not just looking at a superfan. You're looking at the story of Toronto. . . . Every year [Nav] spends $300K of his own money to send kids—mostly from brown, immigrant families—to Raptors games. He does it to show them they belong. . . . When the Finals tip-off, the World is going to see Toronto being Toronto: Diverse, strong, caring. And there'll be a 67-year-old Sikh turbaned guy leading the charge."

In 2021, Nav Bhatia became the first fan ever to be inducted in the Naismith Basketball Hall of Fame. In 2019 not only did the world see Nav Bhatia and Toronto being Toronto, but all of Canada saw it, too. All this is a grand testament to how basketball has been an assimilation accelerator in Canada like no other sport—and also like nothing else in the entire country. The ripple effect is seen in other aspects of Canadian society and in the country's international image.

In 2020, Canada saw an increase in US citizens interested in purchasing a business in Canada, and willing to emigrate there. According to a Canadian agency head, "I think the 'We the North' changed many Americans' perception of what Canada is and serendipitously/inadvertently showcased our diversity." And the increased interest isn't just from the United States. There was a 21 percent spike—right after the Raptors won the 2019 championship—from international buyers interested in purchasing a business in Ontario.

Even in Toronto's small nonimmigrant Black community, the sense of greater belonging was palpable. "We were basketball kids in a hockey country, Black kids in a white neighborhood, hip-hop heads in the home of Celine and the Barenaked Ladies. The Raptors made us feel *seen,*" wrote Kathleen Newman-Bremang for *Refinery29.*

Impossible not to acknowledge the sweetness of it all coming back to Ontario, to where James Naismith grew up and immigrated from. No different from one hundred years ago, when Naismith's game became an entry point for immigrants trying to acculturate, assimilate, and demonstrate belonging in cities all over the United States. The game has again, in a time of maximum global immigration, in a country that takes more immigrants than any other, become not only the entry point of new Canadians but the point of pride for an entire nation to express its rejection of divisive other-ism in favor of united multiculturalism.

Toronto is a basketball immigration model. The game of basketball is a model showing how to dissolve othering and become a proud, cohesive, functioning society within the borders of our shared space. Toronto, and all of Canada, uses the game, its structure, and accessibility to bring different people together in a shared, bordered space called a country.

Could a policy of basketball immigration like Toronto's be studied, replicated, adapted, and implemented in Marseille, Essen, Brighton, Chicago, Phoenix, or Amsterdam? Why not follow the blueprint that has worked for two and a half generations in the nation with the world's most aggressive ingathering of newcomers?

Meanwhile, Toronto is doubling down on its commitment to basketball. In May 2021, construction was finished on the Playground, the largest privately owned basketball complex in the world.

The whole country is doubling down. "In fact, basketball's biggest problem in Canada right now might be accommodating all that new interest. Officials from Canada Basketball recently went across the country speaking to local clubs and organizers. The one thing they heard, over and over again, is 'we need more facilities,'" Glen Grunwald, president and CEO of Canada Basketball told the *National Post*. "We don't have enough time and gyms available to meet the need that's growing here in Canada."

That intense need is the result of the dual interest in the game and its platform for immigration absorption. "We know from our research that we're the most popular sport among young people, the most popular sport among newcomers to Canada," said Grunwald. "We need to be able to meet that demand."

THIS LAND IS YOUR LAND

Jeremy Lin did get it done. He got so much done.

He was the first American of Chinese or Taiwanese descent to play in the NBA. He was the other and he was othered. But most of all, he paved the way for so many others like him to show everyone that the othering can stop now.

He didn't look like a basketball player, except maybe when he won the 2005 California State championship over heavily favored Mater Dei then got voted Northern California player of the year. Yet, he got no major Division I program offers. Harvard let him play. He didn't look like a basketball player there—except maybe when he scored thirty against twelfth-ranked UConn, in a close loss on the road, prompting Hall of Fame coach Jim Calhoun to tell *The Harvard Crimson*, "He's one of the better kids, including Big East guards, who have come in here in quite some time." Still, he didn't look like a basketball player, so he went undrafted. For two years, he ended up on the end of NBA benches in markets with sizable Asian American populations. First the Bay Area with Golden State, then Houston, then New York. Who knew he was even there? Asian Americans knew. And then on February 4, 2012, when the Knicks had absolutely no one else to put in, D'Antoni sent in Lin.

He performed like no other.

In the most dramatic fashion, Jeremy Lin led the Knicks on a twelve-game tear, winning seven straight and nine of twelve, out-dueling some of the NBA's best players including Kobe Bryant, Deron Williams, and John Wall. No player in the history of the NBA since the 1976 NBA-ABA merger has scored more points in their first three career starts, their first four career starts, and their first five career starts. The absolute delirium that ensued in the global media, the entire basketball world, the Asian American community, Madison Square Garden, and the city of New York was dubbed Linsanity.

Linsanity was a watershed moment for Asian Americans. Not since Bruce Lee has so much literature been dedicated to Asian American masculinity, Asian American role models, and the influence and perception of Asian Americans in media and pop culture. Lin triggered an entire market—Asian American and beyond—that basked in the reflected glory of his achievements. Lin got two *Sports Illustrated* covers and the cover of *Time*. He got his own Ben and Jerry's flavor, a Volvo deal, and a Nike deal. Sales traffic to the Knicks online store increased 3,000 percent. Lin had the number-one-selling NBA jersey in February and March 2012, the second-best jersey sales for the entire season. According to the regional sporting goods store Modell's, then the leader in licensed sports apparel sales in New York, they sold more Jeremy Lin merchandise in three days during Linsanity than in any week of merchandise sales for Yankees World Series and Giants Super Bowl championships *combined*.

It wasn't just Asian Americans who were buying in. Everybody wanted in. New York governor Andrew Cuomo and New York

attorney general Eric Schneiderman saw fit to intervene in a ne-
gotiations stalemate between Time Warner Cable and MSG Networks, which had been preventing cable subscribers in New York
City from seeing Knicks games during Linsanity. President Barack
Obama, looking to bolster public confidence, told ESPN's Bill
Simmons on a *Grantland* podcast, "I knew about Jeremy before
you did, or everybody else did. So I've been on the Jeremy Lin
bandwagon for a while."

Jeremy Lin had moved the needle for Asian Americans. He
certainly belonged in the NBA, without a doubt. And if he belonged, so did others, others like him.

But of course, there was othering. There were multiple racial
slurs in sports media on national outlets like Fox Sports and ESPN.
Lin said he'd heard much worse in the Ivy League in college. In-
explicably to many, the Knicks let him go elsewhere at the end of
the Linsanity season. In 2016, a fan set up an entire YouTube
channel—"Jeremy Lin: Too Flagrant Not to Call"—documenting
the double standard of hard fouls called when committed against
other NBA players but not against Jeremy Lin. For too many, he
still didn't look like an NBA player.

Other players with less impressive records of achievement remained in the league. Lin was cut, but he tried to get back in. He
played in China's CBA. He toiled in the G League. The NBA
wasn't calling. Yet for Jeremy Lin, his playing basketball was never
far from his higher calling. When Covid hit, so did an odious, nationwide wave of violent hate-filled anti-Asian attacks. In March
2021, Stop AAPI Hate, Asian American community coalition,
launched a national public service announcement video, "Stop

Asian American Pacific Islander Hate." They needed a lead voice
for it, somebody Asian Americans and all Americans turned to first
and foremost—the one who moved the needle. They called the
basketball player Jeremy Lin.

Basketball continues to be a proven model to elevate a community, to signal that they are part of, not apart from. There may
be nothing more illustrative of this principle than the role basketball plays in the reclaiming of indigenous nationhood on Native
American reservations—a similar but inverse take on the
immigrant-outsider use of the game. The extraordinary primacy
of basketball on so many Native American reservations is impossible to overstate—from the Lakota to the Navajo to the Crow to
the twenty-nine tribes of Washington State, to reservations in Or-
egon and Wisconsin, basketball is central. Their coming together
for basketball is about more than basketball. On March 13, 2020,
when the NBA and NCAA had canceled all basketball games because of Covid, the Native American nationals featuring forty-
three middle school and high school teams from reservations
around the country were playing games in Las Vegas. One of the
coaches explained why: "We're all indigenous people gathered together. Our people believe [in] gathering in strength rather than
separation because our people have been conquered or have lost
major battles because of separation."

Basketball is exactly about bringing us all together, not separat-
ing us. Not them, but we. *We* the North. *We* the People. That's
what basketball means and does for anyone who wants to demonstrate his or her citizenship in a new land, a new society. Basketball
provides a place for the one who does not belong to claim belonging. Basketball at its heart is meant for the masses—the big "we"—

and that goal becomes especially acute when individuals are denied or segregated, kept out or othered. The game of basketball is a model for showing how we dissolve othering and become a society. We must create twenty-first-century institutions where, as long as there is othering, there is a place that says we are you and you are we—a place that says there is no other.

PRINCIPLE
10

URBAN
AND
RURAL

Lloyd would leave at midnight, basketball in hand, and head down to the local park. And after he slipped through a cut in the chain-link fence... he'd stand in the darkness, stand amid the broken bottles and shavings of glass, amid the rocks and debris that would coat a man's hand black with dirt just from dribbling the ball. He would shoot baskets for hours. Just a kid, alone in the world, an island unto himself, trying to make sense of his situation.

—John Valenti, with Ron Naclerio, *Swee'pea*

More than anything, and I understand it clearly now, the jump shot was a matter of aesthetics, an art form for a small town kid—the ballet-like movement, the easy release, the gentle arc over a telephone wire through summer nights of Iowa, while my mother and father peered out the back-porch screen door and looked at each other softly.

—Robert James Waller, "Jump Shots," *The Des Moines Register*, July 6, 1986

These facts are not in dispute. Basketball is as urban as it is rural. The game is as beloved in Kentucky, Kansas, and Indiana as it is in Brooklyn, Compton, and Detroit. Lore and legend, poetry and prose, film and photography have captured hoop dreams born in entirely different physical environments but unified by a shared, common physical fixture: the ten-foot-high hoop and bouncing rubber ball. Take away the barn, the open plain, the village square. Take away the housing project, the crowded street, the sky full of buildings. What's left is the same dream coming from the same action from playing the same game unified by the same common objects.

The urban-rural duality of basketball emanates directly from the duality of Naismith himself: a rural consciousness that created a city game. John Gasaway, author of *Miracles on the Hardwood,* a lively history of Catholic college basketball, sees the development of the game breaking down along urban and rural traditions he calls "parish and plains." Gasaway explains, "The two traditions are the direct result of a creation story that is itself complementary and variegated to its core. Naismith invented what is, among its many perfections, the perfect city sport. He was inspired in part by a game he played in the great outdoors as a child on the farm. Parish and plains."

The game Gasaway refers to is "Duck on a Rock," a simple competition played by boys in the evening that required nothing more than stones, the ability to loft them accurately on an arc, and the timing of one's movements relative to the stones. This was one way young Naismith passed the time growing up in the small-town rural idyll of Bennies Corners, Ontario.

It is there, in rural Bennies Corners, that you see the roots of Naismith's core basketball values—still flourishing in pick-up games in city or country—of self-reliant, self-governing, coachless problem solving.

"Work had its influence as well. When a boy was sent into the field with a team, he was expected to accomplish the task that he had been assigned," Naismith recalled in *Basketball: Its Origin and Development*. "If some emergency arose, he was not expected to go to the house and ask for help; if at all possible, he was expected to fix the trouble himself. Sometimes deep in the woods, a singletree would break, and it was expected that the teamster, whether he be sixteen or sixty, make his own repairs."

One can see the ethos of pick-up basketball forming. One can hear the sound of the in-the-moment situational awareness of fast-break basketball—to adapt and improvise—falling like a tree in those Ontario woods.

Years later, as a man in his thirties, Naismith created a game that was aimed at city life but infused with rural sensibility—a game that naturally flourished in both places.

Toward the end of his life, Naismith observed the geographically agnostic tie that binds all basketball players: "I remember walking across the gym floor one day and seeing a boy toss a ball toward a basket, recover it, and toss it again. An hour later as I came back through the gym, the same boy was still at play. For some time I had been trying to discover what there was about goal-throwing that would keep a boy at it for an hour. I stopped and asked him why he was practicing so long. That boy answered that he did not know, but he just liked to see if he could make a basket every time he threw the ball."

It's the same universal compulsion shared by a kid shooting at a hoop nailed to a tree in a clearing out in the woods, or city kids playing with no lights in the playground after dark, or a girl in her driveway at dusk called into dinner and answering with the plea, "One more shot, Mom." It's the same opportunity, the same hoop dream, separated from place, connected by the same understood human aspiration—make the shot. Naismith was that boy. We are all that boy. And when we meet another boy, wherever he's from, we share this thing meant for both of us, this thing we both do, our common practice.

MAGIC AND BIRD

In the history of the game, perhaps nothing counters the differences between urban and rural better than the symbiotic relationship between country hick Larry Bird and city playground hustler Magic Johnson. The world insisted on their difference. The two men, however, were bonded by a shared ethic of the game so elevated that perhaps only the two of them understood it.

They grew up four hundred miles apart. Magic came from Detroit-inflected Lansing, Michigan. Bird was from the tiny backwoods of French Lick, Indiana. Magic's father worked the assembly line at General Motors, hauling trash on the side to make ends meet. The family of nine brothers and sisters struggled for money but were tight-knit. Bird's family, five siblings, were even lower on the income scale than Magic's. His mother worked hard as a waitress and a cook. His father, a Korean War veteran, couldn't hold down a job, was often self-medicating, and took his own life when Bird was in high school.

Bird was shy and closed. Magic was outgoing and easygoing.

When it came to early-life experiences of race, they found themselves at intersections. Magic was part of a forced busing program to integrate Lansing schools. Still, the whites and Blacks remained separate, except when they came together to fight, which happened a lot. The high school principal chose Magic, because of his good personality, to be a peacemaker. Bird, at age nine, was already playing pick-up with grown Black men who worked at a hotel near his house. For him it was a blissful atmosphere of camaraderie, Kool cigarettes, trash talk, and beer. They were his friends.

Magic also took to basketball early in life, hitting the local court at 6:00 a.m. to practice before elementary school. He was a Lansing playground fixture. Bird practiced alone a lot. It was his outlet. He needed it every day. At thirteen, he visited his aunt in another part of Indiana, got in a pick-up game, and dominated. Everyone there told him he was a star and begged him to play another game. Bird marks it as "the day I fell in love with basketball." Their local legends grew to national prominence throughout their high school careers.

Basketball was the ticket out for both of them. But both stayed close to home. Magic could have gone anywhere, yet he chose Michigan State, a school with little basketball legacy, in nearby East

Lansing. Bobby Knight gave Bird a full ride to Indiana University, but after less than one month in Bloomington, he returned home, overwhelmed. A year later he enrolled at basketball-bereft Indiana State, nestled in the more countrified Terre Haute.

Four years later, they both led their two previously unheralded basketball programs to the 1979 NCAA Tournament Finals. To this day, that game remains the most viewed NCAA Tournament Finals ever. Most people trace the massive growth of March Madness to that one game, to the coming together of Magic and Bird for the whole nation to see.

Their rivalry was dramatized on every level. Their different personality types. Their different urban and rural backgrounds. Their different races.

Magic won that game. Bird never got over it.

That summer, they both got drafted into the NBA, which only widened and added to the elements of their great divide. They went to opposite coasts, Magic to LA and Bird to Boston. Their teams played opposite styles; the flashy "Showtime" Lakers versus the grind-it-out, meat-and-potatoes Celtics. Not to mention, the modern NBA was in large part a league built on the legacy of franchise rivalry between the Lakers and the Celtics.

Night after night, for a decade, the two men tore up the league. Bird won three NBA championships: 1981, 1984, and 1986. Magic won five: 1980, 1982, 1985, 1987, and 1988. They met in the Finals three times, the Lakers winning two. Each man won league MVP three times. Reams of commentary came forward in those years about the racial implications of Magic and Bird for our larger society.

The implications for a struggling league were clear: Bird and Magic saved it. Their rivalry gave Madison Avenue and an enterprising young commissioner, David Stern, what they needed to broadcast the NBA Finals on primetime television for the first time ever in 1987, the last time Magic and Bird met in the Finals. That's because the whole country was into it; they were into Magic and Bird.

The amazing thing is that other than on the court, the two men had never spoken. They were rivals on the national stage for years who only knew each other via the basketball court. And that was not exactly a friendly relationship.

"We're so competitive anyway that there was a dislike there," Johnson recalled, together with Bird, in their 2009 joint interview with NPR's Michele Norris on *All Things Considered*. "I even hated him more because I knew he could beat me." Bird felt similarly: "I always thought you had to keep the edge. You don't want to get too close to a person because you will get a little soft."

In 1985, at the height of their NBA rivalry, Converse asked Johnson and Bird to tape a commercial in French Lick, filming the two of them playing a grudge match one-on-one. They agreed. During the shoot, neither spoke a word to the other. And then it happened. Somehow it was decided the two would have lunch at Bird's house.

"His mom gave me the biggest hug and hello, and right then she had me," Johnson told Norris. "Then Larry and I sat down for lunch, and I tell you, we figured out we're so much alike. We're both from the Midwest, we grew up poor, our families [are] everything to us, basketball is everything to us. So that changed my whole outlook on Larry Bird."

On November 7, 1991, before Magic Johnson told the world

he had been diagnosed with HIV, he privately called a short list of people to tell them first. On that list was Larry Bird.

"We'd been connected to each other since college," explained Johnson. "We were always thinking about each other—what we were doing and how we were doing. I knew that he would want to know and also know from me. And I'm glad I was able to talk to Larry and let him know that I'm gonna be okay, and I knew he was going to be supporting me."

Bird told Norris he'd never forget the moment he got the call. Because in that moment, he felt something he'd never felt before. He didn't want to play basketball.

He remembered hanging up the phone, knowing a Celtics game was hours away. "It was probably one of the worst feelings you could ever imagine," he said. "It was very difficult. We played against each other for a long time. At that time, HIV was known to be a death sentence. Still, I was a gamer, I loved game day; I couldn't wait to get down to the gym. But when I got that call that's the one time, I can honestly tell you I didn't feel like playing."

The playing of basketball between these two men—one from the city and one from the country, like the essence of the game itself—seemed to each somehow less without the influence of the other. They totally shared this game. For all the rivalry, all the perceived difference between them, they were not so different. It wasn't complicated, Bird said to Norris. "Me and Magic? We both liked to pass the ball. We liked to try to make other guys better. And we were winners."

"We're mirrors of each other," Johnson told Mark Medina of the *Los Angeles Times*. "I may smile a little bit more, but the way we play the game of basketball was exactly the same because we would do anything to win. We didn't care about scoring points. We cared about winning the game and making our teammates better. That's why we were able to change not only basketball but able to change the NBA, too."

Change meaning *save*, which is what happens when we find the bridge instead of the divide. We can save things.

DIVIDED WE'RE FALLING

There is a stark and dangerous twenty-first-century divide. Election results, social attitudes, and all kinds of behaviors and feelings are split along these lines: those that live in urban environments and those that live in rural environments.

What do we have in common? Not TV.

Josh Katz's analysis of a *New York Times* heat-map study of the 2016 presidential elections, "'Duck Dynasty' vs. 'Modern Family': 50 Maps of the U.S. Cultural Divide," showed a clear and incontrovertible breakdown along urban and rural zip codes between how people vote and what television shows they watch.

The correlation between viewership and the percentage of people who voted for Donald Trump was higher for *Duck Dynasty*—least popular in the Northeast, most popular in rural parts of Texas, Arkansas, and Louisiana—than it was for any other show. *Deadliest Catch*, the reality show about Alaskan crab fishing, was also extremely popular in rural red America.

Family Guy was more correlated with support for Hillary Clinton than any other show. *Modern Family's* audience pattern was the prototypical example of a city show—most popular in liberal, urban clusters in Boston, San Francisco, and Santa Barbara, and least popular in the more rural parts of Kentucky, Mississippi, and Arkansas. *Orange Is the New Black,* the Netflix drama and critique of the prison system, was popular in urban America.

A follow-up 2019 study led by the Norman Lear Center at the USC Annenberg School built off the *New York Times* heat maps and gathered individual voting history and attitudinal data to prove an even stronger connection between TV preference, political beliefs, and behavior. Urban "blues" have liberal attitudes toward abortion, the environment, guns, marriage, and immigration. Rural "reds" hold conservative views on most issues, including positive attitudes toward police and skepticism about affirmative action, immigrants, and Islam. Blues often get their news from MSNBC, and they typically enjoy watching *Modern Family.* Reds watch the Hallmark, History, and Ion channels far more than others, and their favorite shows include *NCIS* and *Criminal Minds.*

In his 2019 book, *Why Cities Lose,* Stanford political scientist Jonathan Rodden claims that the American form of government is uniquely structured to exacerbate the urban-rural divide. That is, boundary-drawing for single-member Congressional districts in many states being undertaken by the party that predominates in the state government leads to inefficient and disproportionate voter representation. The creation of winner-take-all congressional districts systematically under-represents spatially concentrated voter districts (typically urban) and destructively polarizes politics along urban-rural lines. But it's not only the United States.

In similar majoritarian democracies such as the United Kingdom, Australia, and Canada, clear urban-rural political divides appear, too. Who is pro–European Union? Urban. Who is anti-EU? Rural. And it's not just Western democracies.

Turkey's traditional secular elite has been consistently outvoted by pious small-town voters. Turkey's president, Erdoğan, calls this the split between "white" and "black" Turks. In Israel, the country as a whole has moved toward the right, but the cosmopolitan city of Tel Aviv remains a center of liberalism. Resentment grows in Japan between sparsely populated rural areas and densely populated cities; the former receive disproportionate parliamentary representation and, consequently, federal taxpayer dollars, keeping the conservative Liberal Democratic Party in power for all but four years since 1955. In the Philippines, populist autocrat Rodrigo Duterte came to power after running against the liberal elite of "imperial Manila." In Thailand, all politics over the past decade has become a national clash between Bangkok, the capital city, and the rural north—rural "reds" versus urban "yellows."

This is how wars start. The 2020 US presidential election culminated in a violent insurrection at the Capitol Building in Washington, D.C., in an effort to, among other things, forcibly invalidate the election results. The 2020 US electorate data showed a country more entrenched in its urban–rural polarization than it was four years earlier.

By 2022, NPR reported that "red ZIP codes are getting redder and blue ZIP codes are becoming bluer" as a result of Americans actively relocating to places where they could cluster with other people whose political views matched their own.

But is that divide as true in fact as it is in perception? Magic and Bird thought they were different. Everyone said they were.

But they weren't. Magic and Bird is not a fairy tale but a true story of two men from vastly different urban and rural points of origin sharing basketball as a common value system. Basketball is likely just the beginning of what unites urban and rural.

Upon closer examination, might we find that white West Virginia schoolteachers on strike and Black single moms in Brownsville, Texas, have more in common than they are led to believe? Might we find that different barriers to higher education for urban and rural families lead to the same unreachable, unaffordable result? Might we find that the demoralizing, quiet desperation of the un- and under-employed in the heartland follows the same basic logic of cause and effect as in the projects?

In his January 2021 inaugural address, Joseph R. Biden, the newly elected president of a deeply divided United States, encouraged a path forward by focusing on what unites Americans. He quoted Saint Augustine: "A people was a multitude defined by the common objects of their love."

Let's start with one common object.

PROJECT BACKBOARD

In 2015, Dan Peterson created Project Backboard, a 501(c)(3) organization that renovates public basketball courts and installs large-scale works of art on the playing surfaces.

To date, he's worked with over forty well-known artists to create over fifty strikingly beautiful courts in urban and rural communities across the continental United States and in Puerto Rico.

215

Project Backboard's stated mission in revitalizing basketball courts is to "strengthen communities, improve park safety, encourage multi-generational play, and inspire people to think more critically and creatively about their environment."

"The functional side of this project is about actually making the surface playable," explained Peterson, the free-thinking former college basketballer and law school graduate who did fitness work with the Memphis Grizzlies and a stint with Teach for America. "But the art side," he told our students, "exists to create the energy and excitement that's going to cause this park to actually become a center of community interaction—it's the glue that brings everyone together around a court."

The results are in. It's working.

"What we've discovered," Peterson said, "is the parks become busier, they become safer, they become cleaner." The new court gives people an increased sense of civic pride and engagement. They show up and clean up after themselves and others more.

"And—this is totally unintentional—it seems like the colorized courts tend to have more families and young women out using the space." The art attracts different kinds of people who might not typically come to a basketball court, because the court is cleaner and safer, multiplying the sheer number of people in the community who come more and more often and make it even cleaner, safer, and more communal.

It's no longer just a basketball court, but a multiuse community center where the art and activity attract people who come to read, work out, and hang out. "All usage is great usage," says Peterson. Project Blackboard is knitting communities together.

But Peterson is keen to point to the special power of basketball that created this galvanizing effect. He says that unlike, say, a public library, the activity of basketball creates a deeply personal relationship with its community user. "People have very intimate relationships with their basketball court. I don't have that with my library. I like it, it's cool, but I don't think of it as *my* library, whereas the court I grew up playing on outdoors—like that was *my* court."

Peterson believes this personal bond forms because for so many, the public basketball court is the one space where the community grants equal community membership. Quality multigenerational interaction is the key.

"For me growing up, the first time I really interacted with adults who weren't responsible for my well-being—they weren't teachers, they weren't coaches; they're just community members— was on basketball courts," Peterson recalled. "You're thirteen years old playing pick-up and all of a sudden you've got a forty-year-old guy on your team and a forty-year-old guy on the other team, and some college kids mixed in there and it's the first time where you're really being a community member without the bumpers on. You're learning what it means to be a neighbor. You can't really learn that in a school-type setting."

Public art has become an acknowledged driver of community renewal, quality of life, economic vitality, civic identity, and social cohesion. It is in the combination of public art *and* basketball where Project Backboard has struck gold. As Peterson explained it, the organization helps "people understand that they don't have to be just one type of person—an artist or an athlete— they can be both." He sees the courts "as a canvas for creative expression."

"Playing on courts that look like this may cause you to think

217

more creatively. So, if you're thinking creatively and acting creatively every day, you're going to have more access to your own creativity . . . that's where I think my work could potentially have some sort of long-term impact."

Project Backboard is trying to make a better world, one community at a time, one court at a time, one person at a time. "That is one of the hopes," said Peterson, "that people come into this space and they start imagining 'what if?'"

As Peterson went deeper into his study of art and basketball, he uncovered a language hidden in plain sight. "For one hundred years plus—almost from the time basketball was invented—artists had been using basketball as a symbol and a way to communicate. . . . This was happening almost from the very beginning—I just didn't know about it." A practitioner of his own preaching, Peterson collaborated with artists Carlos Rolón and John Dennis in 2021 to edit a ten-pound, 350-page coffee-table book covering a century of work from over two hundred of the world's leading artists—Salvador Dalí, Andy Warhol, Elaine de Kooning, Faith Ringgold, Barkley Hendricks, David Hammons, Keith Haring, Robert Rauschenberg, and Ai Weiwei, just to name a few. The book is called *Common Practice,* the first comprehensive, illustrated publication to explore the relationship between basketball and contemporary art. Artist Michelle Grabner writes in the book's introduction that the work contained within reflects how "basketball's popularity can underscore a shared life, a common reference point that can refract its rules back onto a world beyond the court."

Not only have Peterson and Project Backboard tapped into a one-hundred-year history of art, basketball courts, and community, but he and his work sit firmly at the center of the zeitgeist—a global movement.

Toronto Raptors vice chairman and president Masai Ujiri, in his role as president of Giants of Africa, committed to building one hundred basketball courts all over Africa, declaring, "These public spaces have the power to unite communities, build togetherness, and improve quality of life for all people." The main stated goals of charitable efforts by Kevin Durant and Steph Curry are to complete from twenty to forty public court renovations, urban and rural, across the United States in the next five years. Art-driven renovations of urban trouble spots in Chicago and the Euclid section of Cleveland, as well as in rural Pine Bluffs, Arkansas, have had noticeable effects in reducing gang violence, vandalism, and litter while creating a positive, active, and elevated sense of community ownership. So-called art courts have gone viral on Instagram, with stunning renovations by creative shops such as ill Studio (Pigalle, Paris), Park Life (New Zealand), and Yinka Ilori (Canary Wharf, London), plus iconic art-courts in Portugal, Manila, and the famed Russian pick-up mecca "Rizhka." These courts are urban *and* rural. However different their architecture, transit systems, and population density may be, urban and rural communities share the ninety-foot court as a space to express communal pride.

The basketball court is where urban and rural literally find common ground. It is where a person who ventures from urban to rural, or vice-versa, can find in the other community an area of common practice. Wherever one goes, when one sees the basketball court it is like seeing a recognizable coat of arms that says, "You may enter here in peace." It is the mezuzah—the sign "upon the [door]posts of thy house, and on thy gates" (Deut. 6:9)—a common object of our trans-urban-and-rural love that signals we pray at the same common altar.

The basketball court is the soul of our shared municipal life. It is the common space where urban and rural can engage, building upon one accepted shared truth that might lead to another, and then another, until being both urban and rural just means being here all together.

PRINCIPLE
11

ANTIDOTE TO ISOLATION AND LONELINESS

I knew when I was teenager that basketball was my friend. I could take my ball and go to the playground, and I didn't need anybody else. I could feel myself doing something that maybe I would never do in reality, but in my imagination, on the court, that was my friend. And it's been my friend for over fifty years.

—Mike Krzyzewski, Hall of Fame college coach, quoted in *Basketball: A Love Story*

Consider Naismith at the time of

his invention: an outsider in a new country, traumatized and displaced following the loss of his parents at an early age. An intellectual wanderer, who, after finishing divinity school, turned away from the ministry and set out alone on his own path. To where? "To do good," he wrote on his Springfield College job application, "wherever I can do this best, there I want to go."

Basketball was a gift he wished someone had given him—a space to easily access where, by yourself or together with others, one can grow and feel closer physically and spiritually to some unity of purpose and meaning. More than a hundred years later, his creation continues to be a magnetic hub of connection, to self and to others.

BASKETBALL DIARIES

Dan Klores's sweeping twenty-hour, sixty-two-part documentary, *Basketball: A Love Story,* interviewed 165 basketball legends. One question posed to each interviewee explored whether their attachment to basketball was one of love or obsession. Among their answers, what emerged consistently was that the game made them feel part of something and less alone in the world. Basketball let them connect when nothing else and no one else could.

After Hall of Fame coach Larry Brown's father died when Larry was young, he looked to the park across the street. "My mom worked, so rather than her worrying about me, I would cross the street and play," Brown shared. "I didn't mind being by myself, and there wasn't a day that went by that I didn't dream about making a last second shot." And when he had to come home, alone in his room, he turned a wire hanger into a hoop, shredded an old sock for a net, and rolled up some white sweat socks for a ball. "That's why I think this sport is so special," Brown said. "You can be there by yourself."

By "there" Brown meant on any basketball court of your own making. "We didn't get a basketball for Christmas because my mom could not afford it," remembered Hall of Famer Spencer Haywood. "So she decided, 'I'm going to make you boys a basketball.'" Spencer Haywood's mom filled a croker sack full of raw cotton and rags and attached a barrel rim to a telephone pole where he played barefoot in the dust bowl adjacent to their shanty in a Mississippi cotton field. "That's when I started to enjoy basketball."

"I've always felt that the greatest thing a person can have is imagination," said Jerry West, Hall of Famer and visage for the NBA logo, who created entire worlds for himself beyond his remote West Virginia existence. "Where I grew up, there was really nothing to do. When I picked that ball up, I could use my imagination to be the hero of every game. As a little boy, that's where my satisfaction came from."

Steve Nash, two-time NBA MVP, said he used the game to

escape the loneliness he felt as a teenager. He felt it was basically therapy to help him deal with his moving from South Africa to British Columbia and not fitting in. Nash said, "Every day from the time I was thirteen till I was forty-one it was my own world: me, the ball, the hoop. I could imagine, conjure, create, and that was at the heart of it all."

The power of the human imagination, unlocked by basketball, is why playing the game by yourself never gets old. No matter the confined space or your own confinement, basketball offers mental liberation. In 2020, during the earliest days of the Covid-19 lockdown, Trae Young posted on Twitter an #InHouseChallenge three-point simulation drill he created in his hallway with socks and laundry baskets. His self-isolation suggestion got over two million views.

The ability to tap into the game by yourself and enter a world of imagination gives relief from psychological isolation as well. Two basketball greats contributed their feelings to Robin Layton's *Hoop: The American Dream*: "I lost myself in basketball," said Naismith Hall of Famer Anne Donovan, who won multiple championships and gold medals as a player and coach. By "lost" she means basketball was where she found herself. "I was a really shy, introverted kid who was always taller than anybody, more gangly than other people. I just found a comfort level and sort of lost myself in the game."

Hall of Famer Rebecca Lobo found the same change in her sense of self. "Basketball is where I learned to love being a tall, young girl." That self-love became transmissible. "Without the sport I would have become a much different woman, and a different mother of three tall girls, than I am now."

Most recently, professional basketball players have taken the lead in publicly discussing mental health issues. Their honest sharing has made them feel less alone in their struggles and lets others struggling with those same feelings know that there is a commonality that connects them. Not surprisingly, it is basketball that has provided the healthy space for them to feel better.

Two of the most upfront voices belong to NBA All-Stars DeMar DeRozan and Kevin Love. At the 2019 Aspen Ideas Festival, in a session titled "Everyone Is Going Through Something," the two men explained basketball's healing power in an interview with psychologist Michael Gervais.

"I know for me when I'm out, that's when anxiety can kick in, you know, you're not sure how to process everything that's going on. You feel so out of control of things. So many emotions run through you. Anger, frustration, sadness, whatever it may be," DeRozan said. "Basketball has always been our escape for us to suppress everything we feel when we're alone."

Kevin Love concurred and added, "It's when we step away from the floor and we lose that control. And also we feel very isolated. And having that isolation and going out in public—being away from anything basketball-related can create [an out-of-control] feeling on an everyday basis. And that in itself is a tough thing to have to go through." What really frightens Love is injury— when the ability to access basketball, what he calls his "safe space" or "happy place," is taken away from him. "Those quiet moments alone are scary," he said.

While Love and DeRozan are public figures, not wanting for attention, loneliness and isolation are a state of mind, invisible but felt by so many. One can be alone but not lonely. One can also be in a crowd or a crowded city and feel like they're in the loneliest place in the world.

Basketball provides an antidote to both.

THE AGE OF LONELINESS

There is a tragic loneliness pervading our age. It's become a matter of life and death.

A study of thirty-seven countries conducted by Jean M. Twenge and colleagues and released in the July 2021 issue of the *Journal of Adolescence* showed that between 2012 and 2018, feelings of loneliness among teenagers, especially girls, skyrocketed—a nearly 100 percent increase—all over the world.

Teen suicide in the United States is not just up, it's become a pandemic. According to an October 2019 report by Sally Curtin and Melonie Heron released by the Centers for Disease Control and Prevention, the suicide rate nationally among people ages ten to twenty-four increased 57.4 percent from 2007 to 2018. By comparison, the report said, the rate had been statistically stable from 2000 to 2007.

In 2021, mass shootings in the United States were up 73 percent, outpacing 2020, which already had the most mass shootings in national history. Almost every mass shooting is linked back to online evidence of the shooters posting hate manifestos or some other digital record of feelings of isolation and alienation. "Violence is a disease and it is contagious," said Dr. Gary Slutkin, former head of the World Health Organization's Intervention Development Unit.

Bottomless feelings of loneliness, isolation, and despair are mental health issues that have led to a national crisis of self-medication: rampant, rising, lethal opioid addiction. In 2019, the number of overdose deaths topped fifty thousand for the first time. In 2020, the CDC reported that drug overdose deaths rose nearly 30 percent, to a record ninety-three thousand (the CDC estimated over one hundred thousand overdose deaths in 2021). Several grim records were set in 2020: the most drug overdose deaths in a year; the most deaths from opioid overdoses; the most overdose deaths from stimulants like methamphetamine; the most deaths from the synthetic opioid called fentanyl.

The brokenness of human connection isn't just a problem in the United States. We have global mental health issues. In Japan, the phenomenon is called *hikikomori*. The Japanese Health, Labor, and Welfare Ministry uses the term to describe people who haven't left their homes or interacted with others for at least six months. Of the more than five hundred thousand Japanese people between the ages of fifteen and thirty-nine who fit that description, 34 percent have spent seven years or more in self-isolation. Another 29 percent have lived in reclusion for three to five years.

At the start of the summer of 2021, China and digital behemoth Tencent launched a "midnight patrol" powered by facial recognition technology aimed at stopping children in China from playing video games between 10 p.m. and 8 a.m. as well as shaming all citizens for wearing pajamas during the day. They want citizens off their devices and out with others. By the end of that summer, the increasingly concerned Chinese government officially banned children under eighteen from online gaming during weekdays and limited play to three hours total on weekends, not including holidays. State-run media referred to gaming as "spiritual opium," a teenage addiction that seriously affects teens' "physical and mental health, leading to a series of social problems."

In April 2020, Finnish NGO HelsinkiMissio Finland launched an urgent anti-loneliness public service campaign, "The Lonely." And Denmark faces such an urgently low rate of reproduction that it sponsored a national ad campaign called "Do It for Denmark," which encourages couples to procreate. Alarmed by the 2017 Jo Cox Commission "Report on Loneliness," showing that more than 14 percent of the UK's 67 million citizens "often" or "always" felt lonely, then prime minister Theresa May established the country's first Minister for Loneliness as a cabinet position, officially placing loneliness atop the national agenda.

Loneliness is an acutely twenty-first-century issue. Right now, we need platforms that help us feel better, that connect us to ourselves and to others in a positive way, and that help us feel less isolated and lonely—platforms that help us feel like we fit in. We need to articulate the problem and make solving it a public health priority. Basketball has served as a space where connection and imagination replace loneliness and isolation. It's also where twenty-first-century public health and public policy can find a way to effectively hold court.

SOCIAL INFRASTRUCTURE VS. SOCIAL DISTANCING

Eric Klinenberg is a terrific sociologist who spends a lot of time looking at maps. In the aftermath of the deadly 1995 Chicago heat wave, he was puzzled by a city map that showed two side-by-side

South Chicago neighborhoods, Englewood and Auburn Gresham, which were both low-income and apparently identical in demographic terms. Despite their similarity, Englewood experienced ten times as many deaths as Auburn Gresham. Klinenberg came to learn that between the two neighborhoods, there was a big gap in "social capital," which is basically how well and how often community members know and come in contact with each other. When the heat became a matter of life and death, social capital made a big difference. In Auburn Gresham, where social capital was strong, people checked on one another and knew where to go for help. In Englewood, where social isolation was more the norm, residents figured things out on their own and consequently fared much worse.

This led Klinenberg to write the highly praised 2018 book *Palaces for the People,* where he argues for the critical societal need for free and accessible public spaces and goods. He calls these spaces "social infrastructure," defined as "the physical conditions that determine whether social capital develops."

"For decades, we've neglected the shared spaces that shape our interactions," says Klinenberg, who believes social infrastructure is just as important as physical infrastructure. "The consequences of that neglect may be less visible than crumbling bridges and ports, but they're no less dire." Just like in the South Chicago study, Klinenberg says when social infrastructure is good, "it fosters contact, mutual support, and collaboration among friends and neighbors." When it's bad, "it inhibits social activity, leaving families and individuals to fend for themselves."

Klinenberg says creating effective social infrastructure need not be the intent of those who enter the space. The community will build on its own, he says, as long as "people engage in sustained, recurrent interaction, particularly while doing things they enjoy." The mix of interaction and joy Klinenberg attributes to social infrastructure is supported by another celebrated scholar, Wharton organizational psychologist Adam Grant, who says inner happiness is directly related to outer interpersonal community.

"Most people view emotions as existing primarily or even exclusively in their heads," Grant wrote in *The New York Times* in 2021. "But the reality is that emotions are inherently social: They're woven through our interactions." He cites the iconic sociologist Émile Durkheim's theory of "collective effervescence," the idea that people feel the greatest bliss doing something together with others. Examples Grant gives include dancing with strangers, collegial brainstorming sessions, religious services with family, and playing on a sports team.

Klinenberg, too, identifies a number of spaces he believes offer the right kind of social infrastructure, including "public institutions, such as libraries, schools, playgrounds, and athletic fields, community gardens and other green spaces. Nonprofit organizations, including churches and civic associations, regularly scheduled markets for food, clothing, and other consumer goods. Commercial establishments, such as cafés, diners, barbershops, and bookstores."

What's the best space, the best kind of activity to create good social infrastructure where life-sustaining bonds are formed, eliminating loneliness and isolation and replacing them with recurring joy?

The acid test came when we were stripped of all locations of social infrastructure and social isolation was imposed on all of us.

The pandemic laid bare so many truths about ourselves and our world. Facing the prospect of stay-at-home orders and strict social distancing, a widespread truth quickly emerged. There was one thing people couldn't do without: basketball.

Strikingly, it was the communal, intimate space—the bodies-with-bodies activity of basketball—that emerged as a pandemic within a pandemic in the time of social distance. It was the only cooperative public activity people would not stop engaging in, even if doing so risked their lives. The human need to enter the cooperative social space of basketball was so strong that public authorities in cities and playgrounds all over the world had to remove rims from backboards. "It wouldn't have stopped if they didn't take the rims down," an exasperated city official told ESPN. They didn't take down soccer goals, they didn't remove tennis nets, they didn't cordon off bocce courts, they didn't police dance classes offered on Instagram. People could live without those things. Basketball was the only recreational activity that required governors, mayors, and other municipal chief executives to issue public statements and expend public resources to prevent citizens from playing. At a press conference, New York governor Andrew Cuomo personally appealed to New Yorkers to stop going to the courts: "I play basketball," he said. "There's no concept of social distancing while playing basketball." Lori Lightfoot, the mayor of Chicago, put out a citywide public service campaign hoping humor would work. "Your Jumper Is Weak. Stay Home," read one of her ads. From the beginning, we should have amended our public health guidelines: "Wear a mask, social distance, wash your hands—AND TAKE DOWN THE RIMS!"

The pandemic seemed to indicate that basketball is the antonym of social distancing. If coronavirus drove us to social distance, signifying the threat to our very existence, then basketball as a construct of social togetherness and social infrastructure is the antidote to isolation; it is literally a sign of life.

"That's why I accepted the invitation to come to your class." Dr. Bessel van der Kolk told my NYU students. "I believe you have struck at the core of something fundamental."

Dr. van der Kolk is a world expert in trauma and has significantly advanced our understanding of trauma and post-traumatic stress disorder (PTSD), which he says exists on such a massive scale that it should properly be considered a normal (not abnormal) human experience. In his watershed bestseller, *The Body Keeps the Score,* he explains that trauma victims live painfully separated from the world "stuck in survival mode . . . focused on fighting off unseen enemies, which leaves no room for nurture, care, and love." They move through the world with "a searing sense of isolation." Their trauma happened in the past, but their body involuntarily responds to the world as if the danger is happening now. Dr. van der Kolk says the way for PTSD sufferers to rewire their internal neurophysiological state is to physically participate in group rhythmic activities that open and engage the part of brain—the ventral vagal complex—that allows the body to experience the pleasures of finding attunement to other people. He explicitly points to basketball as one of those rhythmic activities.

"You learn very powerful things in basketball," Dr. van der Kolk told my NYU students. "The continuous movement and ongoing adjustment to how your body moves to other bodies has a very special quality of getting people in sync with each other, the pleasure of that; a sense of 'I belong here' and 'I'm an important part of a larger thing,' that we all are in the same boat, we're all human beings."

Dr. van der Kolk says our brains are built for social interaction. "Doing things with other people, being in tune with others, is our core pleasure," he told the class. "Yet some of the most fundamental damage that trauma does to people is to create disconnection, a sense of powerlessness, being out of sync with others."

"Basketball," he said, "is indeed a very good metaphor for people who really need to know each other. Basketball has the capacity—continuous adjusting of spatial and temporal relationship with others—to create the conditions for moving in a way where you ask 'How do I really think about where the other person is, what is my relationship to that person, how can I meet them and connect with them?'"

"What you're doing," he said to our class, "is wonderful."

Basketball creates conditions—social infrastructure—that in turn create maximum social capital and collective effervescence. The game is intrinsically about humans sharing physical space in a fun-filled way. Shared, intimate physical space is precisely social infrastructure where empathy gets developed. But here's the kicker. Basketball's empathy-breeding power is not just essential human life support—it's enjoyable!

As public health leaders look to find the cure to loneliness and isolation, a place where there is social infrastructure that can be the difference between Englewood and Auburn Gresham, hopefully they'll study the elements of basketball: cooperative, shared physical space, easy to access, accepting of all, little needed in order to participate, and you can come to it by yourself. And maybe it's simple: We just need a world that puts more rims in more places.

IMAGINE A WORLD

Imagine a world in which the basketball court "wasn't just a place to practice reverse layups" but "the center of social life"—from urban housing projects to coastal fishing villages, bucolic farming communities, and isolated mountain outposts. A world in which basketball courts were such core civic institutions—found clustered next to city halls, courthouses, public markets, and houses of worship—that "people widely (and mistakenly) believed that local governments were required by law to build public courts." And because of this, the basketball court became such a powerful source of social infrastructure that it glued the community together. That the court space started to be used in every conceivable way, from beauty pageants and singing contests to community meetings and annual Christmas and New Year's celebrations that "started at the basketball court and radiated out through the forest paths to people's homes."

That is not an imaginary world. Its the Philippines, as described by author Rafe Bartholomew in *Pacific Rims*, a vivid three-year basketball-adventure ethnography of that basketball-centric country. "Basketball is what knits the social fabric together there," he told our NYU class. "Guys will stop and drop whatever they're doing in the street—they could be working a job—and they'll play a quick, or not so quick, game of pick-up when prompted by not much more than eye contact. Doing that," he continued, "is as natural as saying 'good afternoon' to somebody." Meaning, it's almost *anti-social* to do otherwise.

And thus, in the Philippines, the basketball court is where people gather for their most important occasions: weddings, graduations, debutante balls, funerals. In remote Philippine communities, indoor or "covered courts," which are among the few public buildings, are a critical place of public shelter from tropical storms. Some communities hold driver's license courses at the courts; others hold major public information sessions. In every community, Mikhail Flores reported on ABS-CBN, courts are the venue of choice for "circumcision season," an annual deeply rooted cultural event when boys across the country have their foreskins removed *en masse* as a rite of passage to adulthood. Indeed, the common court-hosted social and communal touchstones are numerous and indelible.

Today, if a local politician wants to demonstrate their commitment to providing services to their electorate, they build a basketball court. That's the standard in all the infrastructure plans. These ubiquitous public courts in the Philippines are successful examples of Klinenberg's "palaces for the people": spaces where an entire nation is bound together, person to person, community to community. Spaces that "foster contact, mutual support, and collaboration among friends and neighbors" where "people engage in sustained, recurrent interaction, particularly while doing things they enjoy." These courts are precisely where every variety of communal "collective effervescence" adds to local, salutary social capital, mounted over time.

In the Philippines everyone knows that whatever's happening with you, you can always go to the court, because it's connected to so much history of shared joy. It's a known, shared space that makes you feel at ease; it connects you to the community and gives you reasons to connect in so many ways. In the Philippines, the basketball court lets so many naturally emerge from their loneliness or isolation.

Call your Minister of Loneliness and tell them we need to not only emphasize the right space, but also advocate that right spaces are the answers to loneliness. If they need to know more, a fact-finding mission to the Philippines would be instructive.

PRINCIPLE
12

SANCTUARY

Playing the game is not counting time nor translating, reducing, calculating in arbitrary material measures, not turning it into something else, possessing or hoarding or exchanging it for money. In other words, not alienating time, not following the dictates of the workaday world that would orphan our bodies from time. In the game, nothing counts about time except its nonstop, swift passing and the way that passage beating inside you is so deep, so sweet and quick like a longed-for, unexpected kiss over before you know you've been kissed but the thrill isn't gone, gets stronger and stronger when time allows you to stand back from it, remember it, it lingers because you're still there as well as here, riding Great Time, what you were and are and will be as long as you're in the air, the game.

—John Edgar Wideman, *Hoop Roots*

This is one of the chief points of this game," wrote Naismith in "Rules for Basketball," the initial 1892 publication of the game's original rules. Basketball "should be so attractive that men would desire to play it for its own sake." Playing the game, he wrote, should result in "the thorough abandonment of every thought but that of true sport."

What did he mean by "the thorough abandonment of every thought but that of true sport?" He meant play. When Naismith first arrived at Springfield College, his supervisor and mentor Luther Gulick taught a well-known Philosophy of Play seminar, which attracted many followers. Gulick's philosophy held that play could be an intentional positive space for individuals to develop positive collective values. And Naismith pushed the idea even further. He wanted a principled intentional game, but he also wanted that game to be a space beyond the machinations of the world, a space of separate and elevated consciousness.

Many sports create that defined safe space to experience self and others, but basketball came from a man who was displaced and who personally knew the value of that kind of space. Naismith wanted to create a sanctuary in all its meanings—safety, refuge, retreat—in order for anyone to feel like they're here and they're okay here.

In 1938, a year before Naismith's passing, Dutch sociologist Johan Huizinga published his seminal work, *Homo Ludens,* explaining that play has always been a safe, sublime, and necessary space for us to find relief from the difficulty of the human condition. Play, as illuminated by Huizinga, delivers a free, voluntary experience, disinterested in material gain and separate from the sprawling incomprehensibility of life. Play gives order to that incomprehensibility with clear rules and limits on time, locality, and duration, where we can live out real human vices and virtues—teamwork, sacrifice, cooperation, selfishness, risk, courage, cowardice, grace under pressure, winning, losing—without the real-life consequences of life and death, profit and loss. Play, according to Huizinga, is freedom itself. What better human sanctuary has ever evolved than pure play?

No need to commercialize it, media-tize it, or reduce it to analytics. It's about being here and yet being apart from being here. Most of all, Huizinga emphasizes, play is intrinsically and necessarily human. We need it. We need that space to understand, integrate, and stabilize our humanity.

Huizinga insists humans understand play at a gut level, even a cellular level: "Any thinking person can see at a glance that play is a thing on its own, even if his language possesses no general concept to express it. Play cannot be denied. You can deny, if you like, nearly all abstractions: justice, beauty, truth, goodness, mind, God. You can deny seriousness, but not play."

If only Huizinga had met Naismith.

The Falconer by Dana Czapnik, a 2019 coming-of-age novel about a teenage girl enamored with basketball in New York City, describes the particular sanctuary-like quality of basketball: "There is no silence like the silence in your own head when you allow it space to be silent. No sirens. No honking. No *ka-klunk ka-klunk*. No shouting from the games on other courts. No music. No playground screams. No stroller wheels. No creeping thoughts. No wondering. No melancholy. No happiness. Just ball on pavement. Silence. Air. *Thwip*. Ball on pavement. Ball on pavement. Feet on pavement. Ball on pavement. Silence. Air. *Thwip* again. . . . There is a meditation in this. A nirvana. I cannot find it anywhere else but here. A ball. A hoop. And me."

Nothing says "the thorough abandonment of every thought but that of true sport," or "play," or "sanctuary," like basketball has for so many, since it first began.

I NEED MY SPACE

"I had my hip replaced. It doesn't matter—I'll still go out and shoot. I'll even limp over to pick up my misses," Mark Cuban told the producers of *Basketball: A Love Story*. "Some people play basketball because they want to. Some people play because they have to. I have to."

People play basketball for lots of reasons. Central among them is the necessary sanctuary it provides. Some, like the writer Sam Anderson, find the game is a sanctuary for a troubled mind. In 2021, in an article for *The New York Times Magazine,* he wrote, "In my life, basketball has always been a deep emotional refuge. When I feel sad or agitated or morally conflicted, I can go shoot one hundred free throws to calm myself down. The game is one of the purest forms of meditation I know."

Others, like the playwright Elizabeth Swados, in her 1978

Tony-nominated musical *Runaways,* cast with twenty-eight actual runaways, use music to express ("The Basketball Song") how basketball provides refuge from domestic abuse: "Here in these hands I hold the planet, bigger than the stars and stranger than the moon . . . when my mama is out looking for a boy to beat, I play basketball. . . ."

After Chamique Holdsclaw's parents, who were struggling with addiction, were institutionalized, she began suffering from depressive episodes. "When the only thing you know," she told our students, "my mom and dad, my leaders, my safety net, they're ripped away from you, it's a shocking thing for a young child." Then she found basketball, and it was an "energy flip" that allowed her to find release and balance. "On the basketball court," she said, "that's when I was able to just breathe freely; that's when I learned to just kind of like let go—it was my safe haven."

Basketball provided a healthy escape from difficult reality, two Hall of Famers told filmmaker Dan Klores. "When you play you forget everything else," said Bernard King, who suffered severe bullying throughout his childhood. "You don't think about any issues, you don't think about any problems, you don't think about friends, you don't think about family, you don't think about anyone. All you think about is the game." Same for Magic Johnson, who to this day battles HIV, which he contracted during his playing days. He told Klores: "When you're on the court you get away from everything, everybody, the world. It's your safe haven, just you and your teammates. If there was anything else going on in my life, when I hit that court, I got two and half hours of joy."

In his memoir *West by West,* Jerry West reflected on how the trauma of losing his older brother David in the Korean War "resulted in the basketball court's becoming my sanctuary and my refuge, the place where I felt most alive, where I was most in control." The court also provided safety from deep psychic and physical pain, levied by an abusive father. Unambiguously, West says, "the game was my way out of hell."

Basketball providing sanctuary from post-traumatic stress is not uncommon. Hall of Famer Paul Pierce rushed back to play with the Boston Celtics after being stabbed in September 2000. He explained why to ESPN's Jackie MacMullan in an interview in August 2018: "I think that's the reason I got back on the court so fast. Me sitting at home thinking about [the stabbing] didn't work. I went to every practice, sat on the sideline for hours, because that's where I felt safe. I didn't want those practices to end because then I had to go back out there in this world that really scared me."

And how important is the sanctuary of basketball when there's a price on your head? Enes Kanter Freedom and his family were subjected to death threats after he spoke out against the Turkish government. "Basketball," Freedom told NBC Sports, "is like my escape. As soon as I step on the court, all I care about is my teammates, basketball and winning. But as soon as I wake up in the morning, the fight begins."

Over time, basketball has proven to be a sanctuary for all kinds of people—whatever their race or gender—to feel safe. Basketball has also helped people find the space to feel safe in the company of other people—no matter *their* race or gender—even and especially when it's otherwise difficult.

The African American writer Damon Young (of *Very Smart Brothas* fame, also a D-I recruit at one point) wrote about basketball's special sanctuary-like quality in "Thursday Night Hoops" from his 2019 essay collection *What Doesn't Kill You Makes You Blacker*. Young observes, "There is nowhere in America I can drive, walk, shit, write, scream, sleep, fuck, eat, sweat, lie, spit, die, conjure, see, touch, sit, dream, drink, run, jump, dunk, dribble, shoot, guard, steal, catch, screen, block, lot, assist, or win without a similar sense of estrangement . . . without knowing that safe superficially black space is enveloped by whiteness." But inside the confines of a regular pick-up game with white people, where he is the only Black person and playing the game alters his consciousness, he finds "for two hours a week I'm able to forget about that." In basketball he lives an experience that temporarily removes him from whiteness and Blackness. Once the basketball game stops, and real life invades, he immediately needs another space.

Perhaps it is true that basketball can provide a sanctuary from the entrenched and unreconciled issue of race in America because the game can provide sanctuary from time itself. It's worth borrowing from the great John Edgar Wideman, who in *Hoop Roots* elucidates and lyricizes on this point like no one else: "Clock time, linear time irrelevant while the game's on. . . . The game trumps time, supersedes it. . . . Time a co-conspirator as you break from clock time you let yourself go where the game flows. Gametime opens like your mouth when you drew your first breath."

SPACE JAMMED

We live in a world that never shuts off. Mobile phones and surveillance cameras track our every move. We are reachable, findable, traceable, GPS-able. Our smart devices see and hear us. Where is the true safe space, where you can, if only for a time, disconnect from the tyranny of digital updating? Such spaces—physical, mental, spiritual—are hard to find.

Unbridled social media never lets up. The title of Jaron Lanier's 2018 peremptory *Ten Arguments for Deleting Your Social Media Accounts Right Now* sounds like an "OK boomer" screed. But the computer scientist and virtual reality pioneer should know. He says these companies are coming for us by investing in keeping us hooked. How broken is the digital world? A 2019 sound-the-alarm book, *The Age of Surveillance Capitalism* by Harvard economist Shoshana Zuboff, outlines the perilous "ubiquitous global architecture of behavior modification that threatens human nature." Zuboff notes that in the last two decades we have undergone "the wholesale destruction of privacy" where "they know so much about us that they can fashion targeting mechanisms"—not just advertising, but "subliminal cues, psychological microtargeting, real time rewards and punishments, algorithmic recommendation tools and engineered social comparison dynamics." Privacy is broken. Our smart devices see us and hear us. They're listening, watching. In state-run societies like China, every face is digitally recognized and every action is digitally tracked. But it's not just China. In New York, the much-photographed sculptural Vessel—at the stupendously expensive (and already financially imperiled) development Hudson Yards—records and owns the images of everyone taking a selfie. The city of Toronto nearly allowed Alphabet, the Google parent company, to develop valuable lakefront property where numberless cameras would capture, collect, and store images and information of all kinds, 24/7. After heated municipal debate, Toronto staved off Google's bid, turning away $1.3 billion of needed development money. Now every developer and every new space confronts this cash-for-privacy-and-data-collection dilemma. Yet much new data-collection development is taking place with no discussion at all.

As the great cultural critic Neil Postman prophesied in 1985 in his ever-relevant *Amusing Ourselves to Death,* in Western societies it's not a governmentally imposed Big Brother that will create technological totalitarianism. We will do it to ourselves. Or, as Postman stated, we may not notice the massive theft of our privacy because, frighteningly, "people will come to love their oppression, to adore the technologies that undo their capacities to think."

Still, the dramatic shrinking of personal space is taking a significant toll. A 2021 Deloitte survey found that 46 percent of Gen Z respondents felt stressed all or most of the time and 35 percent took time off work because of stress and anxiety. They call it "inbox stress"—the inescapable shattering of peace that results from seeing a work email at any and every time of day or night, any day of the week.

With nowhere to run and nowhere to hide, entire new fields of research into psychedelic medicine have been funded at major universities, to explore the value and yearning to take journeys of the mind in order to discover desperately missing portals of escape, balance, serenity, evolution, and enlightenment.

Yet, perhaps there is a more structural approach to sanctuary that society can consider.

THE RIGHT TO SANCTUARY

Shoshana Zuboff, professor emerita of Harvard Business School, has become a sort of digital regulation rock star. She argues in *The Age of Surveillance Capitalism* and in a 2021 *New York Times* opinion piece titled "The Coup We Are Not Talking About" that we live in a new information civilization that is undergoing an "anti-democratic epistemic coup."

This epistemic coup, she wrote in the *Times,* is "the unilateral claiming of private human experience as free raw material for translation into behavioral data" being engineered by "young companies morphed into surveillance empires powered by global architectures of behavioral monitoring, analysis, targeting and prediction." These companies have amassed and continue to amass "unprecedented concentrations of knowledge about us," and they claim the right to all decisions about—and the authority to obtain, manage, and control—that knowledge. Yet, even as they wield such power, they remain unaccountable to any authority other than themselves. They justify their right to own our personal information, says Zuboff, merely by stating that they own the technology that enables them to take it.

Zuboff states plainly, "We may have democracy, or we may have surveillance society, but we cannot have both."

Interestingly, Zuboff compares these formative years of the information civilization to the Gilded Age of Naismith's era. "Our time," she says, "is comparable to the early era of industrialization, when owners had all the power, their property rights privileged above all other considerations." One counter-expression to unchecked monopolistic power that sprang forth then was the game of basketball. What will spring forth now?

Zuboff suggests we need to establish a new fundamental right. While she does not name it outright, what she's essentially advocating for is a right to sanctuary. This would be a new constitutional right that must address the unprecedented twenty-first century harms of the epistemic coup. "Our elemental epistemic rights are not codified in law because they had never come under systematic threat," says Zuboff, "any more than we have laws to protect our rights to stand up or sit down or yawn."

"New legal rights are crystallized in response to the changing conditions of life. During most of the modern age, citizens of democratic societies have regarded a person's experience as inseparable from the individual—inalienable. It follows that the right to know about one's experience has been considered elemental, bonded to each of us like a shadow. We each decide if and how our experience is shared, with whom and for what purpose." Therefore, says Zuboff, "We need legal frameworks that interrupt and outlaw the massive-scale extraction of human experience. . . . We need laws that tie data collection to fundamental rights." This new fundamental right will "define our social order in this century," tying data collection to "public service, addressing the genuine needs of people and communities."

That new fundamental right, the right to sanctuary, is a fundamental principle of basketball. Basketball play, like Huizinga's *Homo Ludens* concept of play, is a social construct intentionally protective of personal freedom, spiritual and psychological autonomy, and anti-algorithmic personal liberty.

In *Numbers Don't Lie*, a discursive socio-historic study of basketball analytics, Yago Colás explores complex questions of who is counting, what is being counted, and why. Colás sees basketball play as "an adventure"—an experience where with every bounce of the ball "we move away from the familiar in space and time and draw closer to what we do not know." This is the anti-predictive model of an analytics-driven existence. This basketball adventurism, as Colás puts it, is the movement "away from the familiar past and present and toward an oncoming future," where "we encounter risks and perils, marvels and wonders, mishaps and misfortunes" but ultimately move "closer to what we do not know."

Isn't that where human truth and knowledge and progress are found? At its core, basketball offers a spiritual and psychological gymnasium to experience one's self away and apart from the prosaic, the commercial, the material. It was meant as a haven for human development, not as a harvest of human exploitation. The "lure" of basketball was to engage in the game in and of itself, not manipulative engagement for third-party purposes. The lure of basketball was the lure of play—the thorough and *safe* abandonment of every thought, not a thorough relinquishing of ourselves and our thoughts for analysis, profit, and control.

In "The Coup We Are Not Talking About," Zuboff warns that absent sanctuary from the epistemic coup, totalitarian conformity will prevail. That's why the fundamental right to sanctuary, like that which is intrinsic to basketball, must be constitutionally recognized and protected. It's the very seed of democracy at stake: the right to be yourself.

Some of the only Jonestown cult members who didn't drink the Kool-Aid in Guyana were part of the cult's basketball team. A group of them had put up a basketball hoop and started a team as a means of establishing some space for themselves amid the oppressive groupthink. As Gary Smith put it in his *Sports Illustrated* piece "Escape from Jonestown," playing basketball was "laced with liberation, a feeling that they were thrusting a middle finger at the holy hypocrite every time they shoveled snow or swept leaves off their concrete patio court and went at it." Stephan Jones, the son of the cult leader Jim Jones and a captain of the basketball team, said that basketball in Jonestown was "such a release, a place to go and let go all of my frustration and rage, a borderline rebellious act." On the day of the 1978 Jonestown mass suicide, the team was traveling for a game and refused to come back to die when ordered to do so. They even tried to warn the rest of the cult membership of their impending doom.

The epistemic coup is not at all different from a cult. It strives to create an algorithmic hive mind and to eliminate any sanctuary spaces beyond its information gathering reach. Digital data gathering devices, filtering our every thought and deed through analytics, are about nothing more than control over freedom. Digital surveillance comes in the guise of technological convenience or expediency or (ironically) democratization, but really, it's limiting us. Do we need an app for everything? Does an app for anything always make experiencing the thing better?

In an interview with Kurt Vonnegut for the November 1995 "Technology" issue of *Inc.,* the writer was asked to discuss his feelings about living in an increasingly computerized world. Vonnegut answered with a story about the time that week he told his wife he'd rather walk a half-mile to the post office to buy a single envelope than push a button on his keyboard to have it delivered to his home. When he returned from his trip to the post office, he told his wife about all the people, places, and things he encountered on his little excursion.

"And I've had a hell of a good time," said Vonnegut, concluding his story. "I tell you, we are here on earth to fart around, and don't let anybody tell you any different."

In all kinds of contexts, we need to question the casual handing over of the right to our own experiences, the forfeit of our fundamental right to sanctuary, to play. And we need to create, as basketball does, intentional sanctuary spaces.

In schools, recess should be not a reward or a privilege but a required developmental time as fundamental as math or science. In restaurants, the move to collect digital devices at the door—so-called digital detox dining—reflects the societal instinct to create a sanctuary space. Discussions about a four-day workweek, or intentional spaces for mindfulness and meditation at the workplace, are expressions of the evolving demand for a fundamental right to sanctuary.

In October 2021, the White House Office of Science and Technology Policy announced an open request for public information that they hope will be a first step in developing a new artificial intelligence bill of rights "to guard against the powerful technologies we have created." What these rights are, how they will be enforced remains to be seen. It's a start.

The rationale to create more of these sanctuary spaces finds a structural forerunner in basketball. The game engages us in being present but also being safe. We get to be human, to be ourselves, taking part in the pleasing motion and relational experience with other humans, thriving in the particular human ecstasy of feeling your own humanity. None of it is judged, tracked, or used to manipulate your next actions or decisions. It's simply a space that lets people be human without having to give up their humanity to do so. Sanctuary is a space that is about the voluntary joy of living instead of the forced work of coping to stay alive.

David Shields, in a wonderfully candid essay "Life Is Not a Playground," writes about his lifelong romance with basketball and how, as an adult, he finds personal sanctuary on courts of every kind while traveling from city to city. He ends with the following: "I once felt joy in being alive and I felt this mainly when I was playing basketball and I rarely if ever feel that joy anymore and it's my own damn fault and that's life. Too bad."

It shouldn't have to be so hard to find sanctuary. Nobody should have to struggle for it. We should make sanctuary a new twenty-first century fundamental right, a stated societal value, a codified constitutional guarantee. We must acknowledge the value of sanctuary spaces to society and how they can heal, protect, and, in a safe way, bring us closer. Make it an agenda item of Health and Human Services. Not one day a week, but every day, like brushing your teeth. A fundamental right, available and protected. Every day.

IF MIKE COULD BE LIKE MIKE

Even Michael Jordan needs his space.

In 1993–94, Jordan "retired" from the NBA for a season, to play baseball with the minor league Birmingham Barons. He was still the most recognizable human on the planet, and still the best basketball player in the world. In that anomalous year, Jordan turned to the one of the oldest, most cherished sanctuary spaces he knew: anonymous pick-up basketball.

In a gem of a short oral history for SI.com Extra Mustard, Dan Gartland relates how others joined Michael at a downtown Chicago sports club, where the members signed their names to a list and waited their turn for "next." Michael Jordan just wanted to play like everybody else. That's it. He signed his name, waited his turn, and played.

Those who played with him said it wasn't complicated:

"Why would he, with all the money in the world, all the cars in the world, all the women in the world, want to spend three hours or four hours in a gym with a bunch of smelly, sweaty guys who just got off their 9-to-5 jobs?" theorized club member Alex duBuclet. "It's the love of the game."

"In the gym, he was just relaxed and himself. It was really cool to see that," said Tom Tuohy, frequently on the court with Jordan. "There's a certain part of gyms that I think is a gym culture where, amazingly, even a guy like him doesn't get bothered. Nobody asks for his autograph.

"Hardly anybody comes up and talks to him unless he's talking just like you would with a regular person. I think that's why he came to that gym and why he went to gyms."

Kendall Gill, a fifteen-year NBA veteran who occasionally played pick-up at the same club, could relate: "That's the way it was for all of us, especially Michael. He got a chance to just be him and be one of the guys. I think that's what he liked about it. He could come in and nobody has the Michael Jordan awe in his eyes. He was just one of the guys who hooped there in the summertime. He was the best one, but still, he was one of the guys."

Sometimes Mike doesn't want to be like Mike. Or maybe he just wants to be Mike, but needs to find the right space where that's okay.

In this way, fundamentally, he's no different from the rest of us.

PRINCIPLE
13

TRANSCENDENCE

The whole world just feels brighter to me. That's how I know it must be something. It ain't just a game. Because I seen my whole world change. Not necessarily the success, or the money. It's just like: I'm seeing people differently. God's got his hand on every court in the world. It's amazing. It makes me emotional, because it's just like, Damn, I didn't know the game could make me think that deep, and feel that deep.

—Kevin Durant, *New York Times Magazine,*
interview by Sam Anderson, June 2, 2021

B asketball, in a very special and compelling way, is about air. It's about weightlessness and defying gravity. When the game is played in the air, we get excited. We see what we may be capable of as a human race. How high can we fly? How long can we stay weightless? They don't call them Air Jordans for nothing. Because when kids and adults put on those shoes, they want to fly, they want to be like Mike. We know we can't fly. We know gravity is part of our earthly condition. "Ah, but a man's reach should exceed his grasp / Or what's a heaven for?" asked the poet Robert Browning in "Andrea del Sarto." Every great society must believe there is something greater to be and do than only what's in front of its face. We must fly. Or, we must dare to dream to fly. That dream is a basketball dream.

In a piece for *Esquire,* John Edgar Wideman explains it beautifully: "When it's played the way it's spozed to be played basketball happens in the air, the pure air; flying, floating, elevated above the floor, levitating the way oppressed peoples of this earth imagine themselves in their dreams."

And as Mojave poet Natalie Diaz put it in her *Top Ten Reasons Why Indians Are Good at Basketball*: "A basketball has never been just a basketball—it has always been a full moon in this terminal

darkness . . . the court is the one place we will never be hungry—
that net is an emptiness we can fill up all day long."

From players to poets, basketball is held as an article of faith.
Beyond evidence and reason, it is expressed as the province of hope.

"Playing basketball in total darkness is an act of devotion, similar to fishing on land," wrote Rick Telander about underserved but hope-filled Brooklyn youth in *Heaven Is a Playground*.

In David Shields's essay "Life Is Not a Playground," he captured the power and purity of the onset of that kind of hope. "There has always been some strange connection for me between basketball and the dark. I started shooting hoops after school in fourth grade, and I remember dusk and macadam combining into the sensation that the world is dying but I was indestructible."

The art critic Dave Hickey's essay "The Heresy of Zone Defense" is a landmark philosophical extrapolation of Julius Erving's timeless defiance of the laws of physics when he went up (over Kareem) and under (behind the backboard, then in front again to score) in Game 5 of the 1980 NBA Finals. For Hickey, watching it in real time was a spiritual experience. "When Erving makes this shot," he writes, "I rise into the air and hang there for an instant, held aloft by sympathetic magic." Hickey sees Erving's magic as a transhuman achievement born singularly from the game's design, illustrating "the triumph of civil society in an act that was clearly the product of talent and will accommodating itself to liberating rules." For Hickey it's basketball's basic immutable principle of the horizontal, elevated goal that separates it, even from fine art, as the beacon of humanity's possibility. In basketball, he says, "Labor must be matched by aspiration. To score, you must work your way down the court, but you must also elevate! Ad astra."

That's why Kierkegaard called the act of believing in something for which there is no proof a *leap* of faith. To go higher, we must get off the ground. Pope Francis couldn't agree more. In 2021, describing the game in an address to the Italian Basketball Federation, the Catholic News Agency quoted the pontiff: "Yours is a sport that lifts you up to the heavens because, as a former player once said, it is a sport that looks upwards, towards the basket, and so it is a real challenge for all those who are used to living with their eyes always on the ground."

The corporeal elevation that the Pope identified had been articulated seventy-six years earlier by future Nobel Prize–winner Ivo Andrić, in his novel *The Bridge on the Drina* (1945): "By catching or throwing a basketball, a man gets transformed, becomes different, lighter and more beautiful, exceeds his own powers and gets closer to the state of weightlessness and high flight, achieving a triumph of his body and, at the same time, a victory of overcoming it."

The game takes human beings to a higher plane of being human. Said Walt Frazier of Earl Monroe after Monroe dropped thirty-two points on him: "I had my hand in his face all night. He shoots without looking."

That's the Earl Monroe whose otherworldly reimagining of what was possible on a basketball court led to a string of supernatural monikers: Black Jesus, Black Magic, the Lord's Prayer. It is no accident that Monroe's name now graces the first-ever specialized basketball-themed public high school, a reimagining of learning, heretofore unimagined—learning through a basketball lens. Because the game, as it was and still is for Monroe, provides a portal for the unimaginable to become real. Opened in the fall of 2021, the Earl Monroe New Renaissance Basketball School transcends the what-was-possible model of education for 440 young people in the South Bronx, letting them transcend along with it.

This is how we get from today to tomorrow. By showing each other, one to the other, that what was not possible yesterday can become real today. Transcendence is a baton handed from one to the next. Pearl was the inspiration for Dr. J. Dr. J was the inspiration for Jordan. Jordan was the inspiration for Kobe and LeBron. And so it goes.

From Anne Myers to Lynette Woodard to Cheryl Miller to Sheryl Swoops to Diana Taurasi and Candace Parker. And so it goes.

Whatever our solutions and plans for the future, they must include a call for what seems to be beyond our reach. If there are traditional constraints that hold us back, then remove them. If we are suffering from institutional failure, then change the institutions. Basketball presents that shift.

I hope you agree with me that these 13 Principles have direct application to the practical world. And that they are mission statements for the twenty-first century that can direct, guide, and animate real-world policies, programs, corporations, and governments. But in every plan, there must be a vision of the as yet unseeable. There must be an imagining of betterness that's beyond our imagination. As it was "evident" to James Naismith "that a new principle was necessary," it is ever clear we must never stop aspiring to be more than we are now. This dream has always been the basketball dream—as Naismith's dream was in the first place, at its origins—even more vibrant and alive today in every player, on every court, found just about anywhere, everywhere in the world. Yes, we know gravity is part of our earthly condition. Yet we must jump in order to fly. It is high time for us to jump.

SOURCES

By James Naismith, Inventor of Basketball

Naismith, James. *Basketball: Its Origin and Development.* Originally published 1941. Reprint, University of Nebraska Press/Bison Books, 1996.

———. *Basketball's Origins: Creative Problem Solving in the Gilded Age.* Edited by Robert S. Cheney. Bear Publications, 1971.

———. *Rules for Basket Ball.* Press of Springfield (Mass.) Printing and Binding Co., 1892. Available at Springfield College Archives and Special Collections. https://cmd16122.contentdm.oclc.org.digital/collection/p15370coll2/id/17727/rec/36.

Introduction

Baccolini, Luca. "La Madonna del basket a Porretta, il prof di New York scrive a Zuppi: 'Sia riconosciuta patrona,'" *la Repubblica,* Mar. 20, 2022. https://bologna.repubblica.it/cronaca/2022/03/20/news/la_madonna_del_basket_a_porretta_il_prof_di_new_york_scrive_a_zuppi_sia_riconosciuta_patrona-342083353.

Harari, Yuval Noah. *21 Lessons for the 21st Century.* Random House, 2018.

Tolentino, Jia. *Trick Mirror: Reflections on Self-Delusion.* Random House, 2019.

Vigarini, Marco. "Il basket ha la sua patrona a Porretta Terme: è il santuario della Madonna del Ponte," *Corriere Della Sera,* Apr. 15, 2022. https://corrieredibologna.corriere.it/bologna/virtus-fortitudo-bologna/22_aprile_15/basket-ha-sua-patrona-porretta-terme-santuario-madonna-ponte-2f540ea6-bca4-11ec-b140-54cb42df7ff0.shtml.

Principle 1: Cooperation

Associated Press. "NBA Names Finals MVP after Celts Great Russell." ESPN, Feb. 15, 2009. www.espn.co.uk/nba/news/story?id=3908460.

Bradley, Bill. *Life on the Run.* Vintage, 1995.

SOURCES

———. *Values of the Game.* Broadway Books, 2000.

Cohen, Ben. "Dr. Fauci Was a Basketball Captain. Now He's America's Point Guard." *The Wall Street Journal,* Mar. 29, 2020. www.wsj.com/articles/dr-fauci-was-a-basketball-captain-now-hes-americas-point-guard-11585479601.

Collins, Jim. *Good to Great: Why Some Companies Make the Leap . . . and Others Don't.* Harper Business, 2001.

Consolazio, Dave. "Here's Why Bill Russell Finally Ended His Basketball Hall of Fame Boycott." *Sportscasting,* Nov. 16, 2019. www.sportscasting.com/heres-why-bill-russell-finally-ended-his-basketball-hall-of-fame-boycott.

Deford, Frank. "The Ring Leader." SI.com, May 10, 1999. www.si.com/nba/2014/08/15/bill-russell-boston-celtics-ring-leader-si-60-frank-deford.

Delizonna, Laura. "High-Performing Teams Need Psychological Safety. Here's How to Create It." *Harvard Business Review,* Aug. 24, 2017. https://hbr.org/2017/08/high-performing-teams-need-psychological-safety-heres-how-to-create-it.

DelVecchio, Steve. "New York Governor Andrew Cuomo Criticizes People Playing Basketball, Not Social Distancing." *Larry Brown Sports,* Mar. 22, 2020. https://larrybrownsports.com/everything-else/new-york-governor-andrew-cuomo-basketball-social-distancing/543145.

Deutschman, Alan. "The Fabric of Creativity." *Fast Company,* Jan. 1, 2004. www.fastcompany.com/51733/fabric-creativity.

Dominus, Susan. "Is Giving the Secret to Getting Ahead?" *The New York Times,* Mar. 27, 2013. www.nytimes.com/2013/03/31/magazine/is-giving-the-secret-to-getting-ahead.html.

Dunk (@dunk). www.instagram.com/Dunk.

Galloway, Scott. "Post Corona: Higher Ed." *No Mercy / No Malice,* Mar. 19, 2021. www.profgalloway.com/post-corona-higher-ed.

Goleman, Daniel. *Emotional Intelligence: Why It Can Matter More Than IQ.* Bantam Books, 2006.

Goleman, Daniel, and Richard E. Boyatzis. "Social Intelligence and the Biology of Leadership." *Harvard Business Review,* Sept. 2008. https://hbr.org/2008/09/social-intelligence-and-the-biology-of-leadership.

Gordon, Devin. "Can 'Athletic Intelligence' Be Measured?" *The New York Times,* Sept. 2, 2020. www.nytimes.com/2020/09/02/magazine/athletic-intelligence.html.

Grant, Adam. *Give and Take: Why Helping Others Drives Our Success.* Penguin, 2014.

Hickey, Dave. "The Heresy of Zone Defense." *Air Guitar: Essays on Art and Democracy.* Art Issues Press, 1997.

Hollander, Dave. "Big Jerk, Bigger Hero." *Slate,* Nov. 24, 2013. https://slate.com/culture/2013/11/rick-barry-free-agency-one-of-the-biggest-jerks-in-basketball-history-is-also-one-of-the-sports-worlds-biggest-heroes.html.

Holmes, Baxter. "Coronavirus Has Stopped Basketball across America." ESPN, Apr. 7, 2020. www.espn.com/nba/story/_/id/29004540/coronavirus-stopped-basketball-america.

Hoops 4 Hope. *Hoops Africa: Ubuntu Matters.* https://hoopsafrica.org/movie.

———. *H4H on BBC Africa.* https://vimeo.com/415684875.

SOURCES

Huizinga, Johan. *Homo Ludens: A Study of the Play-Element in Culture.* Angelico Press, 2016.

Jabr, Ferris. "The Social Life of Forests." *The New York Times,* Dec. 3, 2020. www .nytimes.com/interactive/2020/12/02/magazine/tree-communication -mycorrhiza.html.

Jackson, Phil, and Hugh Delahanty. *Sacred Hoops: Spiritual Lessons of a Hardwood Warrior.* Hyperion, 2006.

Kourlas, Gia, and Angelo Vasta. "How We Use Our Bodies to Navigate a Pandemic." *The New York Times,* Mar. 31, 2020. www.nytimes.com/2020/03/31/arts/dance /choreographing-the-street-coronavirus.html.

Layton, Robin. *Hoop: The American Dream.* powerHouse Books, 2013.

Levitt, Steven D. "Sue Bird: 'You Have to Pay the Superstars.' (People I [Mostly] Admire, Ep. 12)." *Freakonomics,* Feb. 24, 2021. https://freakonomics.com/podcast /pima-sue-bird.

Low, Tobin and Kathy Tu. "Natalie Diaz Talks Love and Basketball," *Nancy,* WNYC (podcast), Apr. 29, 2019. https://www.wnycstudios.org/podcasts/nancy /episodes/nancy-podcast-natalie-diaz-talks-love-basketball.

MacMullan, Jackie, Rafe Bartholomew, and Dan Klores. *Basketball: A Love Story.* Crown Archetype, 2018.

McKinsey, James O. "Return, Reimagine, Reinvent: Organization." McKinsey & Company, 1996. www.mckinsey.com/business-functions/organization/our -insights/return-reimagine-reinvent.

McPhee, John. "A Sense of Where You Are." *The New Yorker,* Jan. 25, 1965. www .newyorker.com/magazine/1965/01/23/a-sense-of-where-you-are.

Middelkoop, Willem. *The Big Reset Gold Wars and the Financial Endgame.* Amsterdam University Press, 2014.

Moore, Wes. *The Other Wes Moore: One Name, Two Fates.* Spiegel & Grau, 2011.

"Russell Shuns Hall of Fame Bid." *The New York Times,* Feb. 10, 1975. www.nytimes .com/1975/02/10/archives/russell-shuns-hall-of-fame-bid.html.

Satterstrom, Patricia, et al. "The Voice Cultivation Process: How Team Members Can Help Upward Voice Live On to Implementation." *Sage Journals* 66, no. 2 (Oct. 5, 2020): 380–425.

Scott, Jelani. "Ja Morant Gifts Desmond Bane Most Improved Player Award," SI.com, "Extra Mustard," Apr. 26, 2022. https://www.si.com/extra-mustard/2022/04 /26/ja-morant-gifts-desmond-bane-most-improved-player-award?utm_source =newsletter&utm_medium=email&utm_campaign=newsletter_axiossports &stream=top.

TMZ Staff. "Chicago Mayor Urges Hoopers to Stay Home with Legendary Diss." TMZ, Apr. 10, 2020. www.tmz.com/2020/04/10/chicago-mayor-urges-hoopers -to-stay-home-with-legendary-diss.

Wideman, John Edgar. *Hoop Roots: Playground Basketball Love and Race.* Houghton Mifflin, 2003.

Wimbish, Jasmyn. "Celtics Legend Bill Russell Accepts Basketball Hall of Fame Ring, Ends 44-Year Boycott with Private Ceremony." CBSSports.com, Nov. 15, 2019. www.cbssports.com/nba/news/celtics-legend-bill-russell-accepts-basketball-hall -of-fame-ring-ends-44-year-boycott-with-private-ceremony.

Woods, Mark. "NBA: At 75, Bill Russell Still Casts Long Shadow over NBA's All-Star Circus." *The Guardian,* Feb. 16, 2009. www.theguardian.com/sport/blog/2009/feb/16/basketball-nba-all-star-weekend.

Zaldivar, Gabe. "How the Hoop Bus Became a Symbol of Community during a Turbulent Time." Culture. *En Fuego,* June 10, 2020. www.enfuegonow.com/culture/hoop-bus-brings-positive-change-to-blm-protests.

Principle 2: Balance of Individual and Collective

Ahmed, Nabil, et al. *Inequality Kills,* Oxfam, Jan. 2022. https://oxfamilibrary.openrepository.com/bitstream/handle/10546/621341/bp-inequality-kills-170122-en.pdf.

Andersen, Kurt. *Evil Geniuses: The Unmaking of America: A Recent History.* Random House, 2020.

Anderson, Sam. *Boom Town: The Fantastical Saga of Oklahoma City, Its Chaotic Founding, Its Apocalyptic Weather, Its Purloined Basketball Team, and the Dream of Becoming a World-Class Metropolis.* Crown, 2018.

———. "What I Learned Inside the N.B.A. Bubble." *The New York Times Magazine,* Sept. 30, 2020. www.nytimes.com/2020/09/30/magazine/nba-bubble.html.

Araton, Harvey. "A Little Solace Amid a Lot of Winning." *The New York Times,* Dec. 3, 2014. www.nytimes.com/2014/12/04/sports/basketball/san-antonio-spurs-gregg-popovich-remains-haunted-by-missed-chances.html.

Arrieta, Armando. "Anand Giridharadas: Stop Spreading the Plutocrats' Phony Religion." *The New York Times,* Oct. 16, 2019. www.nytimes.com/2019/10/16/opinion/anand-giridharadas-global-elites.html.

Bloomberg Billionaire Index. https://www.bloomberg.com/billionaires.

Brooks, David. "How to Actually Make America Great." *The New York Times,* Oct. 15, 2020. www.nytimes.com/2020/10/15/opinion/how-to-actually-make-america-great.html.

Calhoun, Ada. *Why We Can't Sleep: Women's New Midlife Crisis.* Grove Press, 2020.

Chancel, L., Piketty, T., Saez, E., et al. *World Inequality Report 2022.* World Inequality Lab. wir2022.wid.world.

Coffey, Clare, et al. *Time to Care,* Oxfam, Jan. 2020. https://oxfamilibrary.openrepository.com/bitstream/handle/10546/620928/bp-time-to-care-inequality-200120-en.pdf.

Confessore, Nicholas, et al. "Small Pool of Rich Donors Dominates Election Giving." *The New York Times,* Aug. 1, 2015. www.nytimes.com/2015/08/02/us/small-pool-of-rich-donors-dominates-election-giving.html.

Covert, Bryce. "When 'the American Way' Met the Coronavirus." *The New York Times,* Dec. 29, 2020. www.nytimes.com/2020/12/29/opinion/new-york-covid-economy.html.

Ding, Haiyu, and Yijing Zhang. "Op-Ed: Key Takeaways from Davos on China and ESG in a Post-COVID-19 Era." *Chief Investment Officer,* Jan. 27, 2021. www.ai-cio.com/news/op-ed-key-takeaways-davos-china-esg-post-covid-19-era.

Dionne, E. J., Jr., and Kayla Meltzer Drogosz. "United We Serve? The Debate over

SOURCES

National Service." Brookings, July 28, 2016. www.brookings.edu/articles/united
-we-serve-the-debate-over-national-service.

Galloway, Scott. "The Post-Pandemic World Economy." *The Prof G Pod with Scott Galloway.* https://podcasts.apple.com/us/podcast/the-post-pandemic-world
-economy/id1498802610?i=1000501935571.

———. "Why 2021 Will Be a Year of Reckoning for Big Tech." *Fast Company,* Jan. 21, 2021. www.fastcompany.com/90595497/scott-galloway-why-2021-will
-be-a-year-of-reckoning-for-big-tech.

Gay, Roxane. "Is This Where We Are, America?" *The New York Times,* Nov. 20, 2020. www.nytimes.com/2020/11/20/opinion/student-loan-forgiveness-biden.html.

Gelles, David. "'Working People Want Real Change': A Union Chief Sounds Off on the Crisis." *The New York Times,* May 22, 2020. www.nytimes.com/2020/05/22
/business/mary-kay-henry-seiu-corner-office.html.

Giridharadas, Anand. *Winners Take All: The Elite Charade of Changing the World.* Knopf, 2018.

Global Health Security Index 2019: Building Collective Action and Accountability. Nuclear Threat Initiative and Johns Hopkins Center for Public Security, Oct. 2019. www
.ghsindex.org/wp-content/uploads/2019/10/2019-Global-Health-Security
-Index.pdf.

Hamilton, Moke. "Draymond Green Redefines NBA 'Greatness.'" *Basketball Insiders,* June 12, 2016. www.basketballinsiders.com/nba-sunday-draymond-green
-redefines-greatness.

Heller, Nathan. "Politics Without Politicians." *The New Yorker,* Feb. 19, 2020. www
.newyorker.com/news/the-future-of-democracy/politics-without-politicians.

Helliker, Kevin. "Iconoclastic Economics: Dambisa Moyo." Brunswick, Oct. 15, 2020. www.brunswickgroup.com/dambisa-moyo-interview-i17062.

Income, Net. "Spencer Dinwiddie: 'If We Follow Warrior Model, I See Myself as Draymond Green.'" NetsDaily, Oct. 16, 2020. www.netsdaily
.com/2020/10/16/21520260/spencer-dinwiddie-if-we-follow-golden-state
-model-i-see-myself-as-draymond-green.

Jackson and Delehanty. *Sacred Hoops.*

Kight, Stef W. "How Americans Really See Success." *Axios,* Oct. 2, 2019. www.axios
.com/americans-view-success-versus-society-fame-5c1e3a12-444e-438d-8906
-ccfb5beec2c7.html.

Kingson, Jennifer A. "A 'Wake-up Call' to Corporate Executives." *Axios,* Dec. 6, 2019. www.axios.com/wakeup-call-corporate-executives-social-environment
-dd4d66cf-6dd3-46b4-a352-e2359ff0c2e9.html.

Klein, Ezra. "A Radical Proposal for True Democracy," *The New York Times* (podcast), Feb. 23, 2021. https://www.nytimes.com/2021/02/23/opinion/ezra-klein
-podcast-helene-landemore.html.

Klosterman, Chuck. "The Karl Marx of the Hardwood." *Esquire,* Nov. 1, 2005. http://
classic.esquire.com/article/2005/11/1/the-karl-marx-of-the-hardwood.

Kolata, Gina. "Social Inequities Explain Racial Gaps in Pandemic, Studies Find." *The New York Times,* Dec. 9, 2020. www.nytimes.com/2020/12/09/health
/coronavirus-black-hispanic.html.

Kulish, Nicholas. "Giving Billions Fast, MacKenzie Scott Upends Philanthropy." *The

SOURCES

New York Times, Dec. 20, 2020. www.nytimes.com/2020/12/20/business /mackenzie-scott-philanthropy.html.

Kyriakou, Simoney. "Leading Economist: We Are Unlikely to Get a V-Shaped Recovery." FTAdviser.com, Sept. 24, 2020. www.ftadviser.com /investments/2020/09/24/leading-economist-we-are-unlikely-to-get-a-v -shaped-recovery/?page=2.

Landemore, Hélène. *Open Democracy: Reinventing Popular Rule for the Twenty-First Century.* Princeton University Press, 2020.

Levitsky, Steven, and Daniel Ziblatt. "End Minority Rule." *The New York Times,* Oct. 23, 2020. www.nytimes.com/2020/10/23/opinion/sunday/disenfranchisement -democracy-minority-rule.html.

Logan, Greg. "Nash's Focus: Don't Complicate Things." *Newsday,* Jan. 21, 2021. www.newsday.com/sports/basketball/nets/steve-nash-kyrie-irving-nets-1 .50126251.

Malone, Noreen. "The Age of Anti-Ambition" *The New York Times Magazine.* February 15, 2022. https://www.nytimes.com/2022/02/15/magazine/anti -ambition-age.html?utm_source=pocket-newtab.

Markovits, Daniel. *The Meritocracy Trap: How America's Foundational Myth Feeds Inequality, Dismantles the Middle Class, and Devours the Elite.* Penguin, 2019.

Martin, Brian. "The Chris Paul Effect: Franchise-record wins follow wherever he plays," NBA.com, Apr. 7, 2022. https://www.nba.com/news/the-chris -paul-effect-franchise-record-wins-follow-wherever-he-plays?utm_source =newsletter&utm_medium=email&utm_campaign=newsletter_axiossports &stream=top.

Meyer, Theodoric, and Caitlin Oprysko. "The Chamber Embraces Biden. And Republicans Are Livid." *Politico,* Feb. 12, 2021. www.politico.com /news/2021/02/12/chamber-of-commerce-biden-468820?cid=apn.

Miller, Hayley. "Texas Lt. Gov. on Reopening U.S. Economy: 'More Important Things Than Living.'" *HuffPost,* Apr. 21, 2020. www.huffpost.com/entry/texas-dan -patrick-coronavirus-economy_n_5e9f0d70c5b6b2e5b8388499?ncid=newsltushp mgnews.

Moyo, Dambisa. "Op-Ed: How Corporations Can Help Confront Rising Inequality." *Chief Investment Officer,* Feb. 10, 2021. www.ai-cio.com/news/op-ed-corporations -can-help-confront-rising-inequality.

———. "3 Things to Make the World Immediately Better After Covid-19." *The New York Times,* July 31, 2020. www.nytimes.com/2020/07/31/opinion/coronavirus -economy.html.

Moyo, Dambisa, and Astrid Sandoval. "Growth and Prosperity: A Conversation with Economist Dambisa Moyo." McKinsey & Company, Dec. 15, 2020. www .mckinsey.com/business-functions/strategy-and-corporate-finance/our-insights /growth-and-prosperity-a-conversation-with-economist-dambisa-moyo.

Myers, Joe. "8 Quotes on the Future of Capitalism from Davos 2020." World Economic Forum, Jan. 24, 2020. www.weforum.org/agenda/2020/01/quotes-on -the-future-of-capitalism-davos-2020.

Nicas, Jack. "The Man with 17,700 Bottles of Hand Sanitizer Just Donated Them." *The New York Times,* Mar. 15, 2020. www.nytimes.com/2020/03/15/technology /matt-colvin-hand-sanitizer-donation.html.

SOURCES

Packer, George. *The Unwinding: An Inner History of the New America.* Farrar, Straus and Giroux, 2014.

Paddison, Laura. "Just 162 Billionaires Have the Same Wealth as Half of Humanity." *HuffPost,* Feb. 4, 2020. www.huffpost.com/entry/billionaires-inequality-oxfam-report-davos_n_5e20db1bc5b674e44b94eca5.

Patel, Nihar. "Steve Nash, Basketball's Selfless Socialist?" NPR, May 26, 2006. www.npr.org/2006/05/16/5408616/steve-nash-basketballs-selfless-socialist.

Putnam, Robert D. *The Upswing: How America Came Together a Century Ago and How We Can Do It Again.* Simon & Schuster, 2020.

Robbins, Liz. "Nash Displays Polished Look: On the Court, of Course." *The New York Times,* Jan. 19, 2005. www.nytimes.com/2005/01/19/sports/basketball/nash-displays-polished-look-on-the-court-of-course.html.

Ruiz-Grossman, Sarah. "A New Billionaire Was Created Every 30 Hours During the Pandemic: Oxfam," *Huffington Post,* May 23, 2022. https://www.huffpost.com/entry/billionaire-wealth-covid-pandemic-oxfam_n_6283e951e4b04353eb0a526d?utm_source=Sailthru&utm_medium=email&utm_campaign=Morning%20Email%205-23-22&utm_term=us-morning-email.

Safronova, Valeriya. "How Women Are Changing the Philanthropy Game." *The New York Times,* Jan. 30, 2021. www.nytimes.com/2021/01/30/style/mackenzie-scott-prisclila-chan-zuckerberg-melinda-gates-philanthropy.html.

Schulte-Bockum, Marie. "Bruce Brown Is the Nets' 'Swiss Army Knife.'" *The New York Times,* May 28, 2021. www.nytimes.com/2021/05/28/sports/bruce-brown-nets.html.

Sohi, Seerat. "The Draymond Generation: Why Undersized Bruisers Are Ideal in Today's NBA." Yahoo!, Jan. 15, 2021. www.yahoo.com/now/the-draymond-generation-why-undersized-bruisers-are-ideal-in-todays-nba-140009989.html.

Sussman, Anna Louie. "The End of Babies." Sunday Review. *The New York Times,* Nov. 16, 2019. www.nytimes.com/interactive/2019/11/16/opinion/sunday/capitalism-children.html.

TNT Inside the NBA, YouTube, May 14, 2021. https://video.search.yahoo.com/yhs/search?fr=yhs-mnet-001&ei=UTF-8&hsimp=yhs-001&hspart=mnet&param1=3503&param2=84593&p=Chris+Paul+telling+barkely+%22i+can+score%22&type=type9099612-spa-3503-84593#id=1&vid=4b5d064efe28f1574fc44b18edc294ce&action=click.

Twain, Mark, and Charles Dudley Warner. *The Gilded Age: A Tale of Today.* Penguin Classics, 2001.

White, Richard. *The Republic for Which It Stands: The United States during Reconstruction and the Gilded Age, 1865–1896.* The Oxford History of the United States. Oxford University Press, 2017.

Williams-Grut, Oscar. "Ex-Barclays Board Member Says Politics 'Contaminated' by Money." Yahoo! Finance, Jan. 23, 2020. https://news.yahoo.com/davos-2020-barclays-dambisa-moyo-politics-corrupted-money-104652544.html?fr=sycsrp_catchall.

Zarroli, Jim. "There's Rich, and Then There's Jeff Bezos Rich: Meet the World's Centibillionaires." NPR, Dec. 10, 2020. www.npr.org/2020/12/10/944620768/theres-rich-and-theres-jeff-bezos-rich-meet-the-members-of-the-100-billion-club.

SOURCES

Principle 3: Balance of Force and Skill

Aaronstampler. "Stampler's Take: Pop Bears the Blame for the Game 6 Loss." *Pounding The Rock*, Aug. 18, 2013. www.poundingtherock.com/2013/8/18/4630452 /stamplers-take-pop-bears-the-blame-for-the-game-6-loss-spurs-heat.

Anderson, Dave. "Sports of The Times; A Gentle, Good-Natured Goliath." *The New York Times*, Oct. 13, 1999. www.nytimes.com/1999/10/13/sports/sports-of-the -times-a-gentle-good-natured-goliath.html.

Anderson, Sam. *Boom Town*.

Borzello, Jeff. "UCLA Bruins Outlast Michigan Wolverines to Reach Final Four of NCAA Men's Tournament." ESPN, Mar. 31, 2021. www.espn.com/mens-college -basketball/story/_/id/31169600/ucla-bruins-outlast-michigan-wolverines -reach-final-four-ncaa-men-tournament.

Brint, Steven. "Merit Square-Off: The Fight over College Admissions." *Los Angeles Review of Books*, Sept. 13, 2015. https://lareviewofbooks.org/article/merit-square -off-the-fight-over-college-admissions.

Cain, Susan. *Quiet: The Power of Introverts in a World That Can't Stop Talking*. Crown, 2013.

Chotiner, Isaac. "Jalen Rose Has a Problem with Basketball Analytics." *The New Yorker*, June 6, 2019. www.newyorker.com/news/q-and-a/jalen-rose-has-a-problem -with-basketball-analytics.

Colás, Yago. *Numbers Don't Lie: New Adventures in Counting and What Counts in Basketball Analytics*. University of Nebraska Press, 2020.

ESPN News Services. "Sources: Denver Nuggets Star Nikola Jokic to Be Named NBA MVP for Second Consecutive Season," May 9, 2020. https://www.espn .com/nba/story/_/id/33886198/sources-denver-nuggets-star-nikola-jokic -named-nba-mvp-second-consecutive-season.

FairTest. "More Than 1,830+ Schools Do Not Require ACT/SAT Scores from Current High School Seniors Applying For Fall 2022," December 7, 2021, *FairTest*. http://fairtest.org/more-1815-schools-do-not-require-actsat-scores-cur.

Harris, Curtis. "Here's How Wilt Chamberlain Once Scored Zero Points in an NBA Game." *Sporting News*, Mar. 25, 2016. www.sportingnews.com/us/nba/news/wilt -chamblerain-zero-points-lakers-1973-history-scoring-record/12d9amj0dln1173 pmsgy6wm51.

Hinkie, Sam. "To the Equity Partners of Philadelphia 76ers, L.P." Letter of resignation. Apr. 6, 2016.

Jaschik, Scott. "'The Tyranny of the Meritocracy.'" *Inside Higher Ed*, Feb. 3, 2015. www.insidehighered.com/news/2015/02/03/qa-lani-guinier-about-her-new -book-college-admissions.

Kornheiser, Tony. "In the NBA Galaxy, Big Dipper Lit Up the Sky." *The Washington Post*, Oct. 13, 1999. www.washingtonpost.com/wp-srv/sports/nba/daily /oct99/13/tk13.htm.

Lincicome, Bernie. "'The Big Dipper's' Legacy Will Stand as Tall as He Did." *Chicago Tribune*, Oct. 13, 1999. www.chicagotribune.com/news/ct-xpm-1999-10-13 -9910130398-story.html.

Livingston, Bill. "Scoring 100 Points Was Just One of Wilt Chamberlain's Amazing Feats: Bill Livingston." Cleveland.com, Mar. 3, 2012. www.cleveland.com /livingston/2012/03/post_44.html.

Lowery, Wesley. "The Most Ambitious Effort Yet to Reform Policing May Be Happening in Ithaca, New York." *GQ*, Feb. 22, 2021. www.gq.com/story/ithaca -mayor-svante-myrick-police-reform?utm_source=pocket-newtab.

Naismith, James. Heritage Auctions, 1930.

Russell, Bill, and Taylor Branch. *Second Wind: The Opinions of an Opinionated Man.* Random House, 1979.

Principle 4: Positionless-ness

Anders, George. "Is Gen Z the Boldest Generation? Its Job-hunt Priorities Are off the Charts." LinkedIn. February 9, 2022. https://www.linkedin.com/pulse/gen-z -boldest-generation-its-job-hunt-priorities-off-charts-anders/?trackingId=pwWr CQQ1SiG9Yds3hH8gUg%3D%3D.

Ballard, Chris. "Nellie Ball: Don Nelson's Fingerprints Are All Over the 2019 NBA Playoffs." *Sports Illustrated,* May 15, 2019. www.si.com/nba/2019/05/15/nba -playoffs-don-nelson-warriors-blazers-bucks-raptors.

———. "Unlocking Giannis Antetokounmpo: How the Bucks Turned the Greek Freak into the MVP." *Sports Illustrated,* Apr. 3, 2019. www.si.com/nba/2019/04 /03/giannis-antetokounmpo-milwaukee-bucks-mike-budenholzer-mvp-playoffs.

Chau, Danny. "Building Around a Unicorn Is No Fantasy Land." *The Ringer,* Mar. 23, 2018. www.theringer.com/nba/2018/3/23/17153784/giannis-antetokounmpo -nikola-jokic-unicorns-bucks-nuggets.

———. "The Year the Unicorns Took Over the NBA." *The Ringer,* Oct. 7, 2019. www.theringer.com/nba/2019/10/7/20898587/year-of-the-unicorn-nba.

Davidson, Cathy N. *The New Education: How to Revolutionize the University to Prepare Students for a World in Flux.* Basic Books, 2017.

Deloitte Global and Human Capital Trends 2017. "Rewriting the Rules for the Digital Age," Deloitte University Press. https://www2.deloitte.com/content /dam/Deloitte/global/Documents/About-Deloitte/central-europe/ce-global -human-capital-trends.pdf.

Epstein, David. *Range: Why Generalists Triumph in a Specialized World.* Riverhead Books, 2019.

ESPN News Services. "Sources: Denver Nuggets Star Nikola Jokic to be named NBA MVP for Second Consecutive Season," May 9, 2020. https://www.espn.com /nba/story/_/id/33886198/sources-denver-nuggets-star-nikola-jokic-named -nba-mvp-second-consecutive-season.

Global Talent Trends 2022. "The Reinvention of Company Culture," LinkedIn, Jan. 18, 2022. https://business.linkedin.com/content/dam/me/business/en-us/ talent-solutions-lodestone/body/pdf/global_talent_trends_2022.pdf.

Goldpaper, Sam. "Lakers Down 76ers, 123-107, and Capture N.B.A. Crown," *The New York Times,* May 17, 1980. https://timesmachine.nytimes.com/times machine/1980/05/17/111242420.html?pageNumber=17; https://www.nytimes .com/1980/05/17/archives/lakers-down-76ers-123107-and-capture-nba-crown -magic-johnson-scores.html.

Grasso, Justin. *"Sixers' Ben Simmons Isn't Focused on Becoming a Scorer." Fan Nation,* Apr. 28, 2021. www.si.com/nba/76ers/news/sixers-ben-simmons-isnt-focused -scorer.

SOURCES

Harari. *21 Lessons for the 21st Century.*

Hirsch, Edward. "Fast Break." SoCalHoops, Feb. 2, 2002. www.socalhoops.com /prep02/0202/fastbreak0202.htm.

Johnson, Scott Morrow. *Phog: The Most Influential Man in Basketball.* University of Nebraska Press, 2019.

Kerkhoff, Blair. *Phog Allen: The Father of Basketball Coaching.* Masters Press, 1996.

Klein, Ezra. Interview with Zeynep Tufecki: "To Understand This Era, You Need to Think in Systems." *The Ezra Klein Show,* Feb. 2, 2021. www.nytimes. com/2021/02/02/opinion/ezra-klein-podcast-zeynep-tufecki. html?showTranscript=1.

Klores, Dan, director. *Basketball: A Love Story.* ESPN Films, 2018.

McPhee, "A Sense of Where You Are."

McLendon, John B., Jr. "More Than Just the Fellow with the Peach Baskets." *The New York Times,* Oct. 27, 1996. www.nytimes.com/1996/10/27/sports/more-than-just-the -fellow-with-the-peach-baskets.html.

Merlino, Doug. "Fast Break Basketball: How a Black Coach Revolutionized the Game." *Bleacher Report,* Apr. 22, 2011. https://bleacherreport.com/articles/673434-fast -break-basketball-how-a-black-coach-revolutionized-the-game.

Miller, Claire. "Celtics Star Jaylen Brown Wants to Fix American Schools." Fast Company, July 8, 2019. https://www.fastcompany.com/90372453/celtics-star -jaylen-brown-wants-to-fix-american-schools.

Murphy, Kate. "UNC Professor Challenged Top Health Officials about COVID-19 Guidance. She Was Right." *The News & Observer,* Jan. 29, 2021. www .newsobserver.com/news/local/education/article248799220.html.

Peterson, Dan. "Mike D'Antoni Changed the Game." *Kos Magazin,* Apr. 17, 2021. www.kosmagazin.com/dan-peterson-mike-dantoni-changed-the-game.

Russell, Bill. "The Psych . . . and My Other Tricks." *Sports Illustrated,* Oct. 1965; available at https://www.spurstalk.com/forums/showthread.php?t=163286.

Shepherd, Sara. "'Forgotten' No More: Coach and Naismith Protégé John McLendon Broke Color Barriers in Basketball." KUsports.com, Mar. 5, 2017. m.kusports.com /news/2017/mar/05/forgotten-no-more-coach-and-naismith-protege-john-.

Sirius XM NBA Radio. Brian Geltzeiler, May 7, 2022. https://twitter.com/Sirius XMNBA/status/1523014809943519232?s=20&t=lzY1Ee_Hj5l_RhuPlX 3NoA.

Smith, Ben. "How Zeynep Tufekci Keeps Getting the Big Things Right." *The New York Times,* Aug. 24, 2020. www.nytimes.com/2020/08/23/business/media/how -zeynep-tufekci-keeps-getting-the-big-things-right.html.

Thomas, Ron. *They Cleared the Lane: The NBA's Black Pioneers.* University of Nebraska Press, 2004.

Villanueva, Virgil. "'That's Not a Point Guard in That Body. That Is a Power Forward.'—Sam Mitchell Compares Luka Doncic to Magic Johnson and Two More Legends," Basketball Network, May 9, 2022. https://www.basketball network.net/latest-news/thats-not-a-point-guard-in-that-body-that-is-a-power -forward-sam-mitchell-compares-luka-doncic-to-magic-johnson-and-two-more -legends.

SOURCES

Walker, Rhiannon. "The Day Magic Johnson Stepped in at Center and Dropped 42 on Philly," Andscape, May 16, 2018. https://andscape.com/features/the-day-magic-johnson-stepped-in-at-center-and-dropped-42-points-on-philly.

Willmott, Kevin, director. *Fast Break: The Legendary John McLendon*. Television movie, 2017.

Yao, Ming, and Ric Bucher. *Yao: A Life in Two Worlds*. Miramax Books, 2005.

Principle 5: Human Alchemy

Afshar, Vala. "Chef José Andrés Shows Us New Business Model Innovation Where Everyone Wins." ZDNet, Jan. 11, 2021. www.zdnet.com/article/chef-jose-andres-shows-us-new-business-model-innovation-where-everyone-wins.

Barry, Rick, with Bill Libby. *Confessions of a Basketball Gypsy: The Rick Barry Story*. Prentice-Hall, 1972.

Bersin, Josh. "The Big Reset: Making Sense of the Coronavirus Crisis." *Forbes*, Mar. 24, 2020. www.forbes.com/sites/joshbersin/2020/03/24/the-big-reset-making-sense-of-the-coronavirus-crisis/?sh=4ec471d4e1cd.

Blackistone, Kevin. "José Andrés and NBA Players Have Made It Clear: Stadiums Must Serve the Public Good." *The Washington Post*, Dec. 25, 2020. www.washingtonpost.com/sports/2020/12/25/jose-andres-stadiums-arenas-nationals-park.

Bleacher Report (@BleacherReport). "WNBA star Maya Moore sat out the entire season last year and helped overturn the conviction of Jonathan Irons, who was serving a 50-year prison sentence." Twitter, July 1, 2020. https://twitter.com/bleacherreport/status/1278481113204178945?s=21.

Cave, Nick. *The Red Hand Files*, no. 90, Mar. 2020. https://www.theredhandfiles.com/corona-fill-the-time.

Charles, Tina. "How Maya Moore Is Transforming Player Activism." *Sports Illustrated*, Dec. 23, 2020. www.si.com/wnba/2020/12/23/maya-moore-activism-inspiration-of-the-year-tina-charles.

Cohen, Kelly. "Vote Here! Ahead of the Presidential Election, America's Sports Stadiums and Arenas Become Polling Centers." ESPN, Sept. 29, 2020. www.espn.com/nfl/story/_/id/29955004/ahead-presidential-election-america-sports-stadiums-arenas-become-polling-centers.

Goleman, Daniel, and Richard E. Boyatzis. "Social Intelligence and the Biology of Leadership." *Harvard Business Review*, Sept. 2008. https://hbr.org/2008/09/social-intelligence-and-the-biology-of-leadership.

Hartlaub, Peter. "Catching Up with Clifford Ray." NBA.com, May 9, 2014. www.nba.com/warriors/catching_up_ray.html.

Herndon, Astead W. "LeBron James's Effort to Attract More Poll Workers Nets 10,000 Volunteers." *The New York Times*, Sept. 30, 2020. www.nytimes.com/2020/09/30/us/elections/lebron-james-more-than-a-vote-poll-workers.html.

Herring, Chris, and Neil Paine. "*Maya Moore Gave Up More To Fight For Social Justice Than Almost Any Athlete*." *FiveThirtyEight*, June 11, 2020. https://fivethirtyeight.com/features/maya-moore-gave-up-more-to-fight-for-social-justice-than-almost-any-athlete.

Klosterman, "The Karl Marx of the Hardwood."

SOURCES

Kornheiser, Tony. "A Voice Crying in the Wilderness," *Sports Illustrated*, Apr. 25, 1983. https://vault.si.com/vault/1983/04/25/voice-crying-wilderness.

More Than a Vote. store.morethanavote.org.

Morse, Ben. "After Leading Lakers to Victory, LeBron James Looks for WNBA Win over Kelly Loeffler." CNN, Jan. 6, 2021. https://edition.cnn.com/2021/01/06 /sport/lebron-james-kelly-loeffler-la-lakers-atlanta-dream-wnba-spt-intl/index .html.

Obama, Michelle. *Becoming*. Crown, 2018.

Reid, Ron. "The Golden State of Rick Barry," *Sports Illustrated*, Dec. 16, 1974. https://vault.si.com/vault/1974/12/16/the-golden-state-of-rick-barry.

Rhoden, William C. Interview with Wynton Marsalis: "Jazz and Basketball—Wynton Interviewed by NYT." *The New York Times*, May 27, 2009. https://wyntonmarsalis .org/videos/view/jazz-and-basketball-wynton-interviewed-by-nytimes.

Simmons, Bill. *The Book of Basketball: The NBA According to the Sports Guy*. Ballantine/ ESPN, 2009.

Streeter, Kurt. "After Helping Her Husband Gain Freedom, Maya Moore Savors Her Own." Sports of the Times. *The New York Times*, May 17, 2021. www.nytimes .com/2021/05/17/sports/basketball/maya-moore-jonathan-irons-release.html.

Time magazine and World Economic Forum, "The Great Reset." https://time.com /collection/great-reset.

Principle 6: Make It Global

Abrams, Jonathan. "N.B.A. Players Meet with Pope Francis on Social Justice Efforts." *The New York Times*, Nov. 23, 2020. www.nytimes.com/2020/11/23/sports /basketball/nba-pope-francis-protests.html.

Akabas, Lev. "Americans More Active in 2020 as Solo Sports Gain during Pandemic: Data Viz." Sportico.com, Feb. 22, 2021. www.sportico.com/business/ commerce/2021/sfia-report-2020-covid-1234623194.

Arbuckle, Alex. "Fidel Castro Felt Basketball Was Perfect Training for Guerrilla Warfare." *Mashable*, June 5, 1972. https://mashable.com/feature/fidel-castro -basketball.

Badenhausen, Kurt. "How Michael Jordan Will Make More Money Than Any Athlete This Year." *Forbes*, Mar. 30, 2016. www.forbes.com/sites/ kurtbadenhausen/2016/03/30/how-michael-jordan-will-make-more-than-any -other-athlete-in-the-world-this-year/?sh=3ed41a738656.

———. "NBA Team Values 2020: Lakers and Warriors Join Knicks in Rarefied $4 Billion Club." *Forbes*, Feb. 11, 2020. www.forbes.com/sites/ kurtbadenhausen/2020/02/11/nba-team-values-2020-lakers-and-warriors-join -knicks-in-rarefied-4-billion-club/?sh=3a04f6c92032.

Bamberger, Bill. Hoops. www.billbamberger.com/hoops.

Baptista, Eduardo. "Meet MoreFree, the Chinese Streetball Pioneer Who Can't Stop Battling NBA Stars." *RADII*, Oct. 9, 2018. https://radiichina.com/meet-the -man-who-founded-chinas-streetball-scene-battles-nba-stars-and-still-dreams-of -turning-pro.

SOURCES

Bartholomew, Rafe. *Pacific Rims: Beermen Ballin' in Flip-Flops and the Philippines' Unlikely Love Affair with Basketball.* Berkley, 2011.

Belson, Ken. "Money, Arena and India Play Into Sale of the Kings." *The New York Times,* Apr. 17, 2013. www.nytimes.com/2013/04/18/sports/basketball/money -arena-and-india-play-into-potential-sale-of-kings.html.

Buha, Jovan. "Ranking the 25 Greatest NBA Signature Sneaker Lines of All Time." *The Athletic,* May 29, 2020. https://theathletic.com/1833124/2020/05/29 /ranking-the-25-greatest-nba-signature-sneaker-lines-of-all-time/#.

Careem, Nazvi. "NBA No. 1 in China Ahead of Premier League and Champions League in Survey of Internet Users; CSL Not in the Top 10." *South China Morning Post,* May 14, 2019. www.scmp.com/sport/china/article/3010184/nba-no-1 -china-ahead-premier-league-and-champions-league-survey.

Carlos, Juan. "Mayans, Yes Mayans, Love Basketball." ESPN, Dec. 8, 2017. www.espn .com/nba/story/_/id/21699578/mayans-yes-mayans-love-basketball.

Cronin, Ben. "Fiba Looks to China to Make Basketball Most Popular Sport in the World." *SportBusiness,* Nov. 6, 2018. www.sportbusiness.com/news/fiba-looks-to -china-to-make-basketball-most-popular-sport-in-the-world.

Crunchyroll. "How Manga Changed Basketball in Japan—Anime Explained." YouTube, Mar. 29, 2019. www.youtube.com/ watch?v=9CNuuDhRGRY&t=207s.

Deb, Sopan. "Chinese State TV to Air N.B.A. for First Time Since Hong Kong Rift." *The New York Times,* Oct. 9. 2020. www.nytimes.com/2020/10/09/sports /basketball/nba-china-cctv.html.

——. "'This Is My Life!' Why the Philippines Is a Hoops Haven." *The New York Times,* June 5, 2019. www.nytimes.com/2019/06/05/sports/nba -playoffs-basketball-philippines.html.

Dennis. "The 10 Best-Selling Sneakers on StockX." Grailify Sneaker Releases, July 9, 2021. www.grailify.com/en/the-10-best-selling-sneakers-on-stockx.

DePaula, Nick. *"Rui Hachimura and Michael Jordan Have Iconic Plans in Japan."* ESPN, Nov. 7, 2019. www.espn.com/nba/story/_/id/28030199/rui-hachimura-michael -jordan-iconic-plans-japan.

"Elimination of Discrimination against Women and Girls in Sport." United Nations General Assembly, Mar. 20, 2019. https://ilga.org/downloads/Elimination_of _discrimination_against_women_and_girls_in_sport.pdf.

Evans, Pat. "Philippines Showcases International Growth Efforts by NBA During Playoffs." *Front Office Sports,* Oct. 27, 2020. https://frontofficesports.com /philippines-nba-international-growth/?utm_medium=email&utm_campaign=N ew+Ticketing+Reality+Wave+1&utm_content=New+Ticketing+Reality+Wave +1%2BCID_a66d13aa6a8f5795e8af048103d0c3d0&utm_source=FOS+Daily +Newsletter&utm_term=drew+the+largest+viewership.

Filipov, David. "A New Russian Film Takes Us Back to the U.S.S.R. to Celebrate a Soviet Olympic Miracle." *The Washington Post,* Dec. 31, 2017. www .washingtonpost.com/world/europe/a-new-russian-film-takes-us-back-to-the -ussr-to-celebrate-a-soviet-olympic-miracle/2017/12/30/429d3ae4-e708-11e7 -9ec2-518810e7d44d_story.html.

Flum, Alex, and Hanah Yasharaoff. "The Friendship Games: Where Basketball and Diplomacy Meet." *Sports Business Daily,* Sept. 25, 2017. www.sportsbusinessjournal .com/Journal/Issues/2017/09/25/Opinion/Friendship-Games.aspx.

SOURCES

Forgrave, Reid. "Can the N.B.A. Find a Basketball Superstar in India?" *The New York Times,* Oct. 3, 2019. www.nytimes.com/2019/10/03/magazine/india-basketball -nba.html.

Gao, Helen. "From Mao Zedong to Jeremy Lin: Why Basketball Is China's Biggest Sport." *The Atlantic,* Feb. 22, 2012. www.theatlantic.com/international/archive /2012/02/from-mao-zedong-to-jeremy-lin-why-basketball-is-chinas-biggest -sport/253427.

In The Lab. "Ten000Hours. Episode 1: Just Another Day." Facebook, Nov. 29, 2018. https://m.facebook.com/watch/?v=273640796628931&_rdr.

———. "Ten000Hours. Episode 8: Back to Zero (Part 1), Devin Explores China." YouTube, June 14, 2015. www.youtube.com/watch?v=ACqV5LX1jck&list=PLVo caCGI5NRkH6fwZ5fuXLcBD9FTY3JbZ&index=11.

———. "Ten000Hours. Episode 10: The Culture." YouTube, Nov. 4, 2018. www .youtube.com/watch?v=deKLol2zTGE&list=PLVocaCGI5NRkH6fwZ5fuXLcB D9FTY3JbZ&index=3.

"International Charter of Physical Education, Physical Activity and Sport." UNESCO, 26 June 2020. https://en.unesco.org/themes/sport-and-anti-doping/sport -charter.

"International Day of Sport for Development and Peace." United Nations General Assembly, Sept. 18, 2013. https://undocs.org/A/RES/67/296.

"International Day of Yoga." United Nations, June 21, 2021. www.un.org/en /observances/yoga-day.

Ives, Mike. "Unified Korean Team, Victor on the Court, Tries to Win Hearts, Too." *The New York Times,* Aug. 25, 2018. www.nytimes.com/2018/08/25/world/asia/ unified-korean-womens-basketball.html.

KBS News. "[Back Then] Respond, Nonggu Dejanchi . . . Memory of Oppa Army [Video]," YouTube, Jan. 7, 2016. https://www.youtube.com/watch?v=aFe 34FOyhAE.

Keene, Louis. "Enes Kanter Is the Man in the Middle." Intelligencer. *New York Magazine,* Apr. 14, 2019. https://nymag.com/intelligencer/2019/04/enes-kanter -is-at-the-center-of-it-all.html.

Keh, Andrew. "A Court Used for Playing Hoops Since 1893. Where? Paris." *The New York Times,* Apr. 17, 2017. www.nytimes.com/2017/04/17/sports /basketball/a-court-used-for-playing-hoops-since-1893-where-paris.html.

Koster, Kyle. "Pope Francis on Basketball: 'Yours Is a Sport That Lifts You Up to the Heavens.'" *The Big Lead,* May 31, 2021. www.thebiglead.com/posts/pope-francis -basketball-yours-is-a-sport-that-lifts-you-up-to-the-heavens-01f71hwgcf8h.

Krasnoff, Lindsay Sarah. "Background and Issues in Global Sports Today." www .lindsaysarahkrasnoff.com/on-sports.

———. "The Hidden Mystery of Hoops Diplomacy: France vs. China, 1966." *Los Angeles Review of Books,* Sept. 10, 2019. https://lareviewofbooks.org/article /hidden-mystery-hoops-diplomacy.

Lange, David. "European Football Market Size 2006-2019." *Statista,* Nov. 26, 2020. www.statista.com/statistics/261223/european-soccer-market-total-revenue.

Lazar, Louie. "Meet the Jerusalem Old City Basketball Legend Known as Issa 6." *Tablet,* May 2, 2013. www.tabletmag.com/sections/sports/articles/jerusalem- basketball-jesus.

SOURCES

————. "Tibet Is Going Crazy for Hoops." *The Atlantic*, Dec. 17, 2018. www .theatlantic.com/magazine/archive/2019/01/tibet-basketball/576421.

Li, Patrick. "Beijing's 6 Best Indoor and Outdoor Courts for Pick-Up Basketball." *The Beijinger*, May 11, 2016. www.thebeijinger.com/blog/2016/05/11/best -courts-pick-basketball-beijing.

"List of International Days and Weeks." United Nations. www.un.org/en /observances/list-days-weeks.

Little, Andrew. "The Beijing Basketball Court That Became the 'Holy Land' of Chinese Streetball." *RADII*, Sept. 9, 2019. https://radiichina.com/dongdan -basketball-china-streetball.

Longman, Jeré. "For Japan, N.B.A. 101 Is Now in Session." *The New York Times*, Oct. 16, 2018. www.nytimes.com/2018/10/16/sports/nba-japan.html.

————. "Under Fidel Castro, Sport Symbolized Cuba's Strength and Vulnerability." *The New York Times*, Nov. 27, 2016. www.nytimes.com/2016/11/27/sports/under -fidel-castro-sport-symbolized-cubas-strength-and-vulnerability.html.

Loo, Egan. "Two Japanese Boys Chosen for 2nd Slam Dunk Scholarship." *Anime News Network*, June 22, 2008. www.animenewsnetwork.com/news/2008-06-22/two -japanese-boys-chosen-for-2nd-slam-dunk-scholarship.

Markevicius, Marius A. director. *The Other Dream Team*. Lionsgate, 2012.

Marris, Laura. "Camus's Inoculation Against Hate." *The New York Times*, Apr. 16, 2020. www.nytimes.com/2020/04/16/books/review/the-plague-albert-camus- coronavirus.html.

Martinez, Nico. "Basketball Named 3rd Most Popular Sport In The World With Over 2 Billion Fans Worldwide." *Fadeaway World*, Jan. 21, 2021. https://fadeawayworld. net/nba-media/basketball-named-3rd-most-popular-sport-in-the-world-with -over-2-billion-fans-worldwide.

Menkin, Dani, director. *On the Map*. Hey Jude Productions, 2017. www.heyjude productions.com/our-films/on-the-map.

Messitte, Zach. "Forget the All-Star Game. Start Watching Italian Basketball." *The New York Times*, Feb. 16, 2019. www.nytimes.com/2019/02/16/opinion/nba-all-star -game-coppa-italia.html.

"NBA Players, Michele Roberts Meeting with Pope at the Vatican." *Sports Business Journal*, Nov. 23, 2020. www.sportsbusinessjournal.com/Daily/Morning -Buzz/2020/11/23/NBA-Papal.aspx.

"NBA Rosters Feature 107 International Players from 41 Countries." NBA.com, Dec. 22, 2020. www.nba.com/news/nba-rosters-feature-107-international- players-from-41-countries.

Office of the President of Ukraine. Transcript of Ukrainian Presidential Address to United Nations, Apr. 5, 2022. https://www.president.gov.ua/en/news/vistup -prezidenta-ukrayini-na-zasidanni-radi-bezpeki-oon-74121.

Palathingal, Anita. "The Contribution of Sports to the Achievement of the Sustainable Development Goals: A Toolkit for Action." Sustainable Development Goals, 2018. www.sdgfund.org/sites/default/files/report-sdg_fund_sports_and_sdgs_web.pdf.

Peter, Josh. "Native Americans Find 'Escape' from Coronavirus Fears with Basketball." *USA Today*, Mar. 14, 2020. www.usatoday.com/story/sports/2020/03/14/native -americans-find-escape-from-coronavirus-fears-with-basketball/5049247002.

SOURCES

"Pope Francis Blesses Hawks' MLK Jersey." NBA.com, Jan. 15, 2021. www.nba.com /news/pope-francis-blesses-hawks-mlk-jersey.

"Pwc 2021 Sports Outlook." *PwC,* 2020. www.pwc.com/us/en/industries/tmt /library/sports-outlook-north-america.html.

Ramzy, Austin. "Dennis Rodman, Frequent Visitor to North Korea, Is Back." *The New York Times,* June 13, 2017. www.nytimes.com/2017/06/13/world/asia/dennis -rodman-north-korea.html.

Scarano, Ross. "Bill Bamberger's 'Hoops' Photo Series." Air.Jordan, Mar. 5, 2020. https://air.jordan.com/card/bill-bambergers-hoops-photo-series.

Sin, Ben. "Slam Dunk: How Japan's Love of Basketball Can Be Traced Back to a Comic." *Sports Illustrated,* May 7, 2013. www.si.com/extra-mustard/2013/05/07 /slam-dunk-how-japans-love-of-basketball-can-be-traced-back-to-a-comic.

Skinner, Robb. "The Transcendent Power of Sports." United Nations Information Center Washington, Apr. 4, 2018. https://unicwash.org/sports-day.

Smith, Rory, and Tariq Panja. "The Erasure of Mesut Özil." *The New York Times,* Oct. 26, 2020. www.nytimes.com/2020/10/26/sports/soccer/mesut-ozil-arsenal -china.html.

Sourav. "Top 10 Most Popular Sports in the World: 2021 Power Ranking." *Sports Show,* July 28, 2021. https://sportsshow.net/top-10-most-popular-sports-in-the -world.

"Sport as an Enabler of Sustainable Development." United Nations General Assembly, Nov. 26, 2018. https://stillmed.olympic.org/media/Document%20Library /OlympicOrg/News/2018/12/Sport-as-an-enabler-of-sustainable-development -EN.pdf.

Sprung, Shlomo. *"Inside the NBA's Push to Make Basketball the World's Most Popular Sport." Forbes,* Mar. 4, 2019. www.forbes.com/sites/shlomosprung/2019/03/04 /nba-china-ceo-derek-chang-takes-us-inside-nbas-push-to-make-basketball -worlds-most-popular-sport/?sh=78ea46d751b0.

Stein, Marc. "Diego Maradona Loved Basketball. Its Stars Loved Him, Too." *The New York Times,* Dec. 2, 2020. www.nytimes.com/2020/12/02/sports/basketball /diego-maradona-nba-ginobili.html.

Sulc, Brittany Alexandra. "What Is the Most Popular Basketball Shoe of All Time?" *Stadium Talk,* May 3, 2021. www.stadiumtalk.com/s/air-jordans-most-popular -basketball-shoe-21108d1fe8d148e3.

Tartaglione, Nancy. "'Three Seconds': Olympic Basketball Drama Is Russia's Highest -Grossing Movie Ever." Deadline, Jan. 16, 2018. https://deadline.com/2018/01 /three-seconds-going-vertical-movie-record-russia-box-office-olympic -basketball-drama-video-1202243843.

Taylor, Nate. "For Spurs, Every Game Is a Global Summit." *The New York Times,* June 9, 2013. www.nytimes.com/2013/06/10/sports/basketball/for-spurs-every -game-is-a-global-summit.html.

"The 17 Goals | Sustainable Development." United Nations Department of Economic and Social Affairs. https://sdgs.un.org/goals.

"The Closure of the UNOSDP." *Sportanddev.org.* www.sportanddev.org/en/news -and-views/call-articles/closure-unosdp.

"The NBA's Growing Popularity Scores Wins for Sponsors." Nielsen, May 9, 2018.

SOURCES

www.nielsen.com/us/en/insights/article/2018/the-nbas-growing-popularity
-scores-wins-for-sponsors.

Tolajian, Michael, director. *Once Brothers*. ESPN Films, 2010.

"Transforming Our World: The 2030 Agenda for Sustainable Development." United
Nations. https://sdgs.un.org/2030agenda.

"UN Presents a New Toolkit for Action on How Sports Can Contribute to Achieve
SDGs." *Sustainable Development Goals Fund,* July 10, 2018. www.sdgfund.org/un
-presents-new-toolkit-action-how-sports-can-contribute-achieve-sdgs.

Wang, Yanan. "How Yao Ming Subverted Stereotypes and Brought Basketball to
Millions." *The Washington Post,* Apr. 30, 2019. www.washingtonpost.com/news
/morning-mix/wp/2016/04/05/hall-of-famer-yao-ming-redefined-chinaman
-for-the-nba-and-brought-the-game-to-hundreds-of-millions.

Wasilak, Sarah. "The 10 Most Valuable Sneakers to Own (and Resell!) in 2021."
Popsugar, Jan. 13, 2021. www.popsugar.com/fashion/best-sneakers-resell-2021
-48106635.

Webb, Alysha. "How Air Force 1s Became Nike's Best-Selling Sneaker." CNBC,
Nov. 16, 2020. www.cnbc.com/video/2020/11/16/how-air-force-1s-became
-nikes-best-selling-sneaker.html.

Wimmer, Micah. "How Fidel Castro Invented the Euro Step: A Brief Oral History."
Medium, Nov. 29, 2016. https://medium.com/the-shocker/how-fidel-castro
-invented-the-euro-step-a-brief-oral-history-1a68c25a4965.

Wong, Alex. "A Humbling N.B.A. Moment Brings Cheers from Japan." *The New York
Times,* May 6, 2021. www.nytimes.com/2021/05/06/sports/basketball/yuta
-watanabe-raptors-japan.html.

"World Chess Day." United Nations General Assembly, Dec. 18, 2019. https://undocs
.org/A/RES/74/22.

Yang, Gang. "NBA Academy Shandong." *NBA.* https://nbaacademy.nba.com
/location/shandong.

Yee, Vivian. "Basketball Is 'War, Minus the Shooting' in Sectarian Lebanon." *The New
York Times,* May 16, 2019. www.nytimes.com/2019/05/16/world/middleeast
/lebanon-basketball-sectarian-politics.html.

Youngmisuk, Ohm. "LeBron James: Daryl Morey Was 'Misinformed' before Sending
Tweet about China and Hong Kong." ESPN, Oct. 14, 2019. www.espn.com/nba
/story/_/id/27847951/daryl-morey-was-misinformed-sending-tweet-china-hong
-kong.

Principle 7: Gender Inclusive

"A Message from Dawn Staley: Now Is the Time to Grow Our Game. You Can
Help." *USA Today,* Apr. 5, 2021. www.usatoday.com/story/sports/2021/04/05
/dawn-staley-now-time-to-grow-womens-basketball/7085142002.

ABC News Radio, "New ESPN Documentary Explores Basketball's Impact in Racial
Injustice, Gender Equality and Other Key Moments of History." ABC News
Radio, Nov. 9, 2018. http://abcnewsradioonline.com/sports-news/new-espn
-documentary-explores-basketballs-impact-in-racial-i.html.

Abokar, Shafi'I Mohyaddin. "Somalia: Death Threats Fail to Stop Women's Basketball."

SOURCES

Inter Press Service, Oct. 18, 2011. www.ipsnews.net/2011/10/somalia-death -threats-fail-to-stop-womenrsquos-basketball.

AFP. "Women's Basketball Restarts in Somalia after 24 Years." YouTube, May 29, 2014. www.youtube.com/watch?v=hPuXd6VujGk.

Associated Press. "Florida Governor Bans Transgender Women and Girls from School Sports." NBCNews.com, June 2, 2021. www.nbcnews.com/feature/nbc-out /florida-governor-bans-transgender-women-girls-school-sports-n1269238.

Barbieri, Alyssa. "Arizona Women's Basketball Coach Adia Barnes Isn't Apologizing for Impassioned Postgame Speech." USA Today, Apr. 3, 2021. https://ftw.usatoday. com/2021/04/adia-barnes-arizona-wildcats-womens-basketball-coach-postgame -speech.

Beech, Hannah. "'She Is a Hero': In Myanmar's Protests, Women Are on the Front Lines." The New York Times, Mar. 4, 2021. www.nytimes.com/2021/03/04/world /asia/myanmar-protests-women.html.

Boynton, Eric. "South Carolina's Dawn Staley Has No Aspirations to Coach Men at Any Level or in the WNBA." Herald-Journal, Apr. 13, 2021. www.goupstate.com /story/sports/2021/04/13/south-carolina-basketball-coach-dawn-staley-has-no -desire-coach-men-wnba/7207086002.

Buckner, Candace. "Dawn Staley, Another Title in Sight, Won't Stop Speaking Out: 'I Can't Not Do It.'" The Washington Post, Apr. 5, 2021. www.washingtonpost.com /sports/2021/03/19/dawn-staley-south-carolina-basketball-protest.

Campagna, Dan. "Breaking Barriers and Ankles with Jamad Fiin." Emmanuel College Athletics, Home of the Saints, Oct. 16, 2020. www.goecsaints.com/sports/w -baskbl/2020-21/releases/20201016gjmhhy.

Cave, Damien. "'The Most Unsafe Workplace'? Parliament, Australian Women Say." The New York Times, Apr. 5, 2021. www.nytimes.com/2021/04/05/world/australia /parliament-women-rape-metoo.html.

Corbett, Sara. Venus to the Hoop: A Gold-Medal Year in Women's Basketball. Anchor, 1998.

Crouse, Lindsay. "So You Want to 'Save Women's Sports'?" The New York Times, Mar. 24, 2021. www.nytimes.com/2021/03/24/opinion/trans-athletes-womens -sports.html.

Fati's Female Sports Channel. "Muslim Somali Basketball Player // Jamad Fiin." YouTube, Sept. 10, 2020. www.youtube.com/watch?v=rzLvIYcZhac.

Gentry, Dorothy J. "The American Basketball League Helped Pave the Way for the WNBA." Sports Illustrated, May 12, 2021. www.si.com/wnba/2021/05/12 /american-basketball-league.

"Giants of Africa Takes Women's Basketball to Somalia." Giants of Africa. https:// giantsofafrica.org/giants-of-africa-takes-womens-basketball-to-somalia.

Gilbert, Sophie. "The Unending Assaults on Girlhood." The Atlantic, Apr. 1, 2021. www.theatlantic.com/culture/archive/2021/03/girlhood-melissa-febos-lucid -expose-rape-culture/618445.

Global Gender Gap Report 2021. World Economic Forum, Mar. 2021. www .weforum.org/reports/global-gender-gap-report-2021?utm_source=newsletter &utm_medium=email&utm_campaign=newsletter_axiosam& amp;stream=top.

SOURCES

Grarup, Jan. "Basket-Somalia06.Jpg." https://jangrarup.photoshelter.com/image /I0000nsRraP9mgHI.

Harris, Kamala D. "The Exodus of Women from the Workforce Is a National Emergency." *The Washington Post,* Feb. 2, 2021. www.washingtonpost.com /opinions/kamala-harris-women-workforce-pandemic/2021/02/12/b8cd1cb6 -6d6f-11eb-9f80-3d7646ce1bc0_story.html.

Hassan, Mohamed Olad. "Somali Clerics Warn Women against Playing Basketball." *Voice of America,* Dec. 22, 2016. www.voanews.com/a/somali-clerics-warn -women-aginst-playing-basketball/3646679.html.

Hincks, Joseph. "How Turkey's Canan Kaftancioglu Challenged Erdogan's Power." *Time,* Feb. 24, 2021. https://time.com/5941493/kaftancioglu-erdogan-turkey.

In The Know. "Jamad Finn Is Changing the Idea of Who Can Play Basketball." YouTube, Nov. 6, 2020. www.youtube.com/watch?v=CrNoUQfMnGE.

Ismail, Julia. "How a Women's Basketball Team in Somalia Is Completely Changing the Culture." Kulture Hub, Mar. 15, 2021. https://kulturehub.com/womens -somalian-basketball-team.

Kermeliotis, Teo. "Somali Women Defy Danger to Write Basketball History." CNN, Dec. 22, 2011. www.cnn.com/2011/12/22/sport/basketball-somalia-women-al -shabaab/index.html.

Kottasová, Ivana. "Scotland Is Making Tampons and Pads Free." CNN, Nov. 25, 2020. www.cnn.com/2020/11/24/uk/scotland-period-products-vote-scli-gbr-intl /index.html.

Looney, Douglas. "A Blazing Dawn," *Sports Illustrated,* Nov. 19, 1990. https://vault.si .com/vault/1990/11/19/scouting-reports-a-blazing-dawn-dawn-staley-all -5-ft-5-in-of-her-lifts-virginia-to-bold-new-heights.

Maclean, Ruth. "In Nigeria, 'Feminist' Was a Common Insult. Then Came the Feminist Coalition." *The New York Times,* Mar. 12, 2021. www.nytimes. com/2021/03/12/world/africa/nigeria-feminist-coalition.html.

Mertens, Maggie. "Get That Life: How I Became an NCAA Championship-Winning Basketball Coach." *Cosmopolitan,* Mar. 1, 2017. www.cosmopolitan.com/career /a9570900/dawn-staley-ncaa-womens-basketball-coach-get-that.life.

Mire, Hana. "Rajada Dalka—Nation's Hope." *GBGG Productions.* https://gbgg productions.com/?page_id=475.

NBC Sports. "Coach Got Game: Why Dawn Staley Is the Ultimate Player's Coach." YouTube, Apr. 5, 2020, www.youtube.com/watch?v=LQu7lzU5b_Y.

Okeowo, Alexis. "The Fight Over Women's Basketball in Somalia." *The New Yorker,* Sept. 4, 2017. www.newyorker.com/magazine/2017/09/11/the-fight-over -womens-basketball-in-somalia.

Pandey, Erica, et al. "Pandemic Was Devastating for America's Working Women." *Axios,* Mar. 13, 2021. www.axios.com/pandemic-devastating-year-working -women-17e52dea-7fb4-467f-a5c1-1e4632d6fd16.html?utm_source=newsletter &utm_medium=email&utm_campaign=newsletter_axiosdeep dives&stream=top.

Papenfuss, Mary. "California Bill Would Make Kids Sections in Large Stores Gender Neutral." *HuffPost,* Mar. 6, 2021. www.huffpost.com/entry/evan-low-gender -neutral-department-store-kids-section-bill-california_n_60445160c5b69078ac6b b4d5.

SOURCES

Pisani, Joseph. "Mr. Potato Head Drops the Mister, Sort Of." Associated Press, Feb. 25, 2021. http://apnews.com/article/mr-potato-head-goes-gender-neutral-d3c178f2 b9b0c424ed814657be41a9d8?utm_source=newsletter&utm_medium =email&utm_campaign=newsletter_axiosam&stream=top.

Rapp, Timothy. "Dawn Staley Addresses 'Glaring Deficiencies' Between Men's, Women's Tournaments." *Bleacher Report,* Mar. 19, 2021. https://bleacherreport. com/articles/2937180-dawn-staley-addresses-glaring-deficiencies-between-mens -womens-tournaments.

Reuters. "Somali Women's Basketball Team Defy Prejudice." YouTube, Oct. 2, 2020. www.youtube.com/watch?v=Zr5RSvmKiw4.

Rhoden, William C. "Sports of The Times; A Hometown Hero, Always at Home." *The New York Times,* Apr. 13, 1996. www.nytimes.com/1996/04/13/sports/sports -of-the-times-a-hometown-hero-always-at-home.html.

Rich, Motoko. "A Novelist Breaks the Code of Being a Woman in Japan." *The New York Times,* May 9, 2020. www.nytimes.com/2020/05/09/world/asia/mieko -kawakami-breasts-and-eggs.html.

Safronova, Valeriya. "Passports May Soon Include a New Option for Gender Identity." *The New York Times,* Feb. 24, 2021. www.nytimes.com/2021/02/24/style/gender -neutral-x-passport-ids.html.

Sandoz, Joli, and Joby Winans, eds. *Whatever It Takes: Women on Women's Sports.* Farrar, Straus and Giroux, 1999.

Schmidt, Samantha. "A Language for All." *The Washington Post,* Dec. 5, 2019. www .washingtonpost.com/dc-md-va/2019/12/05/teens-argentina-are-leading -charge-gender-neutral-language/?utm_campaign=post_most&utm _medium=Email&utm_source=Newsletter&wpisrc=nl_most &wpmm=1.

Sinclair, Stephanie. "These Girls Are Being Cut and Married in Droves." *The New York Times,* Dec. 10, 2020. www.nytimes.com/2020/12/10/opinion/kenya-covid-child-marriage.html.

Sussman, Anna Louie. "'Women's Work' Can No Longer Be Taken for Granted." *The New York Times,* Nov. 13, 2020. www.nytimes.com/2020/11/13/opinion/sunday /women-pay-gender-gap.html.

Taub, Amanda. "After Sarah Everard's Killing, Women's Groups Want Change, Not More Policing." *The New York Times,* Mar. 21, 2021. www.nytimes. com/2021/03/21/world/europe/sarah-everard-police-uk.html.

Tynes, Tyler. "*The Fires That Forged Dawn Staley.*" SBNation.com, Mar. 29, 2019. www.sbnation.com/2019/3/29/18286470/dawn-staley-womens-basketball-fires -that-forged.

Yilek, Caitlin. "Dawn Staley, South Carolina Women's Basketball Coach, on Representation and Speaking Up for People without a Voice." CBS News, Mar. 18, 2021. www.cbsnews.com/news/dawn-staley-south-carolina-gamecocks -wnba.

Principle 8: No Barrier to Access

ActiveRain. "Realtor Code of Ethics Once Required Discrimination." *Inman,* Apr. 17, 2014. www.inman.com/2014/04/17/realtor-code-of-ethics-once-required

SOURCES

-discrimination/?utm_source=newsletter&utm_medium=email&utm_campaign =newsletter_axiosam-hard-truths&stream=top.

Allen, Mike. "Axios AM Deep Dive: Hard Truths." *Axios,* June 19, 2021. https:// newsletry.com/Home/Axios%20AM/7453d42d-7cbf-4237-c727-08d933125fe6.

Axthelm, Pete. *The City Game: Basketball from the Garden to the Playground.* University of Nebraska Press, 1970.

Baradaran, Mehrsa. *How the Other Half Banks: Exclusion, Exploitation, and the Threat to Democracy.* Harvard University Press, 2015.

Benn, Bradlee, et al. "Elevation: How Organizations Can Accelerate the Rise of Black Leaders." Russell Reynolds Associates, May 25, 2021. www.russellreynolds.com /insights/thought-leadership/elevation-how-organizations-accelerate-rise-black -leaders?rm=Recent+Articles&utm_source=newsletter&utm_medium=email &utm_campaign=newsletter_axiosam-hard-truths&stream=top.

Bhutta, Neil, et al. "Disparities in Wealth by Race and Ethnicity in the 2019 Survey of Consumer Finances." The Fed in Print, Sept. 28, 2020. www.federalreserve .gov/econres/notes/feds-notes/disparities-in-wealth-by-race-and-ethnicity-in -the-2019-survey-of-consumer-finances-20200928.htm?utm_source=news letter&utm_medium=email&utm_campaign=newsletter_axiosam-hard-truths &stream=top.

Bouie, Jamelle. "Beyond 'White Fragility.'" *The New York Times,* June 26, 2020. www .nytimes.com/2020/06/26/opinion/black-lives-matter-injustice.html.

Brown, Courtenay. "Goldman Puts $10 Billion behind Fight to Equalize 'Black Womenomics.'" *Axios,* Mar. 10, 2021. www.axios.com/goldman-investing- inequality-black-women-a7e2c1b9-f9a0-40cd-8e6f-27ec53156236.html.

Cacciola, Scott. "Teammates in Brooklyn, Rivals in M.L.S." *The New York Times,* Apr. 15, 2021. www.nytimes.com/2021/04/15/sports/soccer/durant-harden -nash-mls.html.

Choi, Ann, et al. "Undercover Investigation Reveals Evidence of Unequal Treatment by Real Estate Agents." *Newsday,* Nov. 17, 2019. https://projects.newsday.com /long-island/real-estate-agents-investigation/?utm_source=newsletter&utm _medium=email&utm_campaign=newsletter_axiosam-hard-truths&stream=top.

Chotiner, Isaac. "Jalen Rose Has a Problem with Basketball Analytics." *The New Yorker,* June 9, 2019. www.newyorker.com/new/q-and-a/jalen-rose-has-a-problem -with-basketball-analytics.

Contreras, Russell. "Juneteenth Forces U.S. to Confront Lasting Impact of Slavery Economy." *Axios,* June 19, 2021. www.axios.com/juneteenth-slavery-business -built-us-1d1b522c-f1ee-404a-aaf4-e3c9185952c4.html?utm_source=news letter&utm_medium=email&utm_campaign=newsletter_axiosam&stream =top.

Dyson, Michael Eric. "Be like Mike? Michael Jordan and the Pedagogy of Desire." *Cultural Studies* 7, no. 1, 1993, 64–73.

Eligon, John, and Jenny Gross. "Kansas City STAR Apologizes for Racism in Decades of Reporting." *The New York Times,* Dec. 21, 2020. www.nytimes.com/2020/12 /21/us/kansas-city-star-apology.html.

Frey, Darcy. *Last Shot: City Streets, Basketball Dreams.* Houghton Mifflin, 1994.

Friedell, Nick. "Golden State Warriors' Draymond Green Calls Out Double Standards in NBA's Treatment of Players." ESPN, Feb. 16, 2021. www.espn.com/nba

SOURCES

/story/_/id/30909618/golden-state-warriors-draymond-green-calls-double
-standards-nba-treatment-players.

Garcia, Bobbito, and Kevin Couliau, directors. *Doin' It in the Park: Pick-up Basketball NYC.* Goldcrest Films, 2012.

George, Nelson. *Elevating the Game: Black Men and Basketball.* HarperCollins, 1992.

Gonzalez, John. "The Political Donations of NBA Owners Are Not So Progressive." The Ringer, Sept. 24, 2020. www.theringer.com/nba/2020/9/24/21453818/nba
-owners-political-donations-trump-gop.

Hancock, Bryan, et al. "Race in the Workplace: The Black Experience in the US Private Sector." McKinsey & Company, Feb. 21, 2021. www.mckinsey.com
/featured-insights/diversity-and-inclusion/Race-in-the-workplace-The-Black
-experience-in-the-US-private-sector?utm_source=newsletter&utm_medium
=email&utm_campaign=newsletter_axiosam&stream=top.

"History of Fair Housing." US Department of Housing and Urban Development. www.hud.gov/program_offices/fair_housing_equal_opp/aboutfheo/history?utm
_source=newsletter&utm_medium=email&utm_campaign=newsletter_axiosam
-hard-truths&stream=top.

Kight, Stef W. "Gerrymandering Could Take Power from Booming Communities of Color." *Axios,* Mar. 6, 2021. www.axios.com/hard-truths-deep-dive-politics
-influence-race-ethnicity-gerrymandering-census-7b57b5c6-9225-4515-a29b
-94a76adb7bdd.html?utm_source=newsletter&utm_medium=email&utm
_campaign=newsletter_axiosam-hard-truths&stream=top.

Kolata, Gina. "Social Inequities Explain Racial Gaps in Pandemic, Studies Find." *The New York Times,* Dec. 9, 2020. www.nytimes.com/2020/12/09/health/
coronavirus-black-hispanic.html.

"Korn Ferry Study Reveals U.S. Black P&L Leaders Are Some of the Highest Performing Executives." Korn Ferry, Oct. 8, 2019. www.kornferry.com/about-us
/press/korn-ferry-study-reveals-united-states-black-pl-leaders-are-some-of-the
-highest-performing-executives-in-the-us-c-suite?utm_source=newsletter&utm
_medium=email&utm_campaign=newsletter_axiosam-hard-truths&stream=top.

Markay, Lachlan, and Hans Nichols. "The (Mostly) White Revolving Door." *Axios,* Mar. 6, 2021. www.axios.com/hard-truths-deep-dive-influence-race
-ethnicity-lobbying-9c2ac95c-ec83-4270-a15a-f1a9923dbb83.html?utm
_source=newsletter&utm_medium=email&utm_campaign=newsletter_axiosam
-hard-truths&stream=top.

McCammond, Alexi. "The Struggle to Break into America's Political Donor Class." *Axios,* Mar. 6, 2021. www.axios.com/hard-truths-deep-dive-politics-influence
-race-ethnicity-donors-5a00cc50-35ec-41d5-a2f2-ea26d89eeca8.html?utm
_source=newsletter&utm_medium=email&utm_campaign=newsletter_axiosam
-hard-truths&stream=top.

McCausland, Phil, and Tsirkin, Julie. "Can a Post Office Be a Bank? New Services Test a Progressive Priority." NBC News.com, Oct. 4, 2021. www.nbcnews.com
/politics/politics-news/return-postal-banking-postal-service-tests-new-financial
-services-rcna2502.

McIntosh, Kriston, et al. "Examining the Black-White Wealth Gap." *Brookings,* Feb. 27, 2020. www.brookings.edu/blog/up-front/2020/02/27/examining-the-black
-white-wealth-gap/?utm_source=newsletter&utm_medium=email&utm
_campaign=newsletter_axiosam-hard-truths&stream=top.

SOURCES

Mitchell, Bruce. "HOLC 'Redlining' Maps: The Persistent Structure of Segregation and Economic Inequality." NCRC, Mar. 20, 2018. https://ncrc.org/holc/?utm_source=newsletter&utm_medium=email&utm_campaign=newsletter_axiosam-hard-truths&stream=top.

Moore. *The Other Wes Moore.*

"One Million Black Women." Goldman Sachs. www.goldmansachs.com/our-commitments/sustainability/one-million-black-women/?utm_source=newsletter&utm_medium=email&utm_campaign=newsletter_axiosam&stream=top.

Pandey, Erica. "Corporate America's Revolving Door for Black Employees." *Axios,* Nov. 17, 2020. www.axios.com/corporate-america-black-employee-turnover-rate-91563b14-c87b-435b-b157-0443c586735d.html?utm_source=newsletter&utm_medium=email&utm_campaign=newsletter_axiosam&stream=top.

"Poverty Rate by Race and Ethnicity." Peter G. Peterson Foundation, Sept. 28, 2020. www.pgpf.org/chart-archive/0255_poverty_by_race?utm_source=newsletter&utm_medium=email&utm_campaign=newsletter_axiosdeepdives&stream=top.

Rochester, Shawn D. *The Black Tax: The Cost of Being Black in America.* Good Steward, 2018.

Salmon, Felix. "Why the Racial Homeownership Gap Persists." *Axios,* Dec. 19, 2020. www.axios.com/hard-truths-deep-dive-housing-racial-homeownership-gap-cd7595a2-c5d8-408a-bf03-fdd10f04b0f3.html?utm_source=newsletter&utm_medium=email&utm_campaign=newsletter_axiosam-hard-truths&stream=top.

Shaw, Wesley. "NAR President Charlie Oppler Apologizes for Past Policies That Contributed to Racial Inequality." National Association of Realtors, Nov. 19, 2020. www.nar.realtor/newsroom/nar-president-charlie-oppler-apologizes-for-past-policies-that-contributed-to-racial-inequality?utm_source=newsletter&utm_medium=email&utm_campaign=newsletter_axiosam-hard-truths&stream=top.

Shields, David. *Black Planet: Facing Race Through an NBA Season.* University of Nebraska Press/Bison Books, 2006.

Simmons, Bill, and Bakari Sellers. "Barack Obama on Why the NCAA Should Pay Its Athletes." The Ringer, Dec. 17, 2020. www.theringer.com/video/2020/12/17/22187914/barack-obama-on-why-the-ncaa-should-pay-its-athletes.

Soderbergh, Steven, director. *High Flying Bird.* Extension 765, 2019.

Stansell, Amanda, and Dr. Andrew Chamberlain. "Black at Work: A First Look at Glassdoor Ratings by Race/Ethnicity." Glassdoor, Feb. 18, 2021. www.glassdoor.com/research/black-at-work-employee-satisfaction/?utm_source=newsletter&utm_medium=email&utm_campaign=newsletter_axiosam&stream=top.

Stewart, Shelley, III, et al. "The Economic State of Black America: What Is and What Could Be." McKinsey & Company, June 17, 2021. www.mckinsey.com/featured-insights/diversity-and-inclusion/the-economic-state-of-black-america-what-is-and-what-could-be?utm_source=newsletter&utm_medium=email&utm_campaign=newsletter_axiosam&stream=top.

Struyven, Daan, et al. "Black Womenomics: Investing in the Underinvested." Goldman Sachs Research. *The Bigger Picture,* Mar. 9, 2021. www.goldmansachs.com/insights/pages/black-womenomics-f/black-womenomics-report.pdf.

"What Are Covenants?" Mapping Prejudice. https://mappingprejudice.umn.edu/what-are-covenants.

SOURCES

Wideman, *Hoop Roots: Playground Basketball Love and Race.*

Woodbine, Onaje X. O. *Black Gods of the Asphalt: Religion, Hip-Hop, and Basketball.* Columbia University Press, 2016.

Wright, Richard. *The Republic for Which It Stands.*

Yerak, Becky. "Ex-NBA Player's Group Named Winning Bidder for Bankrupt Ebony Media." *The Wall Street Journal,* Dec. 21, 2020. www.wsj.com/articles/ex-nba-players-group-named-winning-bidder-for-bankrupt-ebony-media-11608591316.

Principle 9: For the Outsider, the Other, and the Masses

Abdul-Jabbar, Kareem. "Why the Toronto Raptors' Title Is a Victory for the NBA, Canada . . . and the US." *The Guardian,* June 17, 2019. www.theguardian.com/sport/2019/jun/17/toronto-raptors-basketball-nba-title-championship.

Andrew-Gee, Eric. "La Ball Province: Quebec Basketball's New Generation of NBA Stars Inspires More to Follow." *The Globe and Mail,* May 28, 2021. www.theglobeandmail.com/canada/article-la-ball-province-quebec-basketballs-new-generation-of-nba-stars.

"Antetokounmpo Features in Greek Pandemic Safety Ad." Associated Press, Dec. 17, 2020. https://apnews.com/article/nba-milwaukee-bucks-giannis-antetokounmpo-coronavirus-pandemic-athens-6a0f52e8d56368a4018075e29f0adb84.

Austen, Ian. "Raptors Fever Takes Toronto, as a Diverse City Embraces a Team That Looks Like It." *The New York Times,* June 10, 2019. www.nytimes.com/2019/06/10/world/canada/basketball-toronto-raptors.html.

Aziz, Omer. "The Raptors Win, and Canada Learns to Swagger." *The New York Times,* June 14, 2019. www.nytimes.com/2019/06/14/opinion/sunday/raptors-warriors-canada.html.

Barshad, Amos. "In Giannis We Trust." *Grantland,* Mar. 6, 2014. https://grantland.com/features/milwaukee-bucks-giannis-antetokounmpo.

Bennett, Donnovan. "Three Reasons Why Basketball Is Gaining Popularity in Canada." Sportsnet.ca, June 30, 2017. www.sportsnet.ca/basketball/nba/three-reasons-basketball-gaining-popularity-canada.

Beschloss, Michael. "Naismith's Choices on Race, from Basketball's Beginnings." *The New York Times,* May 2, 2014. www.nytimes.com/2014/05/03/upshot/choices-on-race-even-from-basketballs-beginnings.html.

Bloomfield, Steve. "How Canada's Liberal Immigration Policy Works—And Why It Could Be a Success Here Too." *Prospect,* Aug. 17, 2017. www.prospectmagazine.co.uk/magazine/how-canadas-liberal-immigration-policy-works-and-why-it-could-be-a-success-here-too.

Burlington Basketball Editor. "Basketball Participation, Success Surges with Canadian Youth and Newcomers." *Burlington Basketball,* Jan. 10, 2018. https://burlingtonbasketball.ca/basketball-participation-surges-with-canadian-youth-and-newcomers.

Chau, Danny. "Giannis Through the Eyes of Milwaukee Refugees." *The Ringer,* May 15, 2019. www.theringer.com/2019/5/15/18624331/giannis-antetokounmpo-milwaukee-bucks-refugees-nba-playoffs.

SOURCES

Cheatham, Amelia. "What Is Canada's Immigration Policy?" Council on Foreign Relations, Aug. 3, 2020. www.cfr.org/backgrounder/what-canadas-immigration -policy.

Chow, Cary. "How Jeremy Lin's Career Mirrors the Current Asian American Movement." *The Undefeated,* May 25, 2021. https://theundefeated.com/features /nba-jeremy-lin-career-mirrors-current-asian-american-movement.

Cooley, Paul. "Basketball's Impact on Refugee Camp, Small Town—And Me, The U.S. Volunteer." ThePostGame.com, Mar. 1, 2019. www.thepostgame.com/basketball -refugees-happy-caravan-greece-sepolia-antetokounmpo.

Doherty, Alison, and Tracy Taylor. "Sport and Physical Recreation in the Settlement of Immigrant Youth." *Leisure/Loisir* 31, no. 1 (2010): 27–55. doi:10.1080/14927713.2 007.9651372.

Dougherty, Jesse, and Jonathan Newton. "'Anywhere but Here.'" *The Washington Post,* Jan. 6, 2018. www.washingtonpost.com/sports/2019/01/18/american-indian -high-school-basketball-star-mya-fourstar-pursues-dream-playing-college -basketball.

Ehrenreich, Ben. "Sea of Troubles." *The New Republic,* Oct. 17, 2019. https:// newrepublic.com/article/155271/europe-migrant-crisis-mediterranean-rescue -boat-alan-kurdi?utm_source=newsletter&utm_medium=email&utm_campaign =newsletter_axiosam&stream=top.

Feschuk, Dave. "The Inside Story of the Raptors' Courtship of Masai Ujiri—A Marriage That Likely Wasn't Prearranged." *Toronto Star,* Apr. 20, 2020. www .thestar.com/sports/raptors/opinion/2020/04/20/the-inside-story-of-masai -ujiris-arrival-from-denver-far-from-preordained.html.

Fletcher, Michael A. "Canada Is Now One of the World's Top Sources of Elite Prep Basketball Recruits." *The Undefeated,* May 15, 2017. https://theundefeated.com /features/canada-world-top-elite-prep-basketball.

Foer, Franklin. *Jewish Jocks: An Unorthodox Hall of Fame.* Twelve, 2012.

Gatopoulos, Derek (@dgatopoulos). "SUBTITLED: Giannis Antetokounmpo in Greek campaign for Covid-19 public safety measures. Here's the ad tweeted by the prime minister ahead of the Christmas holidays." Twitter, Dec. 17, 2020. https://twitter.com/dgatopoulos/status/1339667516872863746?lang=en.

Gibson, Charlotte. "UCLA's Natalie Chou Won't Stand for Anti-Asian Racism Related to Coronavirus." *ESPN,* Mar. 26, 2020. www.espn.com/espnw/voices /story/_/id/28955666/ucla-natalie-chou-stand-anti-asian-racism-related -coronavirus.

"Global Refugee & Migration Crisis." Oxfam, Aug. 2, 2021. www.oxfamamerica.org /explore/emergencies/global-refugee-crisis.

Goodman, Matthew. "City College Routs Kentucky at the Garden in March Madness." *Tablet,* Mar. 12, 2020. www.tabletmag.com/sections/sports/articles /city-college-march-madness.

Goodman, Peter S. "Giannis Antetokounmpo Is the Pride of a Greece That Shunned Him." *The New York Times,* May 3, 2019. www.nytimes.com/2019/05/03/sports /giannis-antetokounmpo-greece.html.

"How a New Campaign Is Trying to Get More Ontario Kids to Sign Up for Hockey." CBCnews. www.cbc.ca/player/play/1909513283928.

"Immigration and Ethnocultural Diversity: Key Results from the 2016 Census."

SOURCES

Statistics Canada, Nov. 25, 2017. www150.statcan.gc.ca/n1/daily-quotidien /171025/dq171025b-eng.htm?indid=14428-1&indgeo=0.

"Is Basketball Shifting Canada's Appeal to Immigrant Entrepreneurs?" StartUp Here Toronto, Aug. 26, 2019. https://startupheretoronto.com/partners/is-basketball -shifting-canadas-appeal-to-immigrant-entrepreneurs.

Islam, Shada. "Europe's Migration 'Crisis' Isn't about Numbers. It's about Prejudice." *The Guardian,* Oct. 8, 2020. www.theguardian.com/world/2020/oct/08/europe -migration-crisis-prejudice-eu-refugee-orban-christian.

Kakissis, Joanna. "Golden Dawn: Greek Court Delivers Landmark Verdicts against Neo-Nazi Party." NPR, Oct. 7, 2020. www.npr.org/2020/10/07/921134005 /golden-dawn-greek-court-delivers-landmark-verdicts-against-neo-nazi-party.

Kedrosky, Paul. "Basketball, Trade, and Immigration." Medium, June 13, 2016. https: //medium.com/@pkedrosky/basketball-and-immigration-568dfef2b629.

Keh, Andrew. "A Court Used for Playing Hoops Since 1893. Where? Paris." *The New York Times,* Apr. 17, 2017. www.nytimes.com/2017/04/17/sports/basketball /a-court-used-for-playing-hoops-since-1893-where-paris.html.

Kennedy, J. Michael. "For Illegal Immigrants, Greek Border Offers a Back Door to Europe," *The New York Times,* July 14, 2012. https://www.nytimes.com/2012 /07/15/world/europe/illegal-immigrants-slip-into-europe-by-way-of-greek -border.html.

Kistler, Emmett. "Harvard Hangs Tight with No. 13 UConn." *The Harvard Crimson,* Dec. 7, 2009. www.thecrimson.com/article/2009/12/7/crimson-harvard-lin -uconn.

Klein, Alan. *Lakota Hoops: Life and Basketball on Pine Ridge Indian Reservation.* Rutgers University Press, 2020.

Lin, Jeremy (@JeremyLin). "Heart." Twitter, May 18, 2021. https://twitter.com/JLin7 /status/1394798832542699521?s=20.

Marsh, Calum. "The World's Largest Privately Owned Basketball Complex Is in Toronto." Complex, May 10, 2021. www.complex.com/sports/the-playground -basketball-complex-interview?utm_campaign=%2B&utm_source=instagram .com&utm_medium=social&utm_content=later-17041111.

Murphy, Blake. "Laeticia Amihere Is the Future of Women's Basketball." *Vice,* Nov. 7, 2017. www.vice.com/en/article/43nqzp/laeticia-amihere-is-the-future-of -womens-basketball-the-16-project.

Newman-Bremang, Kathleen. "The Raptors Shaped My Identity—Now They're Re -Shaping All of Canada's." *Refinery29,* June 6, 2019. www.refinery29.com/en-ca /2019/06/234775/raptors-drake-canadian-identity.

Onishi, Norimitsu. "Will American Ideas Tear France Apart? Some of Its Leaders Think So." *The New York Times,* Feb. 9, 2021. www.nytimes.com/2021/02/09 /world/europe/france-threat-american-universities.html.

Onishi, Norimitsu, and Aurelien Breeden. "Macron Vows Crackdown on 'Islamist Separatism' in France." *The New York Times,* Oct. 2, 2020, www.nytimes .com/2020/10/02/world/europe/macron-radical-islam-france.html.

Opara, Ikem. "There Has Never Been a Better Time to Reimagine Learning." *Policy Magazine,* June 29, 2021. www.policymagazine.ca/there-has-never-been-a-better -time-to-reimagine-learning.

Peter. "Native Americans Find 'Escape' from Coronavirus Fears with Basketball."

SOURCES

Podesta, John. "The Climate Crisis, Migration, and Refugees." Brookings, July 25, 2019. www.brookings.edu/research/the-climate-crisis-migration-and-refugees.

Powell, Michael. "Canada Becomes a Basketball Factory." *The New York Times,* June 8, 2019. www.nytimes.com/2019/06/08/sports/basketball/toronto-basketball.html.

————. "Games on a Reservation Go By in a Blur." *The New York Times,* Mar. 2, 2015. www.nytimes.com/2015/03/03/sports/amid-the-red-rock-a-fever-pitch-for-rez-ball.html.

————. "In Navajo Nation, a Basketball Elder Earns Respect." *The New York Times,* Jan. 1, 2017. www.nytimes.com/2017/01/01/sports/basketball/navajo-nation-raul-mendoza-arizona.html.

————. "Mike Budenholzer Has Come a Long Way from Bucket of Blood Street." *The New York Times,* Apr. 14, 2019. www.nytimes.com/2019/04/14/sports/mike-budenholzer-bucks-holbrook-arizona.html.

Rosen, Charley. *Chosen Game: A Jewish Basketball History.* University of Nebraska Press, 2017.

Senra, Paulo. "ESports on Par with Traditional Sports for Gen Z and Millennials." OverActive Media, Oct. 7, 2019. https://overactive-media-group.prezly.com/esports-on-par-with-traditional-sports-for-gen-z-millennials.

Smith, Gary. "Shadow of a Nation." SI.com, Feb. 18, 1991. https://vault.si.com/vault/1991/02/18/shadow-of-a-nation-the-crows-once-proud-warriors-now-seek-glory-but-often-find-tragedy-in-basketball.

Smith, Gillian. "Playing Together—New Citizens, Sport & Belonging." ICC Insights, July 2014. www.inclusion.ca/pdfs/PlayingTogether_FullR%20Online_Final.pdf.

Smith, Stephen. "Toronto Raptors NBA Championship a Big Win for Canadian Immigration." *CIC News,* June 14, 2019. www.cicnews.com/2019/06/toronto-raptors-nba-championship-a-big-win-for-immigration-0612396.html#gs.7zlygk.

Solutions Research Group. "Landmark SRG Study Profiles Impact of Newcomers." www.srgnet.com/2017/11/01/landmark-study-profiles-impact-of-newcomers-to-canada/.

"Stop AAPI Hate." June 17, 2021. https://stopaapihate.org.

Streep, Abe. "What the Arlee Warriors Were Playing For." *The New York Times,* Apr. 4, 2018. www.nytimes.com/2018/04/04/magazine/arlee-warriors-montana-basketball-flathead-indian-reservation.html.

Summerfield, Patti. "Younger People More Excited for the Return of Basketball." *Media in Canada,* July 17, 2020. https://mediaincanada.com/2020/07/17/younger-people-more-excited-for-the-return-of-basketball.

Tavernise, Sabrina, and Richard A. Oppel Jr. "Spit On, Yelled At, Attacked: Chinese-Americans Fear for Their Safety." *The New York Times,* Mar. 23, 2020. www.nytimes.com/2020/03/23/us/chinese-coronavirus-racist-attacks.html.

Thangaraj, Stanley I. *Desi Hoop Dreams: Pickup Basketball and the Making of Asian American Masculinity.* New York University Press, 2015.

"The Original Nexus of Blacks and Jews in Basketball (Parts 6–7 of 9)." *The Black Fives Foundation,* June 10, 2014. www.blackfives.org/original-nexus-blacks-jews-basketball-parts-6-7.

SOURCES

"Toronto Is Raising the Best Hoops Talent in the World." *The Way We Ball,* episode 3. *Vice* Video. https://video.vice.com/en_us/video/sports-toronto-is-raising-the-best-hoops-talent-in-the-world-twwb-toronto/5a690883177dd45df90a9b08?late st=1&utm_source=vicetwitterus.

"Understanding Canada's Immigration System." Government of Canada, July 30, 2018. www.canada.ca/en/immigration-refugees-citizenship/campaigns/irregular-border-crossings-asylum/understanding-the-system.html.

Vice World of Sports. "Rezball: Basketball in Lakota Nation." YouTube, Dec. 21, 2017. www.youtube.com/watch?v=Ouu5LirxBxo.

Warnica, Richard. "Hockey Blight in Canada: As Basketball's Influence Grows, the Nation's Traditional Game Feels Pressure to Change." *Nationalpost,* Jan. 3, 2020. https://nationalpost.com/news/hockey-blight-in-canada-as-basketballs-influence-grows-the-nations-traditional-game-feels-pressure-to-change.

"Who Invented Basketball?" History.com, June 7, 2014. www.history.com/news/who-invented-basketball.

Williams, Brianna. "Toronto Raptors Fan Joins the Naismith Memorial Basketball Hall of Fame." ESPN, May 21, 2021. www.espn.com/nba/story/_/id/31485265/toronto-raptors-fan-joins-naismith-memorial-basketball-hall-fame.

Willms, Nicole. *When Women Rule the Court: Gender, Race, and Japanese American Basketball.* Rutgers University Press, 2017.

Wolff, Alexander. *Big Game, Small World: A Basketball Adventure.* Warner Books, 2002.

Yang, Gene Luen. *Dragon Hoops.* First Second, 2020.

Principle 10: Urban and Rural

Azzarello, Nina. "Lakwena Brings Bold Basketball Court Art with a Meaningful Message to Pine Bluff, Arkansas." *Designboom,* Jan. 23, 2021. www.designboom.com/art/lakwena-bold-basketball-court-art-pine-bluff-arkansas-01-23-2021.

Basketball for Good (@basketballforgood). www.instagram.com/basketballforgood.

Biden, Joseph R., Jr. "Inaugural Address by President Joseph R. Biden, Jr." The White House, Jan. 20, 2021. www.whitehouse.gov/briefing-room/speeches-remarks/2021/01/20/inaugural-address-by-president-joseph-r-biden-jr.

Bird, Larry, et al. *When the Game Was Ours.* Houghton Mifflin Harcourt, 2009.

Blakley, Johanna, et al. "Are You What You Watch?" *Politico,* 2019. www.politico.com/f/?id=0000016a-4bf0-da8e-adfa-6bf35f120001.

Blow, Charles M. "The 4 Great Migrations." *The New York Times,* Feb. 21, 2021. www.nytimes.com/2021/02/21/opinion/texas-climate-migration.html.

Burnett, John. "Americans Are Fleeing to Places Where Political Views Match Their Own." NPR, February 18, 2022. https://www.npr.org/2022/02/18/1081295373/the-big-sort-americans-move-to-areas-political-alignment.

"Common Practice: Basketball and Contemporary Art." Project Backboard, https://projectbackboard.org/about-1.

Daher, Natalie. "A Brighter Future for Run-Down Basketball Courts." *Bloomberg,* Feb. 7, 2018. www.bloomberg.com/news/articles/2018-02-07/project-backboard-turns-urban-basketball-courts-into-public-art.

SOURCES

Dominicis, Laura De, et al. "The Urban-Rural Divide in Anti-EU Vote: Social, Demographic and Economic Factors Affecting the Vote for Parties Opposed to European Integration." ResearchGate, Dec. 2020. doi:10.2776/696524.

Fournier, Philippe J. "338Canada: The Urban-Rural Divide, Right along Party Lines." *Maclean's,* Sept. 29, 2019. www.macleans.ca/politics/ottawa/338canada-the-urban -rural-divide-right-along-party-lines.

Gasaway, John. *Miracles on the Hardwood.* Grand Central Publishing, 2021.

Gordon, Jeremy. "Rap Soundtracks the Michael Jordan Doc. The N.B.A. Wasn't Always That Way." *The New York Times,* May 3, 2020. www.nytimes.com/2020 /05/03/arts/music/michael-jordan-last-dance-soundtrack.html.

Joyner, Lauren. "GoDaddy Q&A with Project Backboard Founder Dan Peterson." GoDaddy, June 10, 2019. www.godaddy.com/garage/godaddy-project-backboard -dan-peterson.

Kanik, Alexandra, and Patrick Scott. "The Urban-Rural Divide Only Deepened in the 2020 US Election." *City Monitor,* Nov. 13, 2020. https://citymonitor.ai /government/the-urban-rural-divide-only-deepened-in-the-2020-us-election.

Katz, Josh. "'Duck Dynasty' vs. 'Modern Family': 50 Maps of the U.S. Cultural Divide." The Upshot. *The New York Times,* Dec. 27, 2016. www.nytimes.com/interactive /2016/12/26/upshot/duck-dynasty-vs-modern-family-television-maps.html.

Keeley, Sean. "For Project Backboard, Community Change Starts on the Basketball Court." Neighborhoods.com, Feb. 14, 2018. www.neighborhoods.com/blog/for -project-backboard-community-change-starts-on-the-basketball-court.

Landau, Laura. "How Can We Improve Social Infrastructure?" *The Nature of Cities,* June 24, 2019. www.thenatureofcities.com/2019/06/24/how-can-we-improve -social-infrastructure.

Levitsky, Steven, and Daniel Ziblatt. "End Minority Rule." *The New York Times,* Oct. 23, 2020. www.nytimes.com/2020/10/23/opinion/sunday/disenfranchisement -democracy-minority-rule.html.

Medina, Mark. "Magic Johnson on Larry Bird: 'We're Mirrors of Each Other.'" *Los Angeles Times,* Apr. 12, 2012. www.latimes.com/sports/lakers/la-xpm-2012-apr -12-la-sp-ln-la-magic-johnson-on-larry-bird-were-mirrors-of-each-other -20120412-story.html.

Merlino, Doug. *The Crossover: A Brief History of Basketball and Race, from James Naismith to LeBron James.* Doug Merlino, 2011.

Norris, Michele. Interview: "Magic and Bird: A Rivalry Gives Way to Friendship." NPR, Nov. 3, 2009. www.npr.org/templates/story/story.php?storyId=120053152.

Poniewozik, James. "Donald Trump Lost His Battle. The Culture War Goes On." The New York Times, Dec. 14, 2020. www.nytimes.com/2020/12/14/arts/television /donald-trump-culture-war.html.

Rachman, Gideon. "Urban-Rural Splits Have Become the Great Global Divider." Financial Times, July 30, 2018. www.ft.com/content/e05cde76-93d6-11e8-b747 -fb1e803ee64e.

Rich, Motoko, Makiko Inoue, and Hikari Hida. "In Japan, Rural Voters Count More Than Those in Big Cities. It Shows." *The New York Times,* Oct. 28, 2021. www .nytimes.com/2021/10/28/world/asia/japan-election-rural-urban.html.

Rodden, Jonathan. *Why Cities Lose: The Deep Roots of the Urban-Rural Political Divide.* Basic Books, 2019.

SOURCES

Rolón, Carlos. *Common Practice: Basketball.* Skira, 2021.

Valenti, John, with Ron Naclerio. *Swee'pea: The Story of Lloyd Daniels and Other Playground Basketball Legends.* Atria Books, 2016.

Waller, Robert James. "Jump Start." *Old Songs in a New Café: Selected Essays.* Grand Central Publishing, 1994.

Principle 11: Antidote to Isolation and Loneliness

Anderson, Sam. "Kevin Durant and (Possibly) the Greatest Basketball Team of All Time." *The New York Times,* June 2, 2021. www.nytimes.com/2021/06/02 /magazine/kevin-durant-brooklyn-nets.html.

Bahrampour, Tara. "Teens around the World Are Lonelier Than a Decade Ago. The Reason May Be Smartphones." *The Washington Post,* July 20, 2021. www .washingtonpost.com/local/social-issues/teens-loneliness-smart-phones /2021/07/20/cde8c866-e84e-11eb-8950-d73b3e93ff7f_story.html.

Bartholomew. *Pacific Rims.*

Birnstengel, Grace. "What Has the U.K.'s Minister of Loneliness Done to Date?" Next Avenue, Jan. 17, 2020. www.nextavenue.org/uk-minister-of-loneliness.

Buttigieg, Pete. "The Key to Happiness Might Be as Simple as a Library or a Park." *The New York Times,* Sept. 14, 2018. www.nytimes.com/2018/09/14/books /review/palaces-for-the-people-eric-klinenberg.html.

CNN Staff. "China Bans Kids from Playing Online Video Games during the Week." CNN, Aug. 31, 2021. www.cnn.com/2021/08/31/tech/china-ban-video-games -minor-intl-hnk/index.html#recipient_hashed=dce3e9bc6bc08da453a0515ba1b8 efa4acc41fe44998200e22f5aca098898c0f.

Curtin, Sally C., and Melonie Heron. "Death Rates Due to Suicide and Homicide Among Persons Aged 10–24: United States, 2000–2017." U.S. Department of Health and Human Services, Oct. 2019. www.cdc.gov/nchs/data/databriefs /db352-h.pdf?utm_source=newsletter&utm_medium=email&utm_campaign =newsletter_axiosam&stream=top.

DelVecchio. "New York Governor Andrew Cuomo Criticizes People Playing Basketball, Not Social Distancing."

"Everyone Is Going Through Something." Session. Aspen Ideas Festival, June 27, 2019. https://www.aspenideas.org/sessions/everyone-is-going-through-something.

Fernandez, Marisa. "Why We're Failing to Stop Teen Suicide." *Axios,* Oct. 18, 2019. www.axios.com/why-were-failing-to-stop-teen-suicide-0b1b4e63-a4c0-48d2 -b76a-ec55651bd050.html?utm_source=newsletter&utm_medium=email&utm _campaign=newsletter_axiosam&stream=top.

Flores, Mikhail, and Agence France-Presse. "'Not Just Basketball': Circumcisions, Pageants at Philippine Courts." *ABS,* Aug. 29, 2019. https://news.abs-cbn.com /spotlight/08/29/19/not-just-basketball-circumcisions-pageants-at-philippine -courts.

Grant, Adam. "There's a Specific Kind of Joy We've Been Missing." *The New York Times,* July 10, 2021. www.nytimes.com/2021/07/10/opinion/sunday/covid -group-emotions-happiness.html.

SOURCES

Gianatasio, David. "In Finland, Covid-19's Desolation Inspires a Campaign Against Loneliness." Muse by Clio, Apr. 16, 2020. https://musebycl.io/advertising/finland -covid-19s-desolation-inspires-campaign-against-loneliness.

Hobbes, Michael. "It's Not Getting Better for Queer Kids." *HuffPost,* Feb. 10, 2020. www.huffpost.com/entry/its-not-getting-better-for-queer-kids_n_5e41f6ffc5b6 f1f57f172dd6.

Holmes, Baxter. "Coronavirus Has Stopped Basketball across America." ESPN, Apr. 7, 2020. www.espn.com/nba/story/_/id/29004540/coronavirus-stopped-basketball -america.

Kanter, Enes. "Basketball Is My Escape!" Facebook, Oct. 5, 2019. www.facebook .com/watch/?v=919250941779976.

Katz, Josh, and Margot Sanger-Katz. "'It's Huge, It's Historic, It's Unheard-of': Drug Overdose Deaths Spike." *The New York Times,* July 14, 2021. www.nytimes.com /interactive/2021/07/14/upshot/drug-overdose-deaths.html.

Kawaguchi, Shun. "Japan's 'Minister of Loneliness' in Global Spotlight as Media Seek Interviews," *The Mainichi,* May 14, 2021. https://mainichi.jp/english/articles /20210514/p2a/00m/0na/051000c.

Klinenberg, Eric. *Palaces for the People.* Crown, 2018.

———. "Worry Less about Crumbling Roads, More about Crumbling Libraries." *The Atlantic,* Sept. 20, 2018. www.theatlantic.com/ideas/archive/2018/09/worry -less-about-crumbling-roads-more-about-crumbling-libraries/570721.

Klores, Dan, director. *Basketball: A Love Story.*

Kriegel, Mark. *Pistol: The Life of Pete Maravich.* Free Press, 2008.

Kristof, Nicholas. "Let's Wage a War on Loneliness." *The New York Times,* Nov. 9, 2019. www.nytimes.com/2019/11/09/opinion/sunday/britain-loneliness-epidemic .html.

Layton. *Hoop: The American Dream.*

Leland, John. "How Loneliness Is Damaging Our Health," *The New York Times,* Apr. 20, 2022. https://www.nytimes.com/2022/04/20/nyregion/loneliness -epidemic.html.

MacLellan, Lila. "In Japan, Hundreds of Thousands of Young People Are Refusing to Leave Their Homes." Quartz, Sept. 23, 2016. https://qz.com/789082/the -hikikomori-problem-in-japan-hundreds-of-thousands-of-young-people-are -refusing-to-leave-their-homes.

MacMullan, Jackie. "The Courageous Fight to Fix the NBA's Mental Health Problem." ESPN, Aug. 20, 2018. www.espn.com/nba/story/_/id/24382693 /jackie-macmullan-kevin-love-paul-pierce-state-mental-health-nba.

MacMullan, Rafe, and Dan Klores. *Basketball: A Love Story.*

May, Tiffany, and Amy Chang Chien. "Game Over: Chinese Company Deploys Facial Recognition to Limit Youths' Play." *The New York Times,* July 8, 2021. www .nytimes.com/2021/07/08/business/video-game-facial-recognition-tencent .html.

Mental Health America. "Covid-19 and Mental Health: A Growing Crisis." http: //mhanational.org/research-reports/covid-19-and-mental-health-growing-crisis.

SOURCES

Orecchio-Egresitz, Haven, and Hannah Beckler. "Mass Shootings Are up Nearly 73% So Far in 2021 in What Gun Violence Researchers Describe as a Contagion Effect." *Insider,* Apr. 16, 2021. www.insider.com/mass-shootings-increased-in -2021-gun-violence-experts-cite-contagion-effect2021-4.

Pane, Lisa Marie. "US Mass Killings Hit New High in 2019, Most Were Shootings." Associated Press, Dec. 23, 2019. https://apnews.com/article/or-state-wire-ny -state-wire-el-paso-2019-year-in-review-tx-state-wire-4441ae68d14e61b64110 db44f906af92?utm_source=newsletter&utm_medium=email&utm_campaign =newsletter_axiosam&stream=top.

Powerade. "'Rose from Concrete.'" iSpot.tv. www.ispot.tv/ad/7a5C/powerade-rose -from-concrete-featuring-derrick-rose.

Ramachandran, Vignesh. "Stanford Researchers Identify Four Causes for 'Zoom Fatigue' and Their Simple Fixes." *Stanford News,* Feb. 23, 2021. https://news .stanford.edu/2021/02/23/four-causes-zoom-fatigue-solutions.

Slutkin, Gary. "Why We Need to Treat Violence Like a Contagious Epidemic," *The Guardian,* Jan. 13, 2020. https://www.theguardian.com/us-news/commentis free/2020/jan/13/changing-violence-requires-the-same-shift-in-understanding -given-to-aids.

Streeter, Kurt. "'Everything Is Closed Down.' The Lack of Youth Sports Is a Crisis." *The New York Times,* Oct. 12, 2020. www.nytimes.com/2020/10/12/sports/covid -youth-sports-canceled.html.

Sykes, Mike D., II. "Trae Young Has the Internet Shooting Jumpers into Trash Cans with the #InHouseChallenge." *USA Today,* Mar. 18, 2020. https://ftw.usatoday .com/2020/03/trae-young-in-house-challenge-twitter.

Tech Insider. "People Aren't Having Babies in Denmark So They Made This Provocative Ad." YouTube, Sept. 26, 2016. www.youtube.com/ watch?v=bE2YSYxMVyQ.

TMZ Staff. "Chicago Mayor Urges Hoopers to Stay Home with Legendary Diss." TMZ, Apr. 10, 2020. www.tmz.com/2020/04/10/chicago-mayor-urges-hoopers -to-stay-home-with-legendary-diss.

Twenge, Jean M., et al. "Worldwide Increases in Adolescent Loneliness." *Journal of Adolescence,* July 20, 2021. doi:10.1016/j.adolescence.2021.06.006.

van der Kolk, Bessel. *The Body Keeps the Score: Brain, Mind, and Body in the Healing of Trauma.* Viking, 2014.

Wan, William. "Teen Suicides Are Increasing at an Alarming Pace, Outstripping All Other Age Groups, a New Report Says." *The Washington Post,* Oct. 17, 2019. www.washingtonpost.com/health/teen-suicides-increasing-at-alarming-pace -outstripping-all-other-age-groups/2019/10/16/e24194c6-f04a-11e9-8693 -f487e46784aa_story.html?wpisrc=nl_most&wpmm=1.

Yeginsu, Ceylan. "U.K. Appoints a Minister for Loneliness." *The New York Times,* Jan. 17, 2018. www.nytimes.com/2018/01/17/world/europe/uk-britain -loneliness.html.

Young, Trae (@traeyoung). "What I'm doing to keep my shot right while I'm at the Crib." Twitter, Mar. 16, 2020. https://twitter.com/hashtag/ InHouseChallenge?src=hashtag_click.

SOURCES

Principle 12: Sanctuary

Anderson, "Kevin Durant and (Possibly) the Greatest Basketball Team of All Time."

Colás. *Numbers Don't Lie.*

Covert, Bryce. "8 Hours a Day, 5 Days a Week Is Not Working for Us." *The New York Times,* July 20, 2021. www.nytimes.com/2021/07/20/opinion/covid-return-to -office.html.

Czapnik, Dana. *The Falconer: A Novel.* Atria Books, 2019.

Deloitte. "The Deloitte Global 2021 Millennial and Gen Z Survey." www2.deloitte .com/global/en/pages/about-deloitte/articles/millennialsurvey.html.

Donahue, Jack. "Jonestown, a Means of Control and Rebellion Through Basketball." Phi Alpha Theta Pacific Northwest Conference, Western Washington University, Apr. 2021. https://pdxscholar.library.pdx.edu/cgi/viewcontent.cgi?article=1007 &context=pat_pnw.

Gartland, Dan. "The Oral History of Michael Jordan's Pickup Game Against Regular Chicagoans." *Sports Illustrated,* June 17, 2020. https://www.si.com/extra-mustard /2020/06/17/michael-jordan-retirement-pickup-games-chicago-oral-history.

Hawkins, Andrew J. "Alphabet's Sidewalk Labs Shuts Down Toronto Smart City Project." *The Verge,* May 7, 2020. www.theverge.com/2020/5/7/21250594 /alphabet-sidewalk-labs-toronto-quayside-shutting-down.

Huizinga. *Homo Ludens.*

Jackson, Lauren. "Shoshana Zuboff Explains Why You Should Care About Privacy." *The New York Times,* May 21, 2021. www.nytimes.com/2021/05/21/technology /shoshana-zuboff-apple-google-privacy.html.

June, Sophia. "Could Gen Z Free the World From Email?" *The New York Times,* July 10, 2021. www.nytimes.com/2021/07/10/business/gen-z-email.html.

Laidler, John. "Harvard Professor Says Surveillance Capitalism Is Undermining Democracy." *Harvard Gazette,* Mar. 4, 2019. https://news.harvard.edu/gazette /story/2019/03/harvard-professor-says-surveillance-capitalism-is-undermining -democracy.

Lander, Eric, and Alondra Nelson. "Americans Need a Bill of Rights for an AI -Powered World." *Wired.* Oct. 2021. www.wired.com/story/opinion-bill-of-rights -artificial-intelligence.

Lanier, Jaron. *Ten Arguments for Deleting Your Social Media Accounts Right Now.* Henry Holt, 2018.

Leland, John. "This Heroin-Using Professor Wants to Change How We Think about Drugs." *The New York Times,* Apr. 10, 2021. www.nytimes.com/2021/04/10 /nyregion/Carl-Hart-drugs.html.

MacMullan. "The Courageous Fight to Fix the NBA's Mental Health Problems."

Pandey, Erica. "The Rise of Digital Detox Dining." *Axios,* July 28, 2021. www.axios .com/cafes-digital-detox-dining-af487826-714b-4e27-ae89-e27d7a490fb5.html.

Postman, Neil. *Amusing Ourselves to Death: Public Discourse in the Age of Show Business.* Penguin, 2005.

Schafer, Sarah. "Vonnegut and Clancy on Technology." *Inc.,* Nov. 1995. www.inc.com /magazine/19951215/2653.

SOURCES

Shields. "Life Is Not a Playground."

SI Staff. "Escape from Jonestown." *Sports Illustrated,* Dec. 24, 2007. www.si.com /more-sports/2007/12/24/jonestown1231.

Swados, Elizabeth. "The Gathering of Runaways." *The Guide to Musical Theatre,* Mar. 1978. www.guidetomusicaltheatre.com/shows_r/runaways_swados.htm.

West, Jerry, and Jonathan Coleman. *West by West: My Charmed, Tormented Life.* Little, Brown, 2011.

Wideman, *Hoop Roots: Playground Basketball Love and Race.*

Winter, Thomas. "Luther Halsey Gulick: Recreation, Physical Education and the YMCA." *Infedorg,* Jan. 14, 2013. https://infed.org/mobi/luther-halsey-gulick -recreation-physical-education-and-the-ymca.

Young, Damon. "Thursday Night Hoops." *What Doesn't Kill You Makes You Stronger: A Memoir in Essays.* Ecco, 2019, pp. 271–89.

Zarley, David B. "NYU Is Launching a Center for Psychedelic Medicine." *Freethink,* Mar. 6, 2021. www.freethink.com/health/psychedelic-medicine.

Zuboff, Shoshana. *The Age of Surveillance Capitalism: The Fight for a Human Future at the New Frontier of Power.* PublicAffairs, 2019.

———. "The Coup We Are Not Talking About." *The New York Times,* Jan. 29, 2021. www.nytimes.com/2021/01/29/opinion/sunday/facebook-surveillance-society -technology.html.

Principle 13: Transcendence

Anderson. "Kevin Durant and (Possibly) the Greatest Basketball Team of All Time."

Andrić, Ivo. *The Bridge on the Drina.* Originally published 1945. University of Chicago Press, 1977.

CNA Staff. "Pope Francis: Basketball Is a Sport That 'Lifts You up to the Heavens.'" Catholic News Agency, May 31, 2021. www.catholicnewsagency.com/news /247846/pope-francis-basketball-is-a sport-that-lifts-you-up-to-the-heavens.

Diaz, Natalie. "'Top Ten Reasons Why Indians Are Good at Basketball,'" *Indian Country Today,* Sept. 13, 2018. https://indiancountrytoday.com/archive/top -ten-reasons-why-indians-are-good-at-basketball-a-poem-by-natalie-diaz.

Frazier, Walt. Quoted in "Black Magic," by Alex Belth, Apr. 29, 2013. https://deadspin .com/black-magic-484364618.

Hickey. "The Heresy of Zone Defense."

Kierkegaard, Søren. *Kierkegaard's Concluding Unscientific Postscripts to "Philosophical Fragments."* Princeton University Press, 1992.

Shields. "Life Is Not a Playground."

Telander, Rick. *Heaven Is a Playground.* Sports Publishing, 2013.

Wideman, John Edgar. "Michael Jordan Leaps the Great Divide." *Esquire Classic,* Nov. 1, 1990. https://classic.esquire.com/article/1990/11/1/michael-jordan -leaps-the-great-divide.

ACKNOWLEDGMENTS

Dan Klores, for so much. Dan makes whatever he touches better. That's how it was for me and this project. Once I met Dan, things elevated. He immediately understood. He became a friend. His leadership, inspiration, and knowledge enriched and amplified my dream. He is a force in this world like no other, and what a thing it has been for that force to be with me. I continue to watch and learn from the power of his example. And I continue to be grateful.

David Cooper for true, enduring, honest friendship. My collaborator, confidant, thought partner from the beginning and before the beginning. And for anything we do next. Coop is it for me. I'm going nowhere without him.

Sandy Seplow for giving shelter from the storm, so fully, so selflessly, with love, like he does and has before.

Mark Thomashow for endless, generous, kind, wise giving in a way that teaches, humbles, ennobles, and makes me want to be a better person.

Terri Jackson for always, from the get-go, supporting, giving

Acknowledgments

access, being present, thinking big, seeing more, and asking, "Why not?" And for your indomitable leadership.

Meg Barber for believing. For your brave and imaginative visioning, for being a vessel and messenger of what this book tries to say. We've got so much good work to do.

I work at a great institution that encourages and inspires great work. My path of good fortune at NYU includes unwavering support from Vince Gennaro, Bri Newland, Daniel Kelly, and all my gifted colleagues at the Preston Robert Tisch Institute for Global Sport, plus tremendously empowering leadership and guidance from Angie Kamath, Stuart Robinson, Jason Pina, Linda Mills, and Ellen Schall. It's easy to love what I do when I do it with people like them at a place like this.

My Founders Hall family takes such good care of me. Paula Zwillich, Jerry Roman, David Jones, and the whole crew. Much of this was written in the Founders Hall, and every day they would ask me, "How's it going?" Because they wanted to make sure it was going well. We share so much. I share this with you.

Mike Funk, all we do together, specially and happily bonded the way we are, for taking the time to share your essential, insightful, and difference-making input.

Adriana Zavala and Anthony Lopez for your honest, open read; for the depth, intelligence, and caring that made this book better. Always, for our friendship, togetherness, and laughter.

Enormous and continuing gratitude for the generous open door of Kathy Behrens at the NBA, as well as Mark Tatum, Mike Bass, Paul Hirschheimer, and the inimitable Charlie Rosenzweig.

Hesitation-less support from Jay Jay Nesheim, Laura Gentile, and the folks at ESPN Films.

Acknowledgments

To all the class guests who said "Yes" and came and delivered, openly, unguarded, and fully, each adding another layer, another truth to our discovery, and most important, showing students a new kind of learning they hoped was possible. These are the givers, if I have not mentioned you already, in whose debt I shall always remain: Adrian Wojnarowski, Alan Klein, Alexander Wolff, Amadou Gallo Fall, Bela Alarie, Bill Bamberger, Bobbito Garcia, Book Richardson, Brendan Tuohey, Bryan Brewer, Chamique Holdsclaw, Christy Hedgpeth, Dan Peterson, Elizabeth Williams, George Gervin, J'nai Bridges, Jonathan Coleman, Laura Big Crow, Makur Maker, Mark Alarie, Mark Tatum, Michael Powell, More Free, Nate Archibald, Nick Collison, Rafe Bartholomew, Sam Anderson, Sue Bird, Tamika Catchings, Teresa Edwards, Val Ackerman, Walt Frazier, Kevin Couliau, Sam Bobley, Stan Thangaraj, Dana Czapnik, Aria McManus, Ben Osborne, Dennis Page Don Filippo Maestrello, Dan Grunfeld, Natalie White, Manock Lual, Jesse Tipping, CJ McCollum, Julius Erving, Al Harrington, Dr. Bessel van der Kolk, and Kathleen Fitzpatrick.

Special thanks to special people who did special things, whether you knew it or not, to carry me through: Mike Isaac Jr., Walter Shay, Jeff Fernandez (the streak stays alive), Trace Jordan, Anat Lubetsky, John Tintori, Peter Newman, Ted Philipakos, Robert Parisi, Sheila Roth, Dagan Nelson, Holly Bolton, Betsy Elias, Nettie Respondek, Brian Kriftcher, Chris Isenberg, Ryan Peek, DJ Sackmann, Jim Calder, Andre Holland, Mary Berke, Meredith Geisler, Kristin Bernert, Keia Clarke, Leo Doyle, Tobie Langsam, Jeffrey Sammons, G. Gabrielle Starr, Gene Luen Yang, Sarah Flynn, Noah Malale, Josh Benedek, Mike Flaherty, Maura Everett, Eric Silverman, Anthony Hightower, Marc Perman, Lindsay Krasnoff, Ramsey

Acknowledgments

Chamie, Alesha Smith, Luke Tadashi, Jake Fenster, David Earthy, Zach Nadler, and Ian Forde.

Thanks to the patient indulgence of Springfield College archivist Jeffrey Monseau.

There's a business to this thing. It started with Ellen Chodosh—how kind she was—who took me aside, asked me questions, and sent me where I needed to go. Which was to Deirdre Mullane, my nurturing, forthcoming, hands-on agent, who said to Ellen, "I see it, too." My attorney Eric Rayman is such a skillful, clear, and decent man. I am fortunate to rely on his wise counsel. And thank heaven for Matthew Benjamin, my editor, who saw the soul of the book before it was written and then, with great equanimity, compassion, and intelligence, applied his remarkable and indispensable gifts for sculpting, clarity, and cohesion. I cannot imagine a better partner on this journey.

Almost all I do, I do for students. That's what motivates me. But man, was I ever lucky to have these students do what they did for me in the making of this work: Maddie Perlmutter, Mona al-Tamimi, Anna Grace Pelto, Andrew Cohen, Sami Robbins, Ellie Rothman, Dan Sherman, Oscar Argemi, Matthew Oscodar, Will Eimas-Dietrich, Lauren Schwartzer, Jake Steele, Audrey Cunningham, Luke Klores, Ada Zhang, Linda Liu, Rebecca Licht, Cache Minott, Bharath Sai Reddy Chinthapanti, Hayden Peek, Myles Pina, Dani Coronado, and the incomparable, there-will-never-be-another Alyssa Barrett.

And then there's Alessandro Gherardi. Extraordinary. What a mind. What a code of honor. What a contribution you have made to this book and all that led up to it. You are ongoing proof that

Acknowledgments

teaching is learning and learning is teaching. Thank you for both, from the very first class together. More please.

Mom and Dad for instilling in me the quest for meaning where the meaning is found in the quest itself, and the consciousness not to miss it. And for your boundless, tireless love. I stand on your shoulders every single day.

Lola, this book is dedicated to you. The whole thing is really just a lot of words trying to say I want you to have a better world. But I know there's nothing better in this world for me than when I'm spending time with you. You stagger me with your goodness.

Thanks to Alexandra Gratsas for watching me wake up every morning and push the rock. Some days you add your hand to that rock when I need it, or push me when I need that, or leave me to struggle through it when I need that. Each way each day, together, we get up and go up that hill—sometimes we see the top, sometimes not. But what we do see, always, is each other next to each other. Which makes it not a climb but a waltz like when I see you now, this morning, across the room as I type this, and I thank you for another day, together, dancing me to the end of love.